Dangerous Weather

Blizzards

Revised Edition

Dangerous Weather

Blizzards

Revised Edition

Michael Allaby

ILLUSTRATIONS by Richard Garratt

Facts On File, Inc.

For Ailsa
—M.A.

To my late wife, Jen, who gave me inspiration
and support for almost 30 years
—R.G.

Blizzards, Revised Edition

Copyright © 2004, 1998 by Michael Allaby

All rights reserved. No part of this book may be reproduced or utilized in any form or by any means, electronic or mechanical, including photocopying, recording, or by any information storage or retrieval systems, without permission in writing from the publisher. For information contact:

Facts On File, Inc.
132 West 31st Street
New York NY 10001

Library of Congress Cataloging-in-Publication Data

Allaby, Michael.
  Blizzards / Michael Allaby; illustrations by Richard Garratt.—Rev. ed.
    p. cm.—(Dangerous weather)
  Includes bibliographical references and index.
  ISBN 0-8160-4791-X (hardcover: acid-free paper)
  1. Blizzards. I. Title.
QC926. 32.A45 2003
551.55′5—dc21   2003005054

Facts On File books are available at special discounts when purchased in bulk quantities for businesses, associations, institutions, or sales promotions. Please call our Special Sales Department in New York at (212) 967-8800 or (800) 322-8755.

You can find Facts On File on the World Wide Web at
http://www.factsonfile.com

Text design by Erika K. Arroyo
Cover design by Nora Wertz
Illustrations by Richard Garratt

Printed in the United States of America

MP Hermitage 10 9 8 7 6 5 4 3 2 1

This book is printed on acid-free paper.

Contents

Preface

What is a blizzard?

Several years have passed since the first edition of this book was published. Much has happened during those years and the decision to update the book for a second edition gives me a welcome opportunity to report at least some of them. In doing so, I have substantially altered, expanded, and in some places rewritten the original text.

There have been more blizzards, of course. Their severity varies, but every winter there are blizzards in many parts of the world and no matter how the climates of the world may change in years to come, there is little chance that they will disappear. Indeed, they could become worse.

Climate research has also intensified in recent years. Concern over the possibility that humans may be altering the global climate has stimulated funding agencies to increase the resources available for evaluating the likelihood of global warming and its consequences. If we are to understand the extent of this threat—if it is a threat—scientists need to learn much more about the ways the Sun, atmosphere, and oceans interact to produce our day-to-day weather. New discoveries are now being made at an unprecedented rate and, although there is still a long way to go before the global climate is fully understood, we are learning more about it almost every day. This new edition takes account of the most recent relevant findings.

Updating the text has also given me an opportunity to expand it in order to provide more detailed explanations. I have added three new chapters. These describe and explain the "Snowball Earth" theory, avalanches, and the lake effect.

This edition contains more sidebars than in the first edition. These explain concepts from atmospheric science, such as adiabatic cooling and warming, humidity, lapse rates, weather fronts, and latent heat, as well as why the Arctic is warmer than the Antarctic and why warm air can hold more moisture than cold air can.

Measurements are given in familiar U.S. units, such as pounds, feet, miles, and degrees Fahrenheit, throughout the book, but in each case I have added the metric or scientific equivalent. All scientists now use standard international units of measurement. These may be unfamiliar, so I have added them, with their conversions, as an appendix. The appendix also includes the Beaufort scale of wind force and the classification system for avalanches.

The first edition contained no suggestions for further reading. These have been added in this edition. The sources include a number of books that you may find useful, but a much larger number of web addresses. If you have access to a computer, these will allow you to learn more about blizzards, snowstorms, and about climate generally quickly and free of charge.

We have decided to omit the photographs from the first edition and instead to increase the number of diagrams and maps. These provide more useful information than photographs of such subjects as swirling snow, icicles, and abandoned cars. My friend and colleague Richard Garratt has drawn all of the illustrations. As always, I am deeply grateful to him for his skill in translating my crude drawings into such accomplished artwork.

I am grateful, too, to Frank K. Darmstadt, my editor at Facts On File, for his hard work, cheerful encouragement, and patience.

If this "new, improved" edition of *Blizzards* encourages you to pursue your study of the weather further, it will have achieved its aim and fulfilled my highest hopes for it. I hope you enjoy reading the book as much as I have enjoyed writing it for you.

—Michael Allaby
Tighnabruaich
Argyll, Scotland
www.michaelallaby.com

Introduction

It began on New Year's Eve 2000. Across Inner Mongolia, the Autonomous Region of northern China that lies between Tibet and Mongolia, the incessant wind intensified and the temperature plummeted. Snow, whipped up from the ground and mixed with desert sand from the Gobi, produced the worst blizzard for half a century. It lasted for three days in some areas. A young girl climbed down from a school bus, just a short distance from her home, but became disoriented and lost. The temperature was about –58 °F (–50 °C). She froze to death. In all, 39 people died from the cold.

People were affected over a large area, but those most at risk were the 60,000 nomadic herders in the prefectures (districts) of Xilin, Chifeng, and Xingan, whose livelihoods depend on their goats, sheep, cattle, camels, and horses. More than 220,000 animals perished. Some of them were found later, frozen rigid but still standing upright. Their deaths deprived the people of food. The ground was frozen and covered with up to 14 inches (35.6 cm) of snow and ice, so the surviving livestock were unable to graze, but that was not all. The snow and iron-hard ground made it impossible for people to collect dry dung, the fuel with which they heat their homes. They faced starvation, and without heating they had little protection from the bitter cold.

There were relief efforts, of course, organized by the State Ethnic Affairs Commission in collaboration with the China Charity Federation, and the International Federation of Red Cross and Red Crescent Societies launched an appeal.

This was a blizzard.

American and European winter storms

The United States had already suffered from the snow that winter. In late October fierce storms generated blizzards and tornadoes across North Dakota. One blizzard dumped 10.8 inches (27.4 cm) of snow on Grand Forks, breaking the previous record of 8.2 inches (20.8 cm) of snow that fell in a 1926 storm. On the road north of Fargo trucks slithered into at least two snowplows. A month later, more snowstorms swept across the northern plains from Wyoming to Minnesota.

Europe did not escape. Heavy snow and blizzards caused chaos in December 2001. Venetian gondolas lay covered with snow, Greek airports were closed, and in northern Spain roads were blocked by cars and trucks, abandoned when the snow made it impossible to continue. In February 2002 it was England's turn. As the visibility deteriorated and the roads became icy, road accidents multiplied. Military helicopters on their way to rescue the victims of a major road pile-up in Yorkshire had to land because of the bad weather.

The 1996 blizzards

This was not a particularly cold winter and over most of the United States it was drier than usual. There had been much worse weather in 1996. On January 7, Washington, D.C., along with much of the Appalachian and mid-Atlantic states, was deep in snow after the worst blizzard for 70 years. In South Carolina, university students played in the snow and a man jogging near the White House described it as "gorgeous, spectacular, almost awe-inspiring." For most people, though, the blizzards meant huge disruption, and there were at least 65 deaths. Mail deliveries were halted in New York City and there were 20-foot (6-m) drifts at the airports. The United Nations building closed. People skied to work across Times Square. In parts of Virginia and eastern Tennessee, drifts were 30 feet (9 m) deep, they were 24 feet (7 m) deep in eastern Kentucky, and there was even one foot (30 cm) of snow in northeastern Georgia. Shenandoah National Park in Virginia lay under almost four feet (1.2 m) of snow. The blizzard affected 17 states, and states of emergency were declared in nine.

In the course of one night during that spell of bad weather there was a fall of 20–30 inches (51–76 cm) of snow driven into drifts by winds of 25–35 MPH (40–56 km/h). Those were the steady winds, however, and at times there were gusts of up to 50 MPH (80 km/h) as the storm traveled north and east, before eventually moving over the Atlantic.

Hardly had people begun clearing away the snow before new storms developed and brought more, increasing the death toll to more than 100. In Washington, federal government offices had managed to reopen on one day, only to close again the next. By this time the weight of snow was causing damage. A church roof collapsed in Harlem, a supermarket roof collapsed in North Massapequa, New York, a lawn and garden center and a barn collapsed in Pennsylvania, and the roof of a store collapsed in Ontario, Ohio. At Dale City, Virginia, Potomac Mills Mall, one of the biggest shopping malls in the country, had to be closed for a day because the roof was sagging under the weight of snow.

President's Day

The third Monday in February—President's Day—seems to attract blizzards. They struck on that day in 1979 and 1983, and in 2003 there was another. After it ended, some people were calling the 2003 President's Day storm the "storm of the century," which was somewhat premature so early in the 21st century.

Storm of the century or not, it was undoubtedly severe and extensive, although it did not produce blizzard conditions everywhere. It lasted from Saturday, February 15 until Monday February 17—President's Day itself—and affected most of the East Coast of the United States, from Massachusetts to Virginia and Washington, D.C. The storm dumped more than 2 feet (60 cm) of snow in some places and badly disrupted travel along the urban corridor linking Boston, New York, and Philadelphia. Snow was still lying from an earlier spell of bitterly cold weather and gales in January. This made the President's Day storm more disruptive than it might have been otherwise.

The cost of bad weather

Blizzard is a word we may associate with the far north or with Antarctica. Certainly blizzards are more common there—and harmless. The population is sparsely scattered in northern Scandinavia, Siberia, and northern Canada. No one at all lives permanently in Antarctica and the scientists who work there can remain safe and warm indoors when the weather makes outside work impossible.

As the Chinese, European, and American storms show, however, blizzards also happen in lower latitudes and with much more serious consequences. The nomadic people of Inner Mongolia live in tentlike dwellings made from skins, wool, or more commonly from felt stretched over a framework of wooden poles. These are easy to assemble, dismantle, and transport, but they are hardly adequate for subzero temperatures and howling winds when the occupants have no fuel for heating and cooking. The eastern United States and Europe are much more densely populated, and ordinary life for their citizens requires transportation systems, telephone lines, and power supplies, all of which can be disrupted by heavy snow, and the damage to property is often costly. Insurance claims following the 1996 blizzards in the U.S. were estimated at about $585 million (in 1996 dollars).

What makes a snowstorm into a blizzard?

A blizzard is not merely snow, it is snow driven by high winds. It is not even necessary for snow to be falling. Blizzards can occur when light, powdery snow lying on the ground is blown into the air, like a desert dust storm. The word itself is American and the first record of its use dates from 1829. It may have come from *blizzer* or *blizzom*, adjectives that mean "dazzling" or "blazing." In the Civil War, a heavy volley of musket fire was called a blizzard and in 1870 an Indiana newspaper used the word to describe a ferocious snowstorm. That usage caught on and within 10 years or so it became the only meaning of the word.

Today, the National Oceanic and Atmospheric Administration (NOAA) defines a blizzard as a storm with winds of at least 35 MPH (56 km/h), temperatures lower than 20° F (–7° C), and enough falling or blowing snow to reduce visibility to less than a quarter of a mile (400 m).

CONTINENTAL AND MARITIME CLIMATES

A blizzard consists of wind-driven snow. Strong winds can occur any-where, but two conditions are needed to produce snow. First, there must be enough water vapor in the air to condense and form cloud. Second, the water must fall as snow rather than rain. Not everywhere in the world has a climate moist enough for this to happen, and not everywhere is cold enough.

All weather, blizzards included, results from solar radiation and its indirect effect on the air. Warmth from the Sun heats the ground and the surface of the sea, and these warm the air in contact with them. When air is warmed, it expands. This makes it less dense, so it rises, and as it rises it cools again. This is called *adiabatic* cooling. Air that is made to subside warms in the same way (see the sidebar).

The amount of water vapor air can hold depends on the temperature. This is because when a substance cools its molecules lose energy. When water molecules lose energy they travel more slowly and collisions between them are less violent. If they cool—and slow down—sufficiently, encoun-ters between molecules will keep them close together long enough for them to join together into groups. The molecules link by *hydrogen bonds* between the hydrogen atoms of one molecule and the oxygen atoms of its neighbors. The groups then join together in the form of liquid droplets. As air cools, therefore, its water vapor condenses and clouds form. As air warms, water evaporates into it, because the molecules gain enough energy to break free from the hydrogen bonds holding them together.

Seasons and the tilting Earth

If this is all there were to it, the weather would be easy to understand, but rather boring. It would not change much from one day to the next and cer-tainly not from one time of year to another. There would be no seasons.

We have seasons because the Earth is tilted on its axis. At present it is at 23.45° to the vertical; the angle changes from 22.1° to 24.5° over a cycle of about 41,000 years. As it travels through its orbit about the Sun, first the Northern Hemisphere and then the Southern Hemisphere is tilted toward the Sun. As the diagram shows, this alters the amount of sunshine each hemisphere receives, not only in intensity but also in duration. Summer days are longer than winter days, and the Arctic and Antarctic Circles mark the boundary of regions where on at least one day in winter the Sun never rises above the horizon and on one day in summer it never sinks

Adiabatic cooling and warming

Air is compressed by the weight of air above it. Imagine a balloon partly inflated with air and made from a substance that totally insulates the air inside. No matter what the temperature outside the balloon, the temperature of the air inside remains the same.

Imagine the balloon is released into the atmosphere. The air inside is squeezed between the weight of air above it, all the way to the top of the atmosphere, and the denser air below it.

Suppose the air inside the balloon is less dense than the air above it. The balloon will rise. As it rises, the distance to the top of the atmosphere becomes smaller, so there is less air above to weigh down on the air in the balloon. At the same time, as it moves through air that is less dense, it experiences less

Effect of air pressure on rising and sinking air

pressure from below. This causes the air in the balloon to expand.

When air (or any gas) expands, its molecules move farther apart. The amount of air remains the same, but it occupies a bigger volume. As they move apart, the molecules must "push" other molecules out of their way. This uses energy, so as the air expands its molecules lose energy. Because they have less energy they move more slowly.

When a moving molecule strikes something, some of its energy of motion (kinetic energy) is transferred to whatever it strikes and part of that energy is converted into heat. This raises the temperature of the struck object by an amount related to the number of molecules striking it and their speed.

In expanding air, the molecules are moving farther apart, so a smaller number of them strike an object each second. They are also traveling more slowly, so they strike with less force. This means the temperature of the air decreases. As it expands, air cools.

If the air in the balloon is denser than the air below, it will descend. The pressure on it will increase, its volume will decrease, and its molecules will acquire more energy. Its temperature will increase.

This warming and cooling has nothing to do with the temperature of the air surrounding the balloon. It is called *adiabatic* warming and cooling, from the Greek word *adiabatos*, meaning "impassable."

below the horizon. At the other extreme, the Tropics of Capricorn and Cancer mark the limits of regions where on at least one day every year the Sun is directly overhead at noon.

The Tropics are at latitudes 23.5° N and 23.5° S. The Arctic and Antarctic Circles are at latitudes 66.5° N and 66.5° S (90°–23.5°). These circles are the consequence of the Earth's axial tilt. If the Earth were upright they would not exist.

Even if the Earth were not tilted, the poles would still be colder than the Tropics. In fact, they would be colder than they are now, because in summer the tilted axis turns them towards the Sun. They are colder

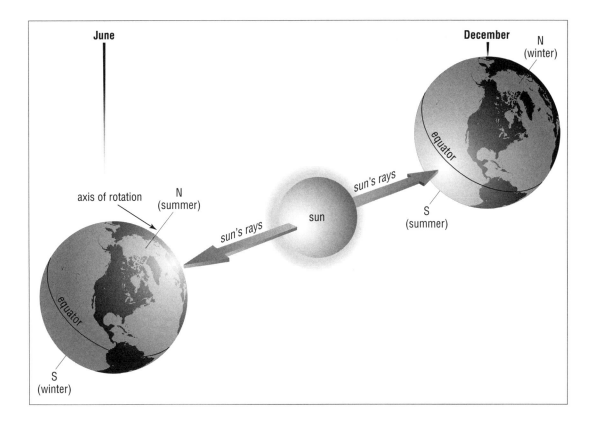

because the light and heat the surface receives is spread over a larger area when the Sun is low in the sky than when it is high, so it is less intense.

How axial tilt produces the seasons

Movements of air and water

Uneven heating of the Earth sets the air in motion. In the lower part of the atmosphere, called the *troposphere*, this produces a general atmospheric circulation (see the sidebar "General circulation of the atmosphere," on page 4). Air moves vertically as well as horizontally, and there are belts around the world where dense air is usually sinking, making the surface pressure high, and other belts where less dense air is rising and surface pressure is low.

This global circulation of air is the first ingredient in the making of weather. The oceans are the second. They warm and cool much more slowly than the land (see the sidebar on specific heat capacity and black-bodies in the section "Cold air and warm water," page 123). In summer, the land heats rapidly and the air above it becomes very warm. If that air moves away from the land and over the ocean, it will be cooled. In winter the opposite occurs.

Ocean water is not the same temperature everywhere, however, because it is also transporting heat. It does so in the form of currents, some carrying warm water away from the equator, others carrying cool water away from the poles. In the large oceans these currents form *gyres*—roughly circular systems of currents that flow counterclockwise in both hemispheres. In each case, the gyres bathe western coasts with cool water and eastern coasts with warm water. This means the eastern coastal regions of continents have a warmer climate than those lying along the west coast, though the effect is fairly small. In Norfolk, Virginia, for example, located at latitude 36.85° N, the average yearly daytime temperature is 68°F (20°C). In San Francisco, at 37.78° N, it is 58°F (15°C).

General circulation of the atmosphere

The tropics of Cancer in the north and Capricorn in the south mark the boundaries of the belt around Earth where the Sun is directly overhead at noon on at least one day in the year. The Arctic and Antarctic Circles mark the boundaries of regions in which the Sun does not rise above the horizon on at least one day of the year and does not sink below the horizon on at least one day in the year.

Imagine a beam of sunlight just a few degrees wide. This beam illuminates a much smaller area if the Sun is directly overhead than it does if the Sun is at a low angle in the sky. The amount of energy in each beam is the same, because they are of the same width, so energy is spread over a smaller area directly beneath the Sun than it is when the Sun is lower. This is why the Tropics are heated more strongly than any other part of Earth and the amount of heat we receive from the Sun decreases the farther we are from the equator.

The Sun shines more intensely at the equator than it does anywhere else, but movements of the air transport some of the warmth away from the

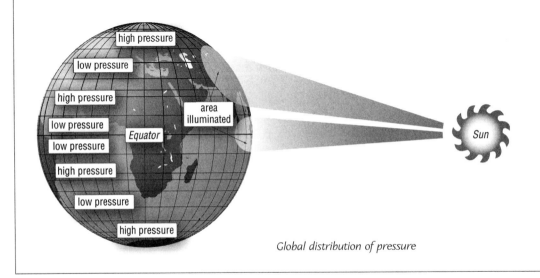

Global distribution of pressure

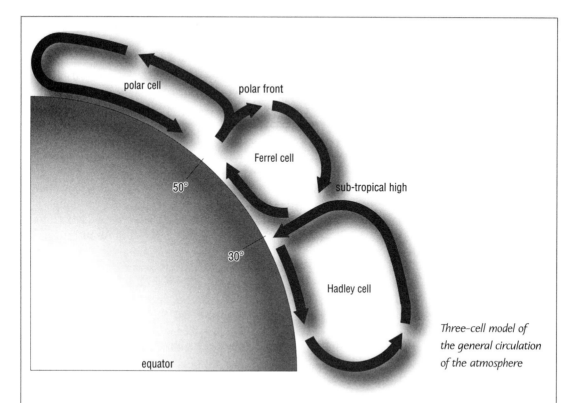

polar cell

polar front

Ferrel cell

sub-tropical high

50°

30°

Hadley cell

equator

Three-cell model of the general circulation of the atmosphere

equator. Near the equator, the warm surface heats the air in contact with it. The warm air rises and, near the tropopause, at a height of around 10 miles (16 km), it moves away from the equator, some heading north and some south. As it rises, the air cools, so the high-level air moving away from the equator is very cold—about –85°F (–65°C).

This equatorial air subsides around latitude 30°N and S, and as it sinks it warms again. By the time it reaches the surface it is hot and dry, so it warms this region some distance from the equator. At the surface, the air divides. This is a region of calm winds, sometimes called the horse latitudes (because when supplies of fresh water ran low on ships carrying horses as cargo, some of the horses died and were thrown overboard). Most of the air flows back toward the equator and some flows away from the equator. The air from north and south meets at the Intertropical Convergence Zone (ITCZ), and this circulation forms a number of Hadley cells.

Over the poles, the air is very cold. It subsides and when it reaches the surface it flows away from the poles. At about latitude 50–60° N and S, air moving away from the poles meets air moving away from the equator. The colliding air rises to the tropopause, in these latitudes about 7 miles (11 km) above the surface. Some flows back to the poles, forming polar cells, and some flows toward the equator, completing Ferrel cells (discovered by the American meteorologist William Ferrel, 1817–91).

Follow this movement and you will see that warm air rises at the equator, sinks to the surface in the subtropics, then flows at low level to around latitude 55°, then rises to continue its journey toward the poles. At the same time, cold air subsiding at the poles flows back to the equator.

If it were not for this redistribution of heat, weather at the equator would be very much hotter than it is, and weather at the poles would be a great deal colder.

Continental and maritime climates

Climates along all coasts are strongly affected by the ocean nearby. They are called *maritime* climates. Proximity to the sea means that precipitation (rain and snow) is spread fairly evenly through the year. In New York City, for example, the amount each month ranges from a minimum of 3.0 inches (76 mm) in November to a maximum of 4.3 inches (109 mm) in August. In Belfast, Northern Ireland, the driest month is April, with an average over 30 years of 1.9 inches (48 mm) of precipitation, and the wettest is July, with 3.7 inches (94 mm). Average temperatures are also fairly equable, in New York ranging from a daytime minimum of 37°F (2.8°C) in January to a maximum of 82°F (27.8°C) in July. In Belfast the average daytime temperature reaches 43°F (6.1°C) in January, and in July and August it is 65°F (18.3°C).

Deep inside continents the climate is drier, because of the great distance to the moist air of the oceans. At Omaha, Nebraska, at about the same latitude as New York City, January is the driest month, with an average of 0.7 inch (18 mm) of precipitation, and June the wettest, with 4.6 inches (117 mm). The weather is also hotter in summer and colder in winter, because places far from the coast benefit much less from the moderating effect the oceans have on air temperatures. Average daytime temperatures in Omaha range from 30°F (–1°C) in January to 86°F (30°C) in July. The temperature range—the difference between the warmest and coolest days—is 45°F (25°C) in New York City and 56°F (31°C) in Omaha. In Berlin, Germany, about 2° south of Belfast, March is the driest month, with 1.3 inches (33 mm) of precipitation, and July the wettest, with 2.9 inches (74 mm). In January the average daytime temperature is 35°F (1.7°C) and in July it is 75°F (23.9°C). Belfast has a temperature range of 22°F (12°C) and Berlin one of 40°F (22°C). These rather dry climates with greater ranges of temperature are called *continental* climates.

Calculating continentality and oceanicity

Most middle latitude climates are of either the maritime or continental type, with some being transitional between the two. There are degrees of *continentality* and *oceanicity*. These can be calculated and given values.

The Conrad formula, devised in 1946 by the American climatologist V. Conrad, produces values for continentality *(K)*. It is: $K = 1.7 A / \sin (\Phi + 10) - 14$, where *A* is the average daytime temperature range (the difference between the maximum and minimum daytime temperatures) and Φ (Greek phi) is the latitude. A fully maritime climate has a value of 0 and a fully continental climate has a value of 100.

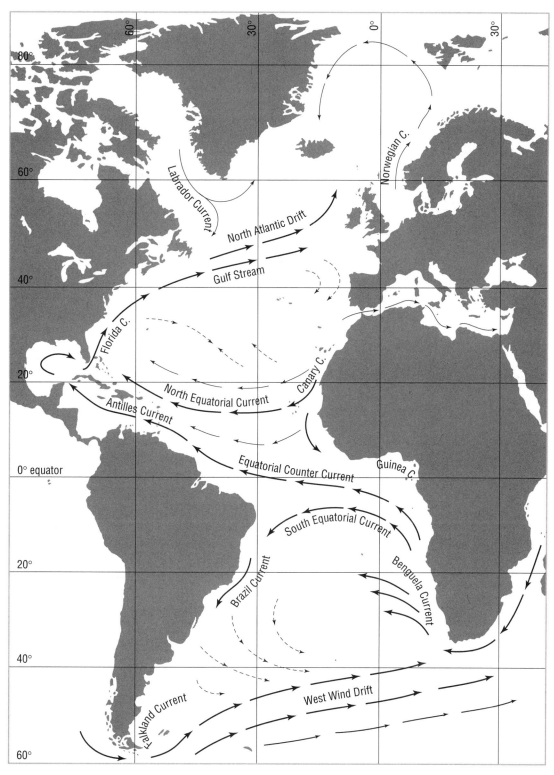

Atlantic Ocean currents

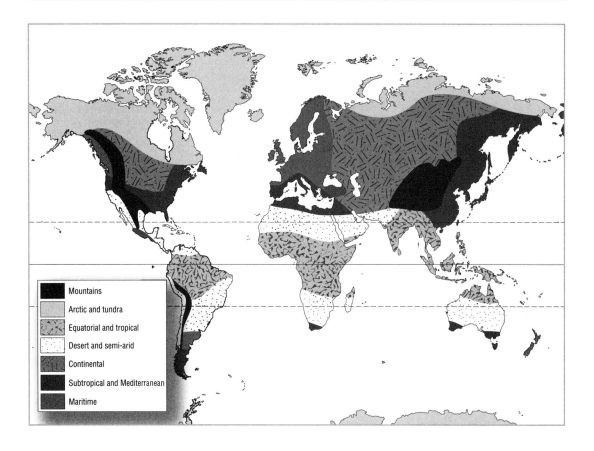

Main climate types

There are several formulas for calculating oceanicity *(O)*. The simplest is: $O = 100 ((T_o - T_a)/A)$ for the Northern Hemisphere and $O = ((T_a - T_o)/A)$ for the Southern Hemisphere, where T_o is the mean monthly daytime temperature in October, T_a is the mean monthly temperature in April, and A is the average daytime temperature range. This gives the result as a percentage: 0 percent indicates an extreme continental climate and 100 percent indicates an extreme maritime climate.

As the map of principal climatic types shows, the middle-latitude climates are bordered to the north by subarctic (with tundra vegetation) and arctic climates (no Southern Hemisphere continent extends far enough south to have a subarctic climate). On the side nearer the equator, middle-latitude climates give way to subtropical and Mediterranean climates.

MOVEMENTS OF AIR MASSES IN WINTER

Each region of the Earth has a particular type of climate, but it is the air that produces all those climates. It might be more accurate to think of particular kinds of air as being associated with climates, rather than geographical regions of the surface. After all, clouds form in air, not on the ground, and it is the movement of air that we feel as the wind. If one area is desert and in another it rains almost perpetually, there must be differences in the air that lies over them.

It may seem strange to think of different kinds of air. After all, air is the same everywhere. It is dustier or more polluted in some places than others, but if you ignore the pollutants, all air is the same mixture of gases, about 78 percent nitrogen and 21 percent oxygen, with trace amounts of carbon dioxide, neon, helium, methane, and about five others. Go to the South Pole, the middle of the Sahara, a South Pacific island, or anywhere else you choose, and this is the air you will breathe (which is just as well if you are planning a trip!).

Cold air, high pressure

Think of what it is like in the middle of a large continent in midwinter. The ground cooled rapidly in the fall and now it is extremely cold and hard as stone. Lakes and rivers are frozen. Air in contact with the surface is at the same temperature as the surface, and that air is dry. Any water on the ground is frozen, so it cannot evaporate, and the amount of water vapor air can hold decreases as the air temperature falls. Between 95°F (35°C) and –23°F (–30.6°C) the amount of water vapor air can hold decreases by half for every 18°F (10°C) decrease in temperature. The sidebar "Why warm air can hold more moisture than cold air can" explains why this is so. Even if liquid water were available, therefore, very little of it could evaporate. Step outdoors in these conditions and the dry air will feel clean and fresh.

When air is cold its molecules have less energy. They move more slowly and crowd closer together, so a given weight of cold air occupies a smaller volume than the same weight of warm air. If the molecules are more tightly crowded together in cold air than in warm air, the cold air must be denser—its mass is greater for each unit of volume. Crowding together leaves no gaps, however. There are no places left without any air because the air has shrunk. Instead, air is drawn down from above and replaced with air flowing into the region at a high altitude. This means a column of air stretching from an area of the surface all the way to the top of the atmosphere contains more air molecules when the air is cold than it does when the air is warm. Because it contains more molecules, it is heavier, and because it is heavier it presses downward more strongly. In other words, its pressure increases at the surface.

Air masses

Continents are large and so this cold, dense, dry air covers many thousands of square miles. Throughout that vast area, all the air is at more or less the same temperature and surface pressure, and contains the same amount of moisture. These shared characteristics also extend vertically. Such a body of air is called an *air mass* and it determines the type of weather people on the ground experience (see the sidebar "Air masses and

Air masses and the weather they bring

As air moves slowly across the surface it is sometimes warmed, sometimes cooled, in some places water evaporates into it, and in others it loses moisture. Its characteristics change.

When it crosses a very large region, such as a continent or ocean, its principal characteristics are evened out and all the air is at much the same temperature and pressure over a vast area and is equally moist or dry. Such a body of air is called an *air mass.*

Air masses are warm, cool, moist, or dry according to the region over which they formed and they are named accordingly. The names and their abbreviations are straightforward. Continental (c) air masses form over continents, maritime (m) ones over oceans. Depending on the latitude in which they form, air masses may be arctic (A), polar (P), tropical (T), or equatorial (E). Except in the case of equatorial air, these categories are then combined to give continental arctic (cA), maritime arctic (mA), continental polar (cP), maritime polar (mP), continental tropical (cT), and

maritime tropical (mT). Equatorial air is always maritime (mE), because oceans cover most of the equatorial region.

North America is affected by mP, cP, cT, and mT air, the maritime air masses originating over the Pacific or Atlantic Oceans, or the Gulf of Mexico. These are shown on the map. As they move from where they formed (their *source regions*) air masses change, but they do so slowly and at first they bring with them the weather conditions that produced them. As their names suggest, maritime air is moist, continental air is dry, polar air is cool, and tropical air is warm. At the surface there is little difference between polar and arctic air, but there are differences in the upper atmosphere.

It is cP air spilling south when the cT and mT move toward the equator in the fall that brings cold, dry winters to the central United States. It is the meeting of mT air from the Gulf and cT air from inland that produces fierce storms in the southeast of the country.

the weather they bring"). If it covers the interior of a continent it is called a *continental air mass*.

Air masses also form over the ocean. These are called *maritime air masses* and they are different from continental air masses. Although they are cold in winter, they are not so cold as continental air masses in the same latitude, because the oceans cool much more slowly than the land. In midwinter the sea is warmer than the air above it. Maritime air is also moister than continental air, partly because it is warmer and can hold more water vapor, but mainly because it is in contact with liquid water. Maritime air produces milder, wetter weather than continental air.

Warm, very moist air can feel oppressive and "sticky." This is because our bodies cool themselves by sweating and allowing sweat to evaporate from the skin. Evaporation absorbs latent heat (see the sidebar on the discovery of latent heat in the section "What happens when water freezes and ice melts," page 99) and this cools the skin. If the air is very moist, however, it may be unable to hold any more water vapor. Consequently, sweat fails to evaporate. It soaks our clothes, trickles down our faces, and no longer cools us as it should, so we feel hot and uncomfortable.

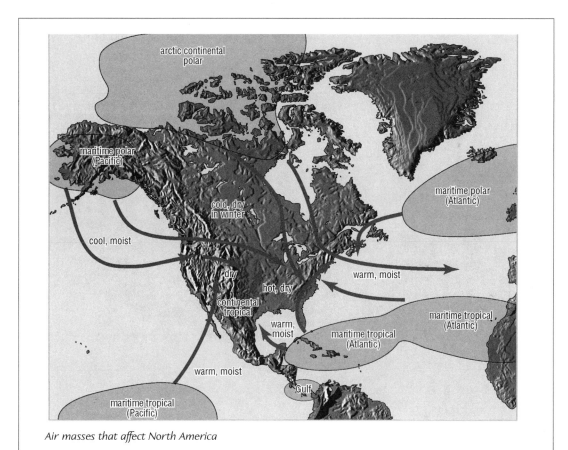

Air masses that affect North America

When air masses move

This makes it sound as though air just sits over a continent or ocean, producing typical climates. Climates are typical, but air masses are constantly on the move. They form, not in stationary air, but in air that is moving most of the time and they acquire their characteristics because of the great distances they must travel.

In the middle latitudes of both hemispheres, air moves mainly from west to east—in the direction of the prevailing winds. To either side of these latitudes, winds generally blow in the opposite direction, from east to west. This can complicate weather forecasting in regions close to the boundaries between these wind systems. Pacific air gives the west coast of North America a maritime climate. Portland, Oregon, for example, has maximum daytime temperatures ranging over 33°F (18.3°C), from 44°F (6.7°C) in January to 77°F (25°C) in July and August and precipitation falls in all months, although July and August are the driest.

Continuing its passage over the continent, the air must travel more than 2,000 miles (3,200 km) before reaching the Atlantic. During this time it loses much of its moisture and becomes continental in character. By the time it reaches Minneapolis it is much drier and brings tempera-

How the characteristics of an air mass change as it crosses the ocean

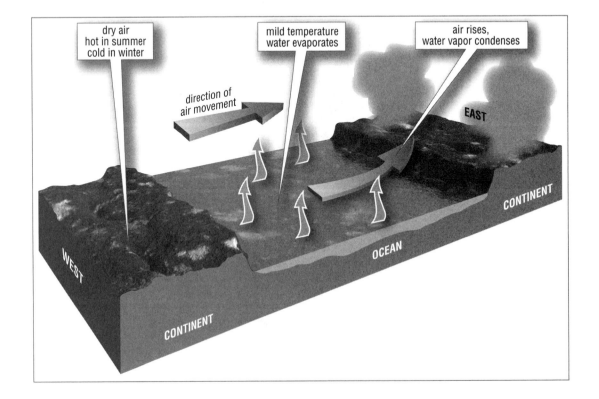

tures ranging through 61°F (34°C), from 22°F (–5.6°C) in January to 83°F (28°C) in July. The maritime air mass from the Pacific has become a continental air mass.

Then it crosses the East Coast. As the map shows, during its 3,000-mile (4,800-km) journey across the Atlantic, the air warms and water starts evaporating into it. It becomes a maritime air mass again, bringing equable, moist conditions to western Europe and losing a substantial proportion of its water vapor when it crosses the coast and is forced to rise.

When air masses meet

A steady progression of air, moving at a constant speed and repeatedly acquiring new characteristics as it crosses continents and oceans, might account for the "average" weather in each region, but it cannot explain certain types of extreme weather. These require an element of conflict— and the atmosphere generates plenty of that.

Not all air masses travel at the same speed. Cold air usually moves faster than warm air. Because of the difference in their densities, masses of air at substantially different temperatures mix very slowly, the warm air tending to form a distinct layer above the cooler. Advancing cold air undercuts the warmer, slower-moving air ahead of it, lifting it above the surface. The boundary where two air masses meet is called a *front* (see sidebar) and it is along fronts that extreme weather is most likely to occur.

Nor is the march of the air masses constant. Dense air may become stuck, remaining in the same place for days or weeks. It is then called a *blocking high* and brings dry, settled weather, extremely cold in winter and hot in summer. Despite blocking the path of other air masses, it does not halt their progress. They are diverted around it.

Eddies can develop in the moving air. These are linked to undulations in the path of the high-level wind known as the *jet stream* (see sidebar). Sometimes these eddies are 1,000 miles (1,600 km) in diameter and last for several days, producing areas of relatively high or low surface pressure called *anticyclones* and *cyclones* (or *depressions*) respectively.

Distribution of pressure

Through all this apparent turmoil, an overall pattern emerges of regions where the surface pressure is usually high and others where it is usually low. *High* and *low* are relative terms, as are *warm* and *cold*. Pressure is "high" if it is higher than that of adjacent air, and the temperature can be

Weather fronts

During World War I, a team of meteorologists led by the Norwegian Vilhelm Bjerknes (1862–1951) discovered that air forms distinct masses. Because each mass differs in its average temperature, and therefore density, from adjacent masses, air masses do not mix readily. He called the boundary between two air masses a *front*.

Air masses move across the surface of land and sea, and so the fronts between them also move. Fronts are named according to the temperature of the air *behind* the front compared with that ahead of it. If the air behind the advancing front is warmer than the air ahead of it, it is a warm front. If the air behind the front is cooler, it is a cold front.

Fronts extend from the surface all the way to the tropopause, which is the boundary between the lower (troposphere) and upper (stratosphere) layers of the atmosphere. They slope upward, like the sides of a bowl, but the slope is very shallow. Warm fronts have a gradient of 1° or less, cold fronts of about 2°. This means that when you first see, high in the sky, the cirrus clouds marking the approach of a warm front, the point where the front touches the surface is about 350–715 miles (565–1,150 km) distant. When you see the first, high-level sign of an approaching cold front, the front is at the surface about 185 miles (300 km) away.

Cold fronts usually move across the surface faster than warm fronts, so cold air tends to undercut warm air, raising it upward along the cold front. If the warm air is already rising, it will be raised even faster along the front separating it from cold air. The front is then called an *ana-front* and there is usually thick cloud and heavy rain or snow associated with it. If the warm air is sinking,

an advancing cold front will raise it less. This is a *kata-front*, usually with only low-level cloud and light rain, drizzle, or fine snow. The diagram on pages 15–16 shows these frontal systems in cross-section, but with the frontal slopes greatly exaggerated.

After a front has formed, waves start to develop along it. These are shown on weather maps and as they become steeper, areas of low pressure form at their crests. These are *frontal depressions*, or *extratropical cyclones*, and they often bring wet weather. Just below the wave crest, there is cold air to either side of a body of warm air. The cold front moves faster than the warm front, lifting the warm air along both fronts until all the warm air is clear of the surface. The fronts are then said to be *occluded* and the pattern they form is called an *occlusion*.

Once the fronts are occluded and the warm air is no longer in contact with the surface, air to both sides of the occlusion is colder than the warm air. Occlusions can still be called cold or warm, however, because what matters is not the actual temperature of the air, but whether air to one side of a front or occlusion is warmer or cooler than the air behind it. In a cold occlusion the air ahead of the front is warmer than the air behind it and in a warm occlusion the air ahead is cooler, but both of these are cooler than the warm air that has been lifted clear of the surface. The diagram shows this in cross-section. As the warm air is lifted, clouds usually form and often bring precipitation. Eventually the warm and cold air reach the same temperature, mix, and the frontal system dissipates. Often, however, another similar system is following behind, so frontal depressions commonly occur in families.

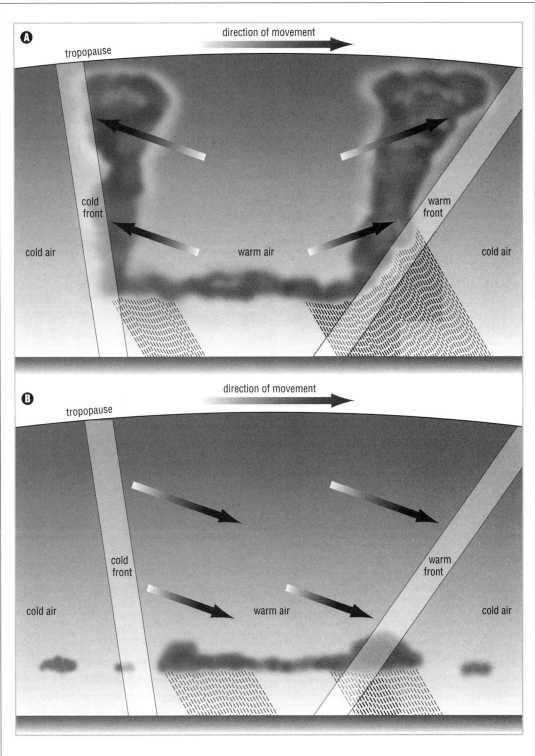

A

direction of movement

tropopause

cold
front

cold air

warm air

warm
front

cold air

B

direction of movement

tropopause

cold
front

cold air

warm air

warm
front

cold air

Frontal depressions

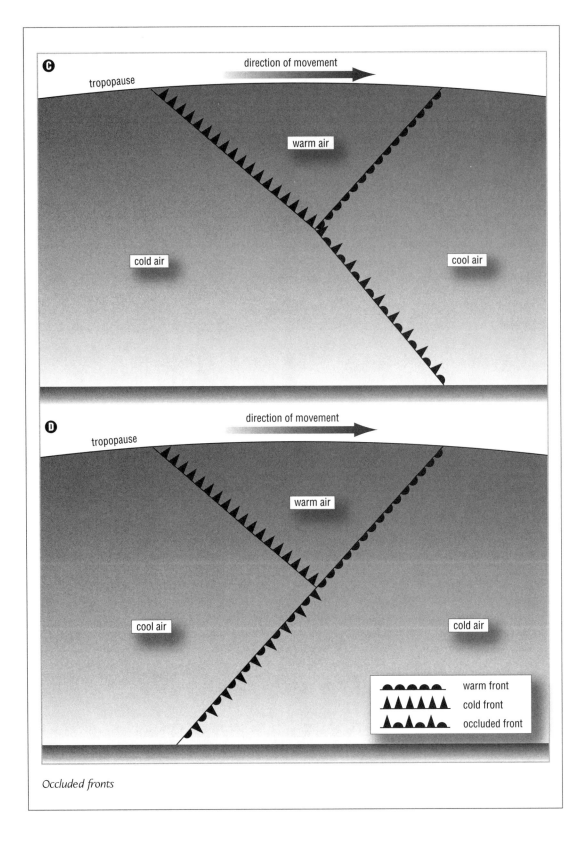

Occluded fronts

Jet stream

During World War II, when high-altitude flying was new, aircrews sometimes found their journey times radically different from those they had calculated prior to takeoff. The effect was not reliable enough to predict, but when flying from west to east they could find their ground speed (their speed in relation to the surface) dramatically increased and when flying in the opposite direction they were just as dramatically slowed. They had discovered what turned out to be a narrow, wavy ribbon of wind blowing at speeds comparable to those of their aircraft. They called it the *jet stream*.

If they approached the jet stream from above or below, pilots found the wind speed increased by about 37–73 MPH for every 1,000 feet of altitude (18–36 km/h per 1,000 m). If they approached from the side, it increased by the same amount for every 60 miles (100 km) of distance from the core of the jet stream. At the center of the stream, the wind speed averages about 65 MPH (105 km/h) but it sometimes reaches 310 MPH (500 km/h).

There are several jet streams. The polar front jet stream is located between about 30° N and 40° N in winter and about 40° N and 50° N in summer. There is an equivalent jet stream in the Southern Hemisphere. The subtropical jet stream is located at about 30° throughout the year in both hemispheres. These jet streams blow from west to east in both hemispheres. In summer there is also an easterly jet at about 2° N extending across Asia, southern Arabia, and into northeastern Africa. This jet stream blows from east to west.

The jet streams are *thermal winds*. That is to say, they are generated by the sharp difference in temperature across the front separating two air masses. This difference is greatest close to the tropopause, which is why the jet streams occur at high altitude—the polar front jet stream at about 30,000 feet (9,000 m) and the subtropical jet stream at about 40,000 feet (12,000 m). The polar front jet stream is associated with the polar front, separating polar air and tropical air. The temperature difference responsible for the subtropical jet stream occurs only in the upper troposphere, on the high-latitude side of the Hadley cells.

The polar jet stream is quite variable and often it is not present at all. The subtropical jet stream is more constant. Consequently, the term *jet stream* often refers simply to the subtropical jet stream and this is the one that is usually shown on maps.

low in air in the "warm" sector ahead of a "cold" front, provided it is lower still in the "cold" air behind the front. The map shows the usual distribution of air pressure over North America.

This is the distribution of pressure that results from the eastward movement of air masses. Over the Pacific, maritime air produces the low pressure in the west. As the air mass crosses the continent and becomes increasingly continental, its pressure increases to produce the two high-pressure regions. Maritime air over the Atlantic produces the low-pressure in the east. The pressure distribution is fairly constant, but it results from the ceaseless movement of air.

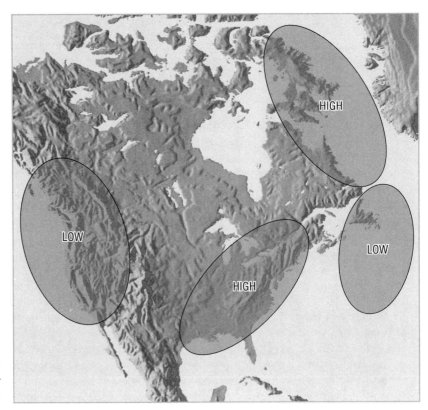

Usual distribution of air pressure over North America

Why warm air can hold more moisture than cold air can

Water molecules (H_2O) are *polar*. That is to say, there is a small positive charge on the hydrogen side of each molecule (H^+) and a negative charge on the oxygen side (O^-). The two charges balance, so the molecule is neutral overall, but the H^+ atoms of one molecule are attracted to the O^- atoms of its neighbors.

In liquid water, this attractive force links molecules together, by *hydrogen bonds*, into small groups. The groups can slide past each other and the bonds are constantly breaking and re-forming.

When its temperature rises, water molecules absorb heat energy. This allows them to move faster and strain against the hydrogen bonds. If they absorb enough energy they are able to break the bonds completely. Single molecules then leave the liquid. Single water molecules moving freely constitute *water vapor*.

If the temperature of the air decreases, the water vapor it contains will also cool. The water molecules then lose energy. If they lose sufficient energy, when water molecules collide they sometimes remain close to each other long enough for hydrogen bonds to form between them. They will then exist as liquid water and some of the water vapor will have condensed.

Consequently, if the air temperature rises, moisture in the air becomes warmer and more of its molecules are able to move freely, as water vapor. If the air temperature falls, water molecules lose energy, hydrogen bonds link them into groups, and the vapor condenses into liquid droplets.

ICE CAPS, GLACIERS, AND ICEBERGS

Blizzards consist of snow blown by the wind, and snow is a form of ice. Water freezes whenever the temperature falls below about 32°F (0°C). It is necessary to use the word *about*, because impurities in the water slightly alter its freezing temperature and so does pressure. Seawater, for example, contains about 35 parts of salt for every 1,000 parts of water. The salt is mainly sodium chloride (NaCl, or common salt) but a variety of other metal salts are also present. With this concentration of salt, the freezing temperature of water, at average sea-level atmospheric pressure, is about 28.5°F (–1.9°C). You can measure this difference in freezing temperature.

The freezing temperature also decreases by 0.014°F (0.008°C) for every one-atmosphere (1,000 millibars, 0.1 megapascals, 14.7 pounds per square inch, 1 kg per square centimeter) increase in pressure. This effect is very small, but extremely important. Atmospheric pressure cannot double, but the weight of other substances can easily amount to much more than 30 lb in^{-2} (2.2 kg cm^{-2}), enough to melt a layer of ice.

The Greenland and Antarctic ice sheets are so thick that their weight is enough to melt the ice at the base, so in some places there is a layer of water between the ice and the underlying rock. This lubricates the ice and greatly accelerates the movement of the glacier.

Where glaciers form

Winter temperatures fall below freezing in many parts of the world, but in some they seldom rise above it. Qaanaaq (formerly Thule), on the coast of northern Kalaallit Nunaat (the modern name for Greenland), has average temperatures that are above freezing from June to September, but they rise to a maximum of only 46°F (7.8°C) and they fall below freezing at night in June and September. In Antarctica temperatures rarely rise above freezing, even in summer, except briefly at the northernmost tip of the Antarctic Peninsula.

In many other parts of the world there are mountains high enough to have temperatures below freezing throughout the year, even in quite low latitudes. In the Himalayan valleys, temperatures in May and June reach about 100°F (37.8°C), but at elevations above 15,000 feet (4,575 m) they remain below freezing all year round. As they climb, mountaineers move from a tropical to an arctic climate, passing through temperate regions on the way. There are also permanent glaciers above 14,000 feet (4,270 m) in

Kenya, on the volcanic peaks of Mounts Kilimanjaro, Kenya, and Ruwen-zori, although the mountain glaciers in tropical Africa have been retreat-ing for more than a century. This is because the snowfall has been insufficient to compensate for natural losses of ice.

The polar ice caps

Where summer temperatures remain below freezing, or rise only briefly to slightly above it, snow does not melt. Each time it snows, the fresh snow lies on top of earlier falls and it stays there. Snow accumulates year after year and century after century. In time, the ground is buried deep beneath an ice sheet. There is some loss. Strong winds below loose snow up from the sur-face. The result is a blizzard, and blizzards may blow snow out over the sea or into an area where summers are a little warmer, and the snow will disap-pear. This type of loss is called *ablation*. Snow can also evaporate directly into very dry air. This direct change from solid to gas is called *sublimation*.

Where snow accumulates long enough it turns into ice, but polar and glacial ice does not form in the same way as the ice cubes you make in a freezer. Freezer ice is water that has been frozen, but over the ice sheets it is not liquid water that falls, but snow. The water is already frozen when it reaches the ground. What changes snow into solid ice is pressure—the weight of snow above it, pressing down. You can see the start of this process where ordinary winter snow has been packed down by people walking or cars driving over it. The snow becomes much more solid than it was when it first fell and you can no longer shovel it the way you shovel fresh snow. You have to chip it away in blocks. It is still snow, however. If the pressure on it had been a great deal heavier the snow would have turned into ice.

The Arctic and Antarctic ice caps and mountain glaciers are made from ice formed in this way. Scientists believe ice began to accumulate in East Antarctica about 35 million years ago and in West Antarctica (see map) perhaps 5 million years later. Not surprisingly, over that long period it has grown very thick. The thickness varies from place to place, but on average it is about 6,900 feet (2,100 m) and in some places the ice is more than 11,500 feet (3,500 m) thick. It makes Antarctica the highest continent in the world, as well as the coldest and driest. Between them, the West and East Antarctic ice sheets—separated by the Transantarctic Mountains—contain a total of more than 11.5 million cubic miles (48 million km³) of ice. That is about 90 percent of all the ice in the world.

Greenland is the largest land area in the Arctic. There, ice covers more than 708,000 square miles (1.83 million km²) to an average thickness of about 5,000 feet (1,525 m).

There is more ice in the Antarctic than in the Arctic, because Antarctica is a continent, whereas most of the area within the Arctic Cir-cle is sea. The Arctic Ocean is affected by warm currents flowing north

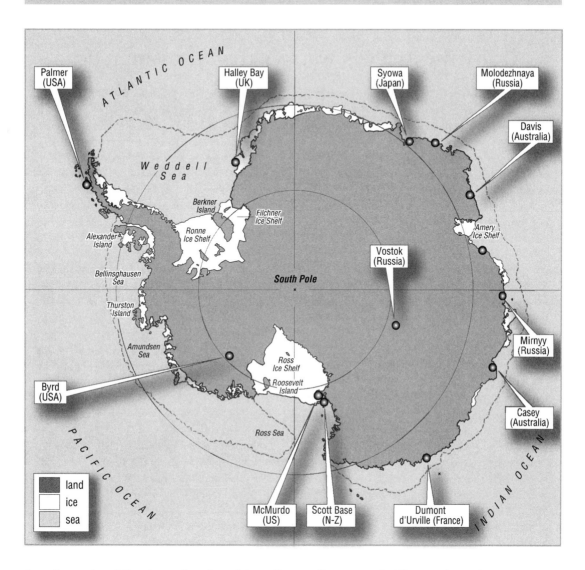

Antarctica

(see the section "Continental and maritime climates," pages 1–8). These prevent temperatures falling as low as those in Antarctica (see the sidebar "Why the Arctic is warmer than the Antarctic," page 22). Between them, the polar ice caps together with mountain glaciers in lower latitudes hold three-quarters of all the freshwater on Earth.

How glaciers move

A large expanse of thick ice is called an *ice sheet* or a *glacier*. The two words mean the same thing and although many people think of a glacier as a river

Why the Arctic is warmer than the Antarctic

Vostok is the name of a Russian research station in Antarctica, located at about 78.75° S. Qaanaaq is a small town in northern Kalaallit Nunaat (Greenland), at 76.55° N.

They are in similar latitudes, but they have very different climates. At Vostok, January is the warmest month, when the average temperature is –26°F (–32°C). The coldest month is August, with an average temperature of –90°F (–68°C). At Qaanaaq, the average temperature ranges from a high of 46°F (8°C) in July to a low of –21°F (–29°C) in February.

Both places are dry, despite all the snow and ice. Qaanaaq has an annual rainfall (it falls as snow in winter, of course, but is converted to the equivalent amount of rainfall) of 2.5 inches (64 mm). Vostok has 0.2 inch (4.5 mm).

The temperature range is similar for both: 64°F (36°C) at Vostok and 67°F (37°C) at Qaanaaq. The difference is that Vostok is much colder than Qaanaaq. This is because Qaanaaq is on the coast, albeit of an ocean that is frozen over for much of the year, and Vostok is in the interior of a large continent. The North Pole is located in the Arctic Ocean and the Arctic Basin is sea, surrounded by Eurasia, North America, and Kalaallit Nunaat.

A large ice sheet covers East Antarctica, where Vostok is located. Air subsiding into the permanent Antarctic high-pressure region flows outward as a bitterly cold, extremely dry wind that blows almost incessantly. This, combined with its elevation—Vostok is 13,000 feet (3,950 m) above sea level, on top of the thick ice—is what gives Vostok its cold, dry climate.

The continent also receives 7 percent less solar radiation than the Arctic does, because in the middle of winter (June) the South Pole is 3 million miles (4.8 million km) further from the Sun than the North Pole is in the middle of its winter (December).

Qaanaaq is at sea level, but its elevation is not the principal reason for its warmer climate. It is warmer because of the sea. Ocean currents carry warm water into the Arctic Basin. The sea is frozen for most of the year, but there are gaps in the ice called *leads* that appear and disappear. Winds move the ice, piling it up in some places and leaving it thin in others. Heat escapes from the ocean where there are open water surfaces, but ice insulates the areas it covers. The sea temperature never falls below 29°F (–1.6°C); below this temperature, the water approaches its greatest density and sinks below warmer water that flows in at the surface to replace it. When the air temperature over the water falls below the temperature of the sea surface, heat passes from the water to the air. This warmer air then moves across the ice. Consequently, air temperatures over the entire Arctic Basin are much higher than they would be if there were land rather than sea beneath the ice.

Antarctica is isolated from other continents. The Southern Ocean surrounds the continent and the West Wind Drift, or Antarctic Circumpolar Current, flows around it from west to east, carrying cold water. There is no land to interrupt the flow and this isolation is an important reason for the extreme Antarctic climate.

The coldest temperature recorded over the ice in the Arctic is –58°F (–50°C), and over most of the Arctic Basin the average temperature ranges between approximately 4°F (–20°C) and –40°F (–40°C). On July 21, 1983, the temperature at Vostok fell to –128.6°F (–89.2°C).

of ice, scientists use them interchangeably. The "river of ice" is a *valley glacier*. Whichever name you use, if it is thick enough the ice will usually flow.

An ice sheet forms in a region where the summer temperature does not remain high enough for long enough to melt all the snow that fell the previous winter. Year by year, the snow accumulates and its weight com-

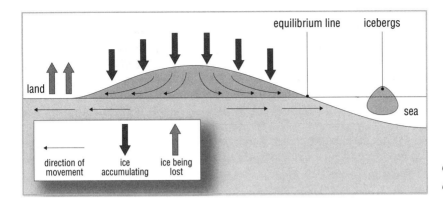

Cross section of an ice sheet

presses the lower layers into ice. The ice is thinner around the edges of this region, because there the summers are a little warmer and more winter snow is lost. There is an *equilibrium line* where the amount of ice the glacier gains each year is equal to the amount it loses. Beyond the equilibrium line the glacier loses ice faster than it gains it. Consequently, the ice sheet grows into a dome, as is shown in the diagram.

The pressure is not distributed evenly inside the ice dome, because the ice mass is greatest at the center and decreases with distance from the center. This deforms the ice so it is squeezed out around the edges. Ice flows past the equilibrium line, growing steadily thinner, until all of it has melted. Provided there is sufficient mass, the ice will deform and flow regardless of the roughness of the underlying rock surface, but it will flow much faster if there is a layer of water beneath the ice to act as a lubricant.

Mountain glaciers begin as *ice fields*—large areas at high elevations that are covered with snow and ice all year round. Once the ice is thick enough to start flowing, it spills out of the ice field and down the side of the mountain, wearing away the rocks and making its own valley. It is then a valley glacier. Many mountain glaciers have been retreating since the late 19th century as the equilibrium line has moved higher.

Glaciers that flow because they melt at the base are known as temperate (or warm). They form well outside the Arctic and Antarctic Circles and move out from large snow and ice fields at higher altitudes, continuing until they reach a level where the temperature is high enough to melt them. Most flow a few inches or a few feet a day, but some can travel as much as 150 feet (46 m) in a day. Not all of the glacier flows at the same speed. Glaciers flow faster at the center than at the sides, where the movement is slowed by friction against the valley walls, faster in the middle than near the head or foot, and the surface flows more slowly than the ice beneath.

It is the movement of the plastic ice—solid ice that changes its shape under extreme pressure—at the base that carries all the overlying ice with it. The ice above the deformed layer is hard and brittle and its flow across an uneven surface makes it break, causing long, deep cracks, called *crevasses*, in the upper layers. The surface of a glacier is very uneven and in places it may consist of a jumbled mass of ice blocks called a *serac*, but there may be liquid water beneath the base. In summer, when some surface snow melts, water may trickle down through crevasses all the way to the rock beneath. Water from melting snow may also run off the ice at the head of the glacier and penetrate beneath the glacier. Some of the glaciers flowing from the Greenland ice sheet are lubricated by water from surface melting that trickles down through crevasses. These glaciers move about 12 inches (30 cm) a day in winter, but about 15 inches (38 cm) a day in summer.

Polar (or cold) glaciers form in high latitudes, where the climate is very much colder and the temperature at the base of the glacier is well below the pressure melting point. The ice will still move, even if there is no melting at its base, provided its weight is sufficient to push the middle and upper layers down the slope, dragging the lower layers with them. Because no melting is involved, polar glaciers flow more slowly than temperate glaciers.

When it meets an obstacle, a moving ice sheet will be pushed hard against it by the weight of ice behind that is still flowing downhill. The forward edge will be forced upward against the obstruction and many mountain glaciers end in an upturned section called a *snout*. Unless the end of the glacier has entered a region where temperatures are above freezing for several months of the year, the obstacle may check the flow only temporarily. In time, as the pressure is sustained and more snow continues to fall and thicken the sheet, the ice will spill over the obstacle and continue on its way.

Ice shelves and icebergs

Eventually the ice sheet arrives at a coast, but this does not halt its progress. Close to the shore, where the water is shallow, the ice presses on along the seabed. When it reaches deeper water it floats (see the section "What happens when water freezes and ice melts," page 99). Ice then extends beyond the coastline and hides it completely. In Antarctica, several ice sheets float out over the sea to form huge ice shelves. The Ross Ice Shelf, over the Ross Sea, is the largest—it it is about the size of France—and the Ronne Ice Shelf, over the Weddell Sea, is almost as large, although it is wrapped around several islands. The Filchner and Larsen Ice Shelves are much smaller. All of these are named after Antarctic explorers. Big ice shelves are between about 550 feet (168 m) and more than 1,000 feet (300 m) thick. There are fewer ice shelves in the Arctic.

Near the coast, an ice shelf rests securely on the land or on the shallow seabed. Further out, however, at a location known as the *grounding line*, the ice loses contact with the solid surface and floats. The shelf is then affected by vertical movements of the water. From time to time, these cause a section to break away from the edge of the shelf as an *iceberg*. In the Antarctic, icebergs are often shaped like tables, flat-topped, up to about 115 feet (35 m) high, and often several square miles in area. A few icebergs form in the Arc-

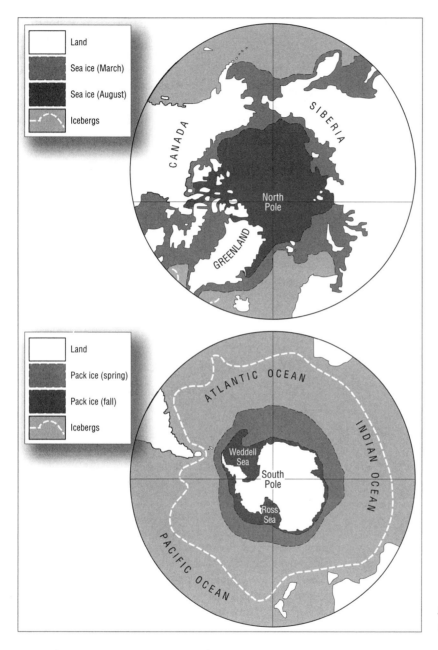

Sea ice, pack ice, and icebergs

tic in the same way and can drift for years in the Arctic Ocean. They are called *ice islands*, and scientific bases have been established on some of them to monitor their movements. Most Arctic icebergs are not like this, however. They are made from ice that has broken away from valley glaciers flowing into the sea from the surrounding lands, rather than ice shelves. This makes them denser than Antarctic icebergs, because they form under greater pressure, and darker in color, because they contain soil and rock scoured from the land surface. Few are more than about half a mile (800 m) long, but they can rise nearly 200 feet (61 m) above the sea surface and extend more than 800 feet (244 m) below it. Freed from the main body of ice, they drift with the ocean currents and sometimes enter shipping lanes. In 1912, a collision with one such iceberg sank the liner *Titanic*. For this reason, their positions are monitored by satellites and reported to ships.

As they enter warmer waters, icebergs start to melt and break into smaller pieces. An iceberg about the size of a house is called a *bergy bit* and one less than 30 feet (10 m) long is a *growler*.

The two maps show how far icebergs can travel in the North Atlantic and around Antarctica before they melt completely. The maps also show the area within which the sea itself freezes, the edge of the sea ice advancing in winter and retreating in summer, but with a considerable area that remains frozen permanently. Winds and waves constantly break up sea ice while it is forming. They carry it this way and that, piling it into various shapes. It is called *pack ice* when it covers a large area. Sailors know when they are approaching pack ice. They see what looks like a white light, called an *ice blink*, above the horizon, caused by light reflected from the ice.

North Atlantic Deep Water and the Great Conveyor

When seawater freezes, the salt is left behind and crystals of freshwater ice form. Later, the crystals start joining together as an oily-looking coating of slush called *frazil ice*, and pockets of salt water are trapped between crystals. At first, though, the ice contains no salt, but the water adjacent to the ice is saltier than water further away, because it contains the "squeezed-out" salt. This added salt makes the water denser and lowers its freezing temperature. It is also at the temperature at which water reaches its maximum density (see the section "What happens when water freezes and ice melts," page 99). This dense water sinks to the ocean floor and flows south as a slow-moving current called the *North Atlantic Deep Water* (NADW), that travels all the way to Antarctica. Its place at the surface is taken by warmer water flowing north.

It is the formation of sea ice in the North Atlantic that drives the system of ocean currents known as the *Great Conveyor*. The Great Conveyor helps regulate the global climate by transporting warm water away from the equator and cold water toward the equator.

Sea ice affects the climate in another way. Farmers and gardeners know that a cover of snow protects the plants beneath it by insulating them. Snow is a poor conductor of heat, so a layer of snow greatly reduces any further cooling of the covered surface. Snow also falls on frozen sea and, because the temperature of the sea ice is already below freezing, it settles. In time it can form a thick layer. This reduces the rate at which the temperature falls in the water beneath the ice.

When the conveyor weakens or fails

The Great Conveyor has flowed reliably throughout recorded history. Quite naturally, we think of it as permanent and reliable. Scientists now believe this long period of stability is unusual, however, and that the pattern of ocean currents changed often in the past. On at least six occasions between 70,000 and 16,000 years ago, for example, vast numbers of icebergs broke away from the thick Laurentide ice sheet covering much of North America and drifted out to sea. The icebergs carried with them rocks and soil scoured from the land and as they melted, these materials sank to the bottom of the ocean. The German oceanographer Hartmut Heinrich recognized them, and in 1988 he described what must have happened. These sudden iceberg releases are called *Heinrich events*.

Icebergs are made from freshwater. When the Laurentide icebergs melted, they covered a large part of the ocean with a surface layer of freshwater that floated on top of the denser salt water. This froze at a higher temperature than salt water, chilled the air crossing it, and brought cold weather to the Northern Hemisphere generally. Europe was especially affected, because the edge of the sea ice shifted, interrupting the formation of NADW. That caused the North Atlantic Drift to cease flowing. The whole of the Gulf Stream turned south in the latitude of Spain, depriving northwestern Europe of the warm water that now bathes its shores.

Scientists know of two such events when temperatures plummeted and ice sheets advanced. Around the edges of the ice the vegetation was typical of alpine and high-latitude environments. It included a pretty alpine plant called mountain avens *(Dryas octopetala)*. Its pollen is found in places that are now much too warm for it to occur naturally, but it has been there for thousands of years and its presence tells scientists that the climate in these places was once much older. These episodes are known as the Older Dryas, from about 12,200 years ago to about 11,800 years ago, and the Younger Dryas, lasting from about 11,000 years ago until about 10,000 years ago. During both Dryas periods the climate was plunged back into the ice age.

READING PAST WEATHER FROM ICE SHEETS

Antarctica is a harsh, unforgiving place. Apart from tourists who stay a day or two, only scientists spend long periods there and, as the map of Antarctica on page 21 shows, most of the research stations are near the coast, within easy reach of the ships that supply them. About 40 of the stations are permanently occupied and there are up to 100 temporary research stations on the continent. Between them they accommodate more than 4,000 scientists and support staff—doctors, dentists, maintenance engineers, carpenters, and so forth—during the summer and fewer than 1,000 during the winter.

The U.S. Amundsen-Scott Station is almost at the South Pole itself, at 89.997° S; the South Pole is at 90° S. Vostok, the Russian station at 78.47° S, is the only other permanent inland station. Opened in 1957, it stayed open all year round until 1994, when it had to close for the winter because tractor trains were unable to deliver fuel to it from the coast. The Vostok staff were compelled to overwinter at the Mirnyy station on the coast, but Vostok reopened the following summer.

Vostok scientists reported the lowest temperature over recorded on Earth, on July 21, 1983. That day their thermometers read –128.6°F (–89.2°C). In the winter of 1997, Vostok scientists reported an even lower temperature, –132°F (–91°C), but the measurement was not confirmed and so the record remains unofficial. Solid carbon dioxide (dry ice) sublimes into the gas at –108.4°F (–78°C), so on those extremely cold days the snow lying on the surface would have consisted of a mixture of water ice and dry ice.

Despite the intense cold at the surface, deep below the ice there are lakes. The biggest of these, Lake Vostok, is about the size of Lake Ontario. It lies beneath Vostok Station and is of great scientific importance, not least because it may contain living organisms that have been isolated from all other organisms for millions of years. There may also be liquid water below the ice covering the surfaces of Europa and Ganymede, two of the moons of Jupiter, and perhaps the Europan ocean supports life. If so, it would be the first extraterrestrial life to be discovered. The sidebar "Lake Vostok, Europa, and Ganymede" on page 29 describes these strange lakes and oceans.

Reading tree rings and ice cores

Vostok is located in a place where the ice sheet is very thick, and the Russian and French scientists who work there use the ice sheet itself to study

Lake Vostok, Europa, and Ganymede

Most of the continent of Antarctica lies buried beneath ice sheets that in places are several miles thick and the climate is far too cold for water to exist at the surface as a liquid. Deep beneath the ice, however, there are more than 70 lakes. The largest of these is Lake Vostok, located below Vostok Station, near the South Geomagnetic Pole and about 1,000 miles (1,600 km) from the geographic South Pole.

The surface of Lake Vostok is 2.4 miles (4 km) below the surface of the ice sheet. It is buried so deeply, and the ice sheet is so ancient, that Lake Vostok has been isolated from the outside world for up to 35 million years. The overlying ice sheet is moving very slowly. This movement carries water out of the eastern side of the lake as ice on the underside of the ice sheet, but replenishes the liquid water at the same rate. The new water comes either from some source beneath the ice, or from melting of the underside of the ice as it makes contact with the lake; at present no one knows. Scientists calculate that none of the water in the lake is less than 400,000 years old and, because it is derived from the base of the ice sheet, it has been isolated much longer than that.

The lake is about 140 miles (225 km) long by 30 miles (48 km) wide, and an average of 3,000 feet (914 m) deep. This is about the size of Lake Ontario.

As soon as the existence of Lake Vostok was confirmed in 1996, scientists agreed that it should remain undisturbed until they had devised a way to sample its water without contaminating it in any way. If the lake harbors living organisms, these will have been isolated for so long that they are of immense scientific interest and importance. Conse-

quently, drilling for an ice core above the lake was halted when the drill was about 492 feet (150 m) above the lake surface. In 1999 a variety of microorganisms were found in ice to the east of the lake that had once been part of the lake water. The water itself has not yet been sampled.

Once a way has been found to sample the Lake Vostok water safely, investigators hope to be able to adapt the method to study an even more tantalizing environment—Europa. Europa is one of the four Galilean moons of Jupiter, so called because it was discovered by Galileo (on January 7, 1610). It was not until the *Voyager* spacecraft photographed it in 1979, however, that people on Earth were able to see Europa's surface clearly. Since then it has been studied closely.

Europa is covered by ice, but the ice is far from smooth. Huge blocks project above the surface and there are deep cracks. These are features produced by tidal forces as Europa orbits Jupiter and suggest that the outer surface is hard and brittle, but beneath the ice there is liquid water—an ocean covering the entire moon. The expansion and contraction due to tidal forces that fractures the ice also releases heat into the water beneath the ice, leading scientists to speculate on the possibility of life. One day it may be possible to land a probe on the surface of Europa and search for traces of living organisms.

Ganymede, another of the Galilean moons of Jupiter, is also covered by ice. Beneath the rigid ice of the outer layer, the ice may be soft and there may even be liquid water. The warmth to melt the ice partly or completely is derived from the gravitational tidal forces generated by Jupiter. Perhaps Ganymede and Europa both support some form of life.

past climates. Two other projects do similar work in the Northern Hemisphere, at a place called Summit, in central Greenland. The United States operates the Greenland Ice Sheet Project 2 (GISP 2), and about 19 miles (30 km) away European scientists operate the Greenland Ice Core Project (GRIP). All these research projects involve drilling vertically deep into the ice and removing cores for examination. The sidebar "Vostok, GISP, and GRIP" on this page describes these projects and their results in more detail.

With many tree species (but not all) you can tell the age of a tree by counting the annual growth rings. Each spring and early summer the tree produces new cells. These are large, with thin walls, and they are pale in color. In late summer the tree produces smaller cells, with thicker walls, which are dark in color. As new growth around the outside thickens the trunk and branches, the older cells die and form the heartwood of the tree. Their history survives, however, as narrow bands of pale wood separated by rings of dark wood, one pair of pale and dark rings for each year of the tree's life. These are the tree rings, or annual growth rings, that you see whenever a tree trunk or large branch is severed.

By counting the rings it is possible not only to calculate the age of the tree, but also the growing conditions each year, because trees grow faster, producing wider rings, in good weather than they do in bad weather. It is not necessary to fell the tree in order to examine its rings. A drill with a cylindrical cutter can take a thin core of wood that serves just as well.

Vostok, GISP, and GRIP

Vostok is the name (the word means "east") of a Russian research station in Antarctica, at the geomagnetic South Pole, 78.46° S, 106.87° E, and at an elevation of 11,401 feet (3,475 m), on the surface of the East Antarctic ice sheet (see the map on page 21). The station was opened on December 16, 1957. Work began in 1980 on drilling through the ice sheet at a point near the station that is 11,444 feet (3,488 m) above sea level. A core of ice was removed from the borehole. In 1985 drilling reached a depth of 7,225 feet (2,202 m). It was impossible to drill this hole deeper, but drilling of a second hole began in 1984. In 1989 this became a joint Russian-French-U.S. project. In 1990 the hole (and core) reached a final depth of 8,353 feet (2,546 m). A third hole, started in 1990, reached 11,887 feet (3,623 m) in 1998.

The Vostok ice cores contain a record of climate that goes back about 420,000 years. So far, analysis has revealed the record over the last 200,000 years.

The Greenland Ice Sheet Project (GISP) is a U.S. program, sponsored by the National Science Foundation (NSF), to retrieve ice cores from the Greenland ice sheet. The first core reached bedrock at a depth of about 9,843 feet (3,000 m), and in 1988 the NSF Office of Polar Programs authorized the drilling of a second hole, GISP2. This was completed on July 1, 1993, after the drill had penetrated 5 feet (1.55 m) into the underlying bedrock. The ice core was 10,018.34 feet (3,053.44 m) long. Ice at the base of the core is about 200,000 years old and analysis of the GISP2 core has yielded a detailed record of climate over more than 110,000 years.

The Greenland Ice Core Project (GRIP) is a European program organized through the European Science Foundation and funded by the European Union and Belgium, Denmark, France, Germany, Iceland, Italy, Switzerland, and the United Kingdom. Drilling began in January 1989, and on August 12, 1992, it reached bedrock at 9,938 feet (3,029 m), where the ice is about 200,000 years old.

GISP2 and GRIP are located close to Summit, the highest point on the Greenland ice sheet, chosen to provide the longest cores, at 72.6°N, 38.5°W. The map on page 31 shows its location.

Ice cores are very like this, only thicker, and they can be dated in the same way, because each year's accumulation of snow is compressed into a layer that can be seen as a band. This banding allows scientists to mark each core with a scale of years before they take samples for analysis. These samples include the ice itself, tiny air bubbles trapped in the ice, and solid particles that fell onto the ice and were then buried.

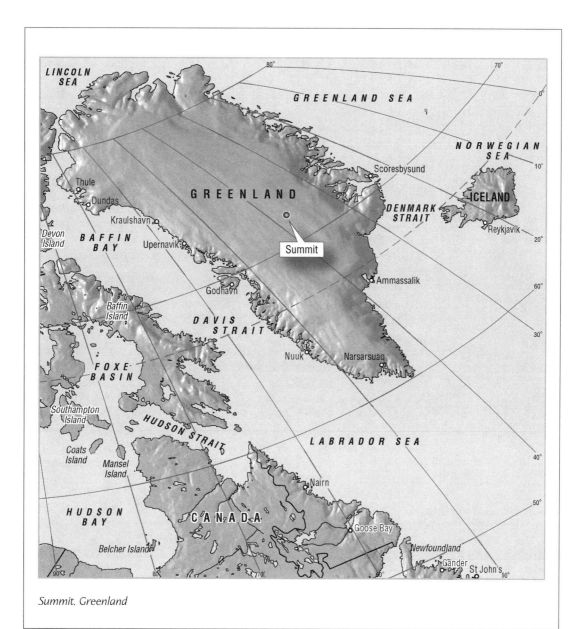

Summit, Greenland

Oxygen isotopes

Ice is made from water, and every water molecule comprises one atom of hydrogen and two of oxygen, but not all oxygen atoms are identical. There are three common isotopes of oxygen, written as ^{16}O, ^{17}O, and ^{18}O. Ordinary oxygen is 99.76 percent ^{16}O, 0.04 percent ^{17}O, and 0.20 percent ^{18}O. Chemically the atoms are exactly the same, because their nuclei possess the same number of protons (eight) and it is the protons, carrying positive electromagnetic charge, that give an element its chemical properties. Their nuclei contain different number of neutrons, however. Neutrons carry no charge, so they have no chemical influence, but they add mass to the nucleus, and the higher the isotope number the heavier is the atom.

Scientists analyzing ice cores are interested only in ^{16}O and ^{18}O. In the atmosphere today there is about one atom of ^{18}O to every 500 atoms of ^{16}O, but in water and ice these proportions may be different. Water molecules containing ^{16}O (written as $H_2{}^{16}O$) are lighter than $H_2{}^{18}O$ molecules and because of this they evaporate at a slightly lower temperature. In warm weather, therefore, when the rate of evaporation is high, the atmosphere contains a greater proportion of ^{16}O and, as this water falls in precipitation, so does the rain and in polar regions the snow. The lower the proportion of ^{18}O compared with ^{16}O in the ice, the colder the air was when the original snow fell.

When snow is compacted into ice, countless tiny bubbles of air are trapped in it. These are also recovered from the ice and analyzed. Scientists believe the proportion of ^{18}O in air depends on the proportion in seawater. This is because evaporation removes $H_2{}^{16}O$ faster than it removes $H_2{}^{18}O$, so that evaporation depletes the seawater of ^{16}O and therefore increases the proportion of ^{18}O. If some of the water vapor then condenses and falls as snow, and becomes incorporated into the polar ice sheets, the seawater will remain enriched in ^{18}O. Water that evaporates later will also be enriched in ^{18}O and enriched water vapor will alter the proportion of the two isotopes in air bubbles, containing water vapor, trapped in the ice. By examining the oxygen trapped in air bubbles, scientists can calculate the size of the ice sheets at the time the snow fell.

Ice sheets and sea levels

Ice sheets grow by accumulating water that has evaporated from the sea. This alters the sea level, because when water is taken from the sea its level falls, so the oxygen in ice cores also provides information about past sea levels. If the present East and West Antarctic Ice Sheets were to melt, for example, seas throughout the world would rise, probably by up to 200 feet (61 m). Then, over thousands of years, the ocean floors would sink under the additional weight of water, lowering sea level by about 65 feet (20 m), and Antarctica itself would rise because the weight of the ice had been removed. Sea levels are affected by factors other than the size of the ice sheets, but none produces effects so quickly.

Even with global warming, no one supposes this will happen in the foreseeable future. The East Antarctic Ice Sheet lies on solid rock and is very stable. It accounts for about two-thirds of the ice in Antarctica and is separated from the West Antarctic Ice Sheet (WAIS) by the Transantarctic Mountains. The WAIS extends from the coast to cover offshore islands and to cover large bays in the Ross and Weddell Seas with ice shelves. Some of the ice shelves have grown smaller in recent decades—especially the Larsen Ice Shelf extending from the northern part of the Antarctic Peninsula, just outside the Antarctic Circle. This has no effect on sea level, because shelf ice is already in the sea and does not add any more water to it if the ice melts. The WAIS has been gradually growing thinner for the last 10,000 years, but scientists believe this trend may have reversed and that the ice sheet is now becoming thicker.

Trapped greenhouse gases

Air bubbles have still more to tell. As well as oxygen and nitrogen, the principal constituents of our atmosphere, they contain carbon dioxide and methane. These are so-called *greenhouse gases* that absorb long-wave radiation and warm the atmosphere (see the section "Will climate change bring fewer blizzards?" on page 173). If the bubbles contain more or less of them than the air does today, it suggests that when they became trapped between snow crystals the air was warmer or cooler than it is now. This is only part of their story, however. Although scientists are confident that if we add more of these gases to the air the climate will grow warmer, it does not follow that in the distant past warming and cooling were caused by changes in the concentration of them. The changes may have been a response to climate change, rather than its cause.

Apart from certain bacteria, all living things obtain the energy they need by oxidizing carbon, a chemical reaction that releases energy and produces carbon dioxide that is returned to the air. The process is respiration (not to be confused with breathing, which is the means we use to take oxygen into and remove carbon dioxide from our bodies). Plants obtain carbon by the process of photosynthesis and animals by consuming the carbon in plants or in other animals.

Ordinarily, the amount of carbon dioxide removed from the air by photosynthesis is equal to the amount returned to the air by respiration, so the atmospheric concentration of carbon dioxide remains constant. If living conditions suddenly improve, however, plants will grow more vigorously and use more carbon dioxide. For a time, the atmospheric concentration will fall. The balance will be restored when animals increase in number, because more food is available and respiration catches up with photosynthesis. In deteriorating conditions, plants will grow less well and there will be less food for animals. As the total quantity of living material (called the *biomass*) becomes smaller, respiration by organisms that decompose formerly living matter will overtake photosynthesis and surplus carbon dioxide will accumulate in the atmosphere. The carbon dioxide content of the air is difficult to interpret, but it can give clues to climates of the past.

Methane is easier to understand. It is released by certain groups of bacteria, some of which live in the digestive system of animals but most of which live below the surface in waterlogged mud. Oxygen poisons them if it occurs free, as a gas, so they inhabit only airless places. They thrive best in warm conditions, so the warmer the climate, the more active they will be and, therefore, the more methane they will release.

Dust

Ice sheets also collect not only air but dust. This, too, contains clues to past climates. Air always contains dust, but the amount varies. Rain and snow wash dust particles from the air. That is why the air often feels much fresher after a rain shower. Individual dust particles rarely remain airborne for more than a few hours before being washed to the ground, but they can stay aloft much longer in dry weather.

When the Sun is low in the sky, around dawn and sunset, its light has to pass through a greater thickness of air than it does when the Sun is higher. If there are enough dust particles in the air they will scatter the shorter blue, green, and yellow wavelengths of light so only red light passes and the sky looks red in the direction of the Sun. The dust indicates dusty air, which is therefore dry, and dry air means fine weather. In middle latitudes, weather systems usually travel from west to east, so if you see a red sky at sunset, in the west, the dry air causing it will reach you in a few hours and the following day will be fine (unless the system is moving so fast that the fine weather passes you during the night). A red sky at dawn, on the other hand, means the dry air is to the east and has already passed, so there is no guarantee of a fine day to follow. This, of course, is the origin of the old saying: "Red sky at night, shepherd's delight; Red sky in the morning, shepherd's warning." It is one piece of weather lore that is fairly reliable.

Eventually, all the dust falls to the ground. Rain and snow simply bring it down faster, often before it has had time to travel very far. Once an ice sheet covers land, dust can no longer be blown up from the surface, so dust in the air over an ice sheet has probably traveled a long way. For that to happen, the air must be dry over a large part of the planet. Dust falling on an ice sheet sticks to the ice crystals and in time is buried beneath later falls of snow. In this way it becomes incorporated in the ice and can be detected in ice cores. If these show that the amount of dust increased during a particular period, it strongly suggests the global climate during that period was relatively dry.

Over the world as a whole, dry weather means cold weather. When temperatures are low, less water evaporates, so there is less cloud and, therefore, less rain and snow. If the weather remains cold for a long time, the ice sheets and glaciers will expand. They take water from the sea, causing the sea level to fall, and the fall in sea level exposes more dry land. Overall, more land is exposed than is covered by the ice sheets themselves, and the combined effect of an increased land area and generally dry climates is to allow more dust to be blown into the air.

Volcanic ash

The dust trapped in ancient ice provides another clue to past weather, but the type of dust also provides valuable clues. Volcanic eruptions inject vast quantities of ash into the air, and volcanic ash can be identified. This knowledge is valuable, because volcanic eruptions sometimes affect the climate. Much of the volcanic ash is washed to the ground in a matter of days, like any other dust, but a really violent eruption can throw minute particles into the stratosphere, where they remain for months or even years. They consist mainly of sulfur dioxide, which reacts to form microscopically small droplets of sulfuric acid. While they are there, these particles reflect incoming sunlight, cooling the surface beneath them, and stratospheric air currents can spread this volcanic blanket right around the world, producing a marked cooling in the climate. When Mt. Pinatubo, in the Philippines, erupted in June 1991, within three weeks a belt of sulfuric acid particles covered 40 percent of the world and reduced surface temperatures for several years, but some past eruptions have had a much greater effect. The eruption of Mt. Tambora, in what is now Indonesia, threw about 35 cubic miles (146 km^3) of dust and fragments into the air. That eruption was in 1815, and because of the particles it threw into the stratosphere, 1816 became known as the year with no summer. Mt. Krakatau, which erupted in 1883, ejected about five cubic miles (21 km^3) of material and caused magnificent red sunsets the following year, as well as a slight fall in temperature.

Ice cores record the evidence of past volcanic activity, and this can be related to changes in climate. Usually these are small, but if the climate was already starting to cool, a violent eruption might accelerate the process.

Sediments, pollen, corals, and beetles

Lakebed and seabed sediments store information much like that contained in ice sheets, but most sediments have accumulated over a shorter period and their record is not so long. Sediments contain the crushed shells of aquatic animals—microscopic marine animals called *foraminiferans* are especially important. The shells are made from calcium carbonate ($CaCO_3$). The animals obtain the carbonate from the water, where it is present as bicarbonate (HCO_3), formed when atmospheric carbon dioxide (CO_2) dissolves. The reactions are:

$$CO_2 + H_2O \rightarrow H_2CO_3 \ (1)$$
$$H_2CO_3 \rightarrow HCO_3 + H \ (2)$$

One of the oxygen atoms in $CaCO_3$ is derived from the water, and therefore the $CaCO_3$ will record the ^{16}O:^{18}O ratio in the water at the time the carbonate formed. If the proportion of ^{18}O is high it means that ice was accumulating around the poles and depleting the water of ^{16}O. A fall in the ^{18}O content indicates that the ice sheets were melting.

Pollen grains, which are covered in a coat so tough they survive in the soil almost indefinitely, can be identified as coming from a particular kind of plant and most plants grow only in certain climates. Many small animals survive only within a narrow temperature and humidity range. Beetles are especially useful in this respect and so are some marine animals. Corals, for example, build reefs only in clear water, about 30–200 feet (9–61 m) deep, at a temperature between 68°F and 82°F (20–28°C). Some fossil reefs are much thicker than 200 feet (61 m), suggesting they continued to grow upward as the sea level slowly rose.

Corals, the wing cases (elytra) of beetles, and pollen grains are valuable indicators of past climates. Much can also be read from the landscape itself. Valleys and lakes made by glaciers are not difficult to recognize. Yet none of these provides the continuous record over more than 100,000 years that can be read from ice cores.

Scientists who study very ancient climates are called paleoclimatologists. The weather leaves many clues. The more we know about past climates the better we will be able to calculate ways in which the climates of the world may change in years to come. We will learn how resistant to change climates are and what is most likely to trigger changes. How it changes will determine whether severe winter storms and blizzards come to afflict wider areas in the future, or whether they retreat until they survive only in history books.

POLAR DESERTS, WHERE BLIZZARDS ARE COMMON

Blizzards happen suddenly in polar regions. Most of the time the sky is clear blue and the light reflected by the snow is dazzling, so travelers wear dark glasses or goggles to protect their eyes. The air is almost still. Then, without warning, the wind starts to blow, quickly picking up to 30 MPH (48 km/h) or more, with frequent gusts at more than twice that speed. Loose snow is whipped up from the surface into a great whirling cloud. Everything is white, the sky merging with the land so it is impossible to tell where one ends and the other begins. Visibility is reduced to a few yards and for the traveler there is no alternative but to stop. Landmarks have vanished; all directions look the same, and although the compass might indicate the direction in which to proceed, it cannot reveal obstacles, such as deep crevasses. A fall into a crevasse could be fatal—although scientists working in this environment are trained to avoid such hazards.

Close to the geomagnetic poles, even a magnetic compass must be used with care. As the two maps show, the magnetic poles are a long distance from the geographic poles. Compass needles align themselves with the geomagnetic field and point to magnetic north, so the two poles may be in entirely different directions.

Blizzards faced by explorers

In winter, of course, blizzards are even more bewildering, because they happen in twilight or total darkness. The only consolation they bring is that Antarctic winter blizzards bring a rapid rise in temperature of up to 32°F (18°C), but very few people venture far from shelter in winter. In summer, blizzards are cold. The temperature falls.

Once a blizzard starts, there is no telling how long it may last. Some fade after a few hours, others continue for days. At the end of their ill-fated march to the South Pole in 1912, a blizzard that lasted nine days confined the three survivors of the Scott Expedition to their tent, where their frozen bodies were found some months later. In the Antarctic winter of 1989, a party set out to cross the continent. They encountered strong winds, sometimes reaching 90 MPH (145 km/h), for almost the entire journey, and temperatures fell to –49°F (–45°C.) One storm lasted for 60 days. On another occasion, the party endured a 17-day-long blizzard.

Adélie Land, the region of Antarctica nearest Tasmania, has been called the home of the blizzard. At Byrd Station (80° S 120° W; see the map of Antarctica on page 21) the winds are strong enough to produce blizzards for about 65 percent of the time, and for nearly one-third of the time they reduce visibility to zero.

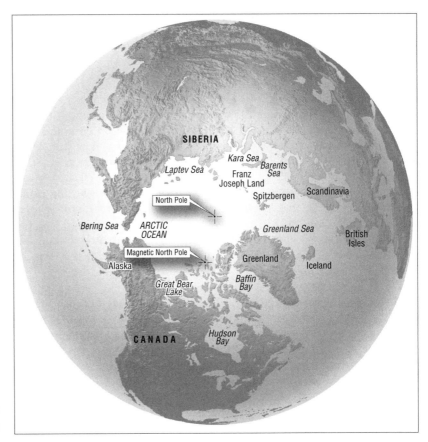

Magnetic and geographic North Poles

The difference between the Arctic and the Antarctic

Snow covers the ground and most of the sea throughout the year inside the Arctic and Antarctic Circles, so the raw material for blizzards is always present. As the map of the Arctic shows, comparatively little land lies north of the Arctic Circle. This fact helps to keep the Arctic much warmer than Antarctica (see the sidebar "Why the Arctic is warmer than the Antarctic" on page 22). Whenever the temperature in the sea beneath the pack ice falls below 29°F (–1.7°C), heat transferred from the ice and open water warms it again, so 29°F (–1.7°C) is as cold as the sea can become, even during the long winter night.

At the North Pole itself, the night lasts 176 days and at Spitzbergen it lasts 150 days. There is no record of average air temperatures at the North Pole. Temperatures at Spitzbergen (78.1° N) range from 19°F (–7°C) in winter to 45°F (7.2°C) in summer. Staff at the Amundsen-Scott Station

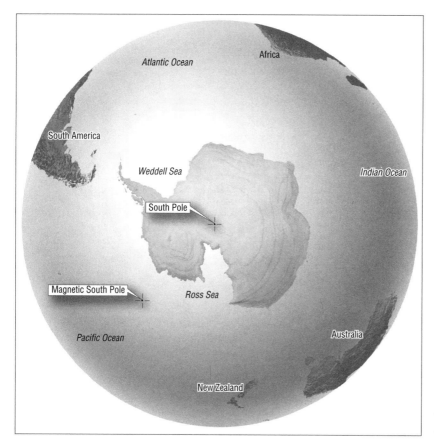

Magnetic and geographic South Poles

record temperatures at the South Pole. These range from an average –75.9°F (–60°C) in winter to –17.4°F (–27.5°C) in summer.

Northern Canada and Greenland have arctic climates. As map (b) on page 40 shows, to the south of this permanently frozen region, a broad belt crossing Canada east of the Rockies has a subarctic climate, where temperatures rise above freezing in summer, supporting tundra vegetation comprising mainly lichens, herbs, and scattered dwarf shrubs and trees.

Deserts, despite being covered with snow

Where the snow, compacted into ice, lies more than a mile thick it is reasonable to suppose snow must fall frequently and heavily. It does not and, despite the ice sheets, not everywhere is covered by snow. In the northern tundra the winter snow is not deep, except where it has drifted,

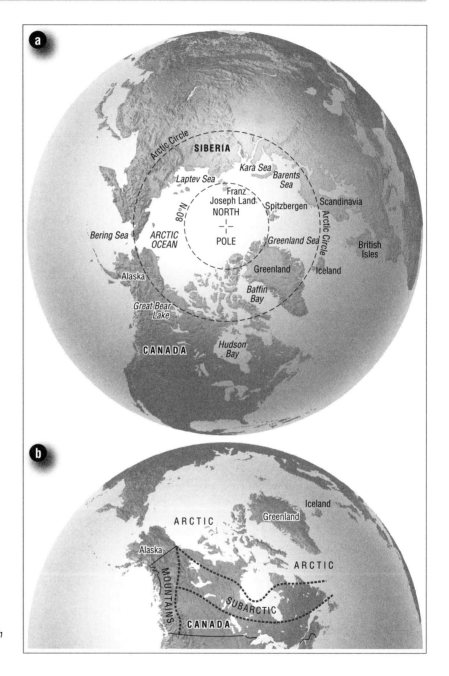

(a) The Arctic. (b) North American Arctic.

and the ground is exposed over large areas. In Antarctica, dry valleys where there is no snow cover a total area of about 2,200 square miles (5,700 km²), and even where snowfalls are frequent, the amounts are usually small. Both the northern and southern polar regions are dry deserts. Snow accumulates in them because the temperature never remains above freezing for long enough in summer to melt all of the snow that fell during winter.

Snow is much bulkier than rain, because of the pockets of air held between its grains, and some kinds of snow are bulkier than others. When snow is expected, forecasters often estimate the amount that is expected to fall in a particular area, giving a figure in inches. This figure represents a depth of snow and the information is helpful if you need to go out or have to clear the drive, but if the amount of precipitation in two places is to be compared it is best to convert snowfall to its rainfall equivalent. This is because big, bulky snowflakes might fall in one place while loose, powdery snow falls in the other, and the two types of snow represent markedly different amounts of water. Converting the amounts allows water to be compared with water and there can be no confusion.

Deserts form wherever the amount of rain or snow that falls is less than the amount that can evaporate from the surface during the same period. Obviously, this depends on the air temperature, but deserts occur anywhere in the world if the annual precipitation is less than 10 inches (25 mm). For comparison, the average annual precipitation in New York City is 43 inches (1,092 mm), and in Dublin, on the other side of the Atlantic Ocean, it is 29.7 inches (754 mm). The histogram shows these beside the average annual rainfall at Touggourt, Algeria, in one of the driest parts of the Sahara. Touggourt has an average of 2.9 inches (74 mm) of rain a year. Qaanaaq (Thule), however, on the northwest coast of Greenland, receives only 2.5 inches (63 mm) of precipitation a year and the South Pole receives an average 2.8 inches (71 mm), in both cases as rainfall equivalent. Of the snow falling at the South Pole, 1.2 inches (30 mm) is lost by sublimation (changing directly from ice to vapor) and being blown away by the wind (this process is called *ablation*). Both places are drier than the Sahara.

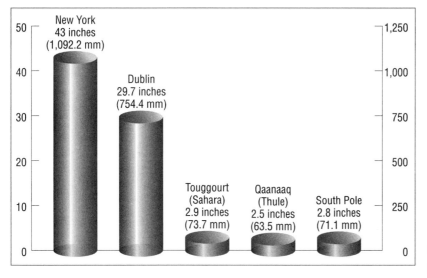

Average annual precipitation

Warm air can hold more water vapor than cold air, so the colder the air, the drier it will be (see the sidebar "Why warm air can hold more moisture than cold air can" on page 18). Polar air is chilled until it is extremely dry, and that is why the polar regions are deserts.

Gales and extratropical hurricanes

Blizzards are mainly caused by loose snow that is blown into the air by the wind. In Greenland, areas of low atmospheric pressure (depressions) passing near the coast generate winds that draw very cold air from the high ground inland, down the glaciated valleys. Depressions also develop in the Southern Ocean and cause gales around Antarctic coasts. Polar depressions are circular, like tropical cyclones, and less than about 300 miles (480 km) across. They produce violent storms with steady winds of 45 MPH (72 km/h) or so, gusting to 70 MPH (113 km/h), and are sometimes called *extratropical hurricanes.*

Other winds, capable of reaching gale force, are caused by the very low polar temperatures. Ice sheets are not simply vast areas of flat ice. Because the ice flows outward from the center (see the section "Ice caps, glaciers, and icebergs" on page 19), ice sheets are domed. Their sides may not slope very steeply, although in some places they do, but a shallow gradient is enough to start air moving. Over the center of the dome temperatures are at their lowest. Being so cold, the lower layer of air is dense and the surface pressure is high. The air cannot rise, because above about 12,000 feet (3,660 m) there is warmer air, often at about 45°F (7°C). This is know as a *temperature inversion* and air can rise through it only if it is warmer than the overlying layer. Instead, the cold, dense air flows downhill. Winds are strongest when the air pressure at the top of the dome is higher than the pressure lower down the slope, so the topographical and pressure gradients incline in the same direction. Air will also flow against the pressure gradient, however—down the slope and into an area of higher pressure.

A wind composed of dense air flowing down a slope is called *katabatic.* Over much of Antarctica the prevailing winds are katabatic and flow from the south. They produce waves in the snow, like sand dunes, some more than six feet (1.8 m) high, and it is these winds that cause blizzards, especially when they are funneled through high-sided valleys.

LOUIS AGASSIZ AND THE GREAT ICE AGE

Each year the seasons follow one another. Spring may arrive a little early or late, summer may be warmer or cooler than it was last year, winter may bring more or less snow than usual, but the progression is orderly and the variation small. Over the course of a human lifetime, the climate remains fairly constant. When you look at the world around you and talk to elderly people about their childhood memories, there seems no reason to suppose that the weather ever really changes. True, people will sometimes tell you that when they were children the summers were warmer or the winters colder, but that is because memory plays tricks. We remember things that stand out. One or two exceptional summers or winters can come to seem typical, simply because we forget about the very ordinary weather in the years separating them.

Until quite recently, that is the way everyone thought things were. They supposed that the kind of weather we experience now is no different from the weather the Romans knew, or people who lived in Old Testament times, or the weather that had existed for countless thousands of years.

The puzzle of the erratic rocks

In Europe, however, there was a puzzle not to do with the weather as such, but with certain rocks. A century ago, geologists were busily classifying rocks and reconstructing landscapes of the past, but these particular rocks did not fit. They were boulders and piles of gravel, lying at the surface or buried just beneath it. Boulders are common enough, but usually they are similar to the solid rock nearby and from which they have clearly been broken. These rocks, however, were nothing like the neighboring rocks, but closely resembled rock formations found hundreds of miles away. Geologists call them *erratics*, and the puzzle was how they came to be where they were found. For a long time it was assumed they had been washed down from the uplands by the biblical flood.

There was one clue, but it did not make much sense either. There is often a jumble of rocks, called a *moraine*, at the lower end or to the side of a glacier. Moraines include rocks that look as though they been transported from far away. Perhaps the erratics had been transported in the same way.

The difficulty was that no one knew how glacial moraines occur. If you look at a glacier or stand on one, what you see is a solid mass of ice with a very rough, broken surface. The ice is not moving. At least, you cannot see it move, although now and then you may hear strange creaking noises emanating from it. Nevertheless, by early in the 19th century some scientists were speculating that glaciers do, in fact, move. If so, this might mean that moraines are made from material the moving glacier has scoured from its bed and sides and then pushed ahead of itself or to the sides, and that the erratics had also been deposited by glaciers that had since disappeared. At that point, however, no one had been able to prove even that glaciers move.

Agassiz and his vacations on the ice

That proof came in about 1840, not from a geologist but from a zoologist. Louis Agassiz (1807–73), then the professor of natural history at the University of Neuchâtel, Switzerland, was already a distinguished ichthyologist (a scientist who studies fish) and a leading authority on fossil fish. He was Swiss and therefore familiar with glaciers when, in 1836 and 1837, he spent his vacations studying them with friends. They built a hut on the Aar glacier to use as a base and called it the "Hôtel des Neuchâtelois."

Boulders and smaller rock fragments lay along the sides of the glacier, looking for all the world as though they had been torn away by the ice. When Agassiz and his friends examined them closely, they found some of the rocks marked with parallel grooves. These marks—the technical term is *striations*—could have been caused by stones made from hard rock that had been partially embedded in the ice and had been dragged over softer rock.

Between vacations Agassiz wrote up the notes he had made and each year he returned. In 1839 he came across another hut. Agassiz found it almost a mile (1.6 km) away from the place where it was known to have been erected in 1827. The glacier must have carried the hut to its new position—how else could it have traveled a mile in 12 years? To check this, in 1840 Agassiz drove a line of stakes directly across the glacier, from one side to the other, fixing them in the ice as firmly as he could. A year later, when he returned, the line was no longer straight. It now made a U shape, and the whole line had moved from its original position. Friction between the rocks and ice at the sides of the glacier slowed its movement there, but ice near the middle of the glacier moved faster.

Glaciers flow

Agassiz had shown conclusively that glaciers flow. This being so, the moraines that pile up at the ends of glaciers *(terminal moraines)* or line their sides *(lateral moraines)* were explained. Glaciers scour away rock, carry it with them, and deposit some of it at their ends, at a level where the air temperature is high enough to melt the ice.

The erratic boulders and gravel deposits that had proved so puzzling looked just like glacial moraines. If glaciers had carried them to their present positions, however, those glaciers had long since disappeared. No one could remember seeing them and there was no historical record of them. Glaciers retreat when temperatures rise, because the point at which the ice melts advances to higher elevations on the mountainside. Conversely, when temperatures fall, glaciers advance. Assuming they really were glacial in origin, the position of the erratics marked the lower boundaries of something much more significant than a few individual glaciers. Agassiz first concluded that at one time, not very far in the geological past, the whole of Switzerland had lain beneath a single ice sheet. He extended his study of glacial deposits to other parts of northern Europe, visiting Scotland in 1840, and came to realize that much of Europe had once been covered by an ice sheet resembling the one that still covered Greenland.

He published his discoveries in 1840 in a book called *Études sur les glaciers* (Studies of glaciers). His idea was not entirely original. As long ago as 1787, Bernard Kuhn had suggested that erratics in the Swiss Jura region might have been transported by glaciers. James Hutton visited the same area in 1794 and reached the same conclusion. Hutton was the Scottish natural philosopher who pioneered the geological concept of *uniformitarianism*—the forces and processes that produced the landscapes we see today are still acting. In 1824 Jens Esmark found evidence of extensive glaciation in Norway, and in 1832 A. Bernhardi suggested that the polar icecap had once extended all the way to southern Germany. Shortly after Agassiz published his book, Jean de Charpentier, a Swiss superintendent of mines, published his own version of the same theory. It was Agassiz who produced the hard evidence and convincing argument, however, and over the next 30 years his idea of what he called the "Great Ice Age" gradually came to be accepted by scientists.

In 1846 King Friedrich Wilhelm IV of Prussia paid for Agassiz to deliver a series of lectures in the United States, mainly about fossil fish, the subject Agassiz had studied for so long. The lectures proved very popular. He extended his visit, then decided to remain permanently, eventually becoming an American citizen. In the years that followed, Agassiz traced the boundaries of the ice sheet that had once covered a large part of North America, establishing that his Great Ice Age had affected the whole of the Northern Hemisphere. The map shows the area covered by the North American ice sheet when it was at its most extensive, and also the area covered by sea ice at that time. In 1848 Agassiz was appointed professor of zoology at Harvard University, and in 1859 he achieved one of his ambitions with the founding at Harvard of what is now called the Agassiz Museum of Comparative Zoology.

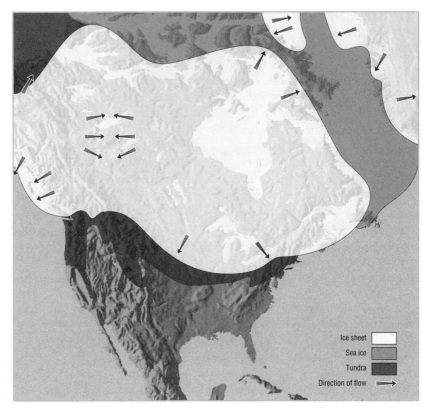

Maximum extent of the Wisconsinian ice sheet in North America

Uniformitarians and catastrophists

New ideas are often controversial. This one was no exception, which is why it came to be accepted only gradually. When Agassiz proposed it, a fierce argument among scientists had been raging for years, between *catastrophists* and *uniformitarians*. Catastrophists held that the history of the Earth is dominated by sudden, violent events. Uniformitarians, on the other hand, believed that change is gradual and continuous, so that processes we can observe today have operated throughout history and can explain fully the formation of the world we see around us.

This view was developed principally by James Hutton (1726–97), who is sometimes called "the father of geology." Although he based his idea on careful observation and deduction, it aroused little interest—possibly because his writing was very hard to follow—until his friend the Scottish geologist John Playfair (1748–1819) popularized it in his *Illustrations of the Huttonian Theory of the Earth* (1802). Another Scottish geologist, Charles Lyell (1797–1875), also became a vigorous supporter of Hutton. He set forth a uniformitarian history of the Earth in *The Principles of Geology*, published in three volumes between 1830 and 1833 and revised regularly until 1875. Lyell believed the erratics had been transported by icebergs and ice rafts during the Great Flood.

Georges Cuvier (1769–1832), at the Natural History Museum in Paris, was the leading proponent of catastrophism. Agassiz had worked under Cuvier and was himself a catastrophist. He suggested the Great Ice Age had destroyed all life on Earth, and his idea of a Great Ice Age contradicted the uniformitarian view that the Earth had been very hot when it first formed and had been cooling steadily ever since.

Not one ice age, but many

Agassiz went much too far, of course. Ice ages cause some extinctions, but surprisingly few. They certainly do not wipe out all life. He was also wrong on another point. His Great Ice Age was not unique. It occurred during what is now called the *Pleistocene epoch*, which began about 2 million years ago and ended about 10,000 years ago, but it was but one of several ice ages, or episodes of glacial advance. North America and Europe experienced five ice ages during the Pleistocene (these are sometimes subdivided to make more). They differed in extent and severity and were separated by warmer periods called *interglacials*. Climates were warmer than those of today during some interglacials. About 100,000 years ago, for example, during the Ipswichian interglacial, rhinoceros, hippopotamus, and elephants lived where London, England, is today, and the average temperature was about 4.5°F (2.5°C) warmer than it is now. Even the ice ages were not unrelieved periods of bitter cold. They were interrupted by *interstades*—episodes of warmer conditions that were shorter and cooler than interglacials (see the sidebar on page 48 for a list of the known Pleistocene glacials and interglacials.)

Scientists believe we are now living in an interglacial, called the *Flandrian* in Britain and Europe and usually known as the *Holocene* in North America, and that one day it will end and the ice will return. The Flandrian began about 10,000 years ago, as the ice sheets retreated at the end of the final ice age of the Pleistocene, known in North America as the Wisconsinian and in Britain as the Devensian (and elsewhere in northern Europe as the Weichselian). This also marked the end of the Pleistocene epoch. We are now living in the Holocene (or Recent) epoch.

At their greatest extent, the Pleistocene ice ages buried a substantial part of the world beneath ice. The map of the world shows the approximate size of the ice sheets, and the names of the biggest. Siberia was not covered by a single, continuous sheet, but this was due to the extremely dry Siberian climate, not warm temperatures. Between the continental ice sheets, the sea was covered in ice shelves and pack ice, so it would have been impossible to tell where continents ended and the sea began.

Pleistocene Glacials and Interglacials

Approximate date (thousand years BP)	North America	Great Britain	Northwest Europe
10–present	*Holocene*	*Holocene (Flandrian)*	*Holocene (Flandrian)*
75–10	Wisconsinian	Devensian	Weichselian
120–75	*Sangamonian*	*Ipswichian*	*Eeemian*
170–120	Illinoian	Wolstonian	Saalian
230–170	*Yarmouthian*	*Hoxnian*	*Holsteinian*
480–230	Kansan	Anglian	Elsterian
600–480	*Aftonian*	*Cromerian*	*Cromerian complex*
800–600	Nebraskan	Beestonian	*Bavel complex*
740–800		*Pastonian*	
900–800		Pre-Pastonian	Menapian
1,000–900		*Bramertonian*	*Waalian*
1,800–1,000		Baventian	Eburonian
1,800		*Antian*	*Tiglian*
1,900		Thurnian	
2,000		*Ludhamian*	
2,300		Pre-Ludhamian	Pretiglian

BP means "before present" (present is taken to be 1950). Names in italic refer to interglacials. Other names refer to glacials (ice ages). Dates become increasingly uncertain for the older glacials and interglacials, and prior to about 2 million years ago, evidence for these episodes has not been found in North America; in the case of the Thurnian glacial and Ludhamian interglacial, the only evidence is from a borehole at Ludham, in eastern England.

There is less land at high latitudes in the Southern Hemisphere than there is in the Northern Hemisphere, so the effects were smaller there, but an ice sheet did cover the western side of South America. The world then did not look quite as it does today. Sea levels had fallen everywhere and shallow seas became dry land. Australia was joined to parts of what is now Indonesia, and Alaska was joined to Asia across the Bering Strait.

Ice ages also occurred in earlier times, although the evidence for them is much sparser than for those of the Pleistocene. The ice sheets advanced at least twice between 950 and 615 million years ago. Glaciers left traces in North Africa around 440 million years ago, but no one knows how large an area they covered. There is reason to suppose that an ice age occurred about 2.3. billion years ago, affecting what are now North America, South Africa, and Australia.

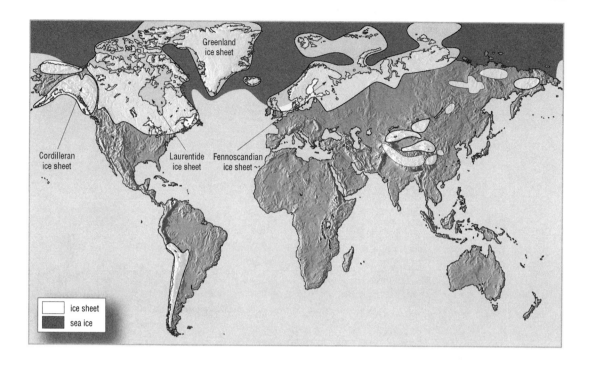

Why do ice ages happen?

Earth during the Great Ice Age

No one really knows what causes ice ages to begin and end, but there is strong evidence in favor of an idea proposed in 1920 by a Serbian climatologist, Milutin Milankovitch (1879–1958). He spent 30 years studying cyclical variations in the rotation of the Earth and its orbit about the Sun. These are very regular, so he could relate them to dates over the past 650,000 years when the cycles were at particular stages. When he did so, he found that the cycles corresponded precisely with the known ice ages.

There are three cycles, shown in the diagram. The first concerns the orbital path Earth follows. Planetary orbits are elliptical, not circular, and the Sun is at one of the two foci of the ellipse. This means the distance between Earth and the Sun varies through the year and, therefore, so does the amount of solar radiation we receive. At present, there is 6 percent difference between the maximum and minimum. Over a cycle of 100,000 years, the shape of the orbital path changes. The ellipse becomes more elongated, so Earth moves further from the Sun. At the extreme of this cycle, the difference between maximum and minimum radiation is 30 percent.

The axis of the Earth's rotation is not vertical in relation to solar radiation. Earth is tilted, at present by about 23.5°. Over a 40,000-year cycle,

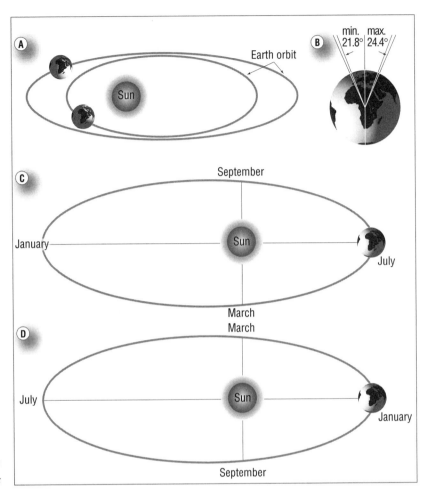

The three Milankovitch cycles

the angle changes, from a minimum of 21.8° to a maximum of 24.4°. This alters the amount of radiation received in high latitudes and, therefore, the extent of the polar ice sheets and sea ice.

The axis also wobbles, describing a small circle, like a toy gyroscope. This is called *precession*, and over a cycle of 21,000 years it alters the time of year of the equinoxes, the dates when the axis is perpendicular to the solar radiation. It also alters the time of year when the Earth is closest to the Sun *(perihelion)*. At present perihelion is in January, but 10,500 years ago it was in July. This affects the warmth of summers and winters.

By itself, each of these cycles has a very small effect on the amount of radiation the Earth receives, but every so often they coincide. When this happens, the Earth receives markedly more or less radiation. The times when the cycles produced minimum radiation coincide with the onset of ice ages, those when radiation reached a maximum with inter-glacials.

The Little Ice Age

Much more recently than the end of the Pleistocene, in about 1550, average temperatures fell by about 2°F (1°C) throughout the Northern Hemisphere and they did not start rising again until about 1860. This period is called the "Little Ice Age." It brought very severe winters, and glaciers everywhere advanced. Year after year, the winter snow failed to melt in southwest Greenland. Everyone living in a Norse colony there died, because the pack ice cut them off from the rest of the world. Some scientists suspect that the climatic warming over the last century may be a continuing recovery from the Little Ice Age.

The Little Ice Age, too, may have been triggered by the Sun. In 1893 an English solar astronomer, Edward Walter Maunder (1851–1928), discovered that the total number of sunspots reported between 1645 and 1715 was smaller than the number seen nowadays in an average year, and that there had been a period of 32 years during which not a single sunspot was recorded. Maunder was then superintendent of the solar division at the Royal Greenwich Observatory, London, and had been checking old records. For centuries astronomers have been interested in sunspots—dark patches that appear on the visible surface of the Sun—and have noted their appearance. Maunder wrote several papers on the subject, suggesting that such changes in the Sun might produce effects on Earth. The period he identified became known as the *Maunder minimum*, but no one took very much notice until the 1970s, when the matter was taken up by the American solar astronomer John A. Eddy.

Sunspot activity affects the rate at which radioactive carbon-14 (^{14}C) is formed in the upper atmosphere and so a historical record of sunspot activity is preserved by the ^{14}C in the growth rings of trees. The ^{14}C record is reliable for the last 5,000 years, and Eddy used it to reveal several earlier Maunder minima. Then he noted that the 1645 to 1715 Maunder minimum coincides fairly closely with the coldest part of the Little Ice Age. The earlier ones also match glacial advances and, during recorded history, periods of very cold weather. Solar maxima, when sunspot activity was high, coincide with warm periods.

Between them, Milankovitch and Maunder have made a convincing link between changes in the amount of radiation we receive from the Sun and the climates of Earth. It is the returning warmth of the Sun that melts the winter snow and heralds summer, but we know now that its output varies and that the orbit and rotation of the Earth also alter the amount of radiation we receive. From time to time in the past, the winter snow has failed to melt and blizzards have continued through what should have been summer. It has happened before and scientists are confident that one day—although probably not in the next thousand years—it will happen again.

SNOWBLITZ

Ice ages can end very quickly. When the temperature starts to rise and the ice begins to melt, the process accelerates. Meltwaters flow as rivers. These carry away fine particles, and where the river meets the sea or slows as it crosses level ground, the particles settle and accumulate as sediment. By examining the sediment, scientists can tell how rapidly it was deposited and, from that, how long it took for the ice age to give way to temperate conditions. The entire transition was often completed in a matter of decades, perhaps in as little as 20 years.

Times of very rapid change are not always good times to be around. Change is disruptive, even when the eventual outcome is a good one, and events can get out of control. During the last ice age, a tongue of the Laurentide ice sheet covering much of North America extended south from British Columbia and dammed the Clark Fork River, near the border between Washington and Idaho. Behind the ice dam, the river formed a huge lake, about 3,000 square miles (7,770 km^2) in surface area and in places 2,000 feet (610 m) deep.

Then, about 15,000 years ago, as the ice age approached its end, suddenly the dam broke. All of the water in the lake, all 500 cubic miles (2,083 km^3) of it, emptied within 48 hours. A wave rushed across the lower land at more than 50 MPH (80 km/h), carrying all before it. The glacial lake no longer exists, but to this day, 15,000 years later, the land has not recovered from the onslaught. It forms the Channelled Scabland, 13,000 square miles (33,670 km^2) of a landscape so harsh that space scientists study it to help them plan for the unmanned landings on Mars.

Do ice sheets form from the top down or bottom up?

Ice ages may end abruptly, but most scientists believe they start gradually. If an ice age were to commence now, several centuries might pass before our descendants knew for certain what was happening. On the other hand, there is a possibility that ice ages might begin just as rapidly as they can end. In that case we would soon be aware of the climatic change, and within a century or two, what are now the temperate regions north of latitude 50° N might be covered in permanent snow, turning into an ice sheet as further snowfalls thickened it. In 1974 the British science writer and TV presenter Nigel Calder gave this fast onset of an ice age the name *snowblitz*. (An extremely heavy and prolonged snowstorm is also sometimes called a snowblitz.)

The idea that this might happen began in the 1970s, when some climate scientists began to question the way ice sheets develop. Until then the conventional view had been that ice ages begin in the mountains. As the global temperature falls, it is the mountains that freeze first. Snowfields accumulate on relatively level parts of the mountains. As these grow thicker and the lower layers are compressed into ice, the ice spills out. It flows down the mountain as valley glaciers and then spreads across the plain at the foot of the mountain (see the section "Ice caps, glaciers, and icebergs" on page 19). Gradually, the ice sheet spreads over the plain until it meets and merges with other ice sheets originating on other mountains. If this is how ice ages develop, it is a very slow process. The transition from an interglacial climate to a full ice age would take centuries, and more probably thousands of years.

But perhaps this is not the way it happens. Perhaps ice sheets grow from the bottom up rather than from the top down. If that were the case, the ice sheets would grow very much faster.

Albedo

It is all to do with *albedo* and *positive feedback*. Albedo is a measure of reflectiveness. In hot weather we often wear light-colored clothes, and cold-weather clothes are usually dark. Pale colors are pale because they reflect most of the light falling on them. Dark colors absorb light—and that is what makes them dark. Light is electromagnetic radiation at wavelengths of 0.4–0.7 μm (one micron or micrometer, symbol μm, is one-millionth of a meter, or about 0.00004 inch). Radiant heat is also electromagnetic radiation, but at wavelengths of 0.8 μm–1 millimeter (0.000003–0.04 inch). Our eyes are not sensitive to radiation at these wavelengths, so we cannot see it. Nevertheless, pale colors reflect it and dark colors absorb it, just as they do visible light. Because of this, less heat penetrates light-colored clothes than penetrates dark ones. It makes little difference with garments as thin as a T-shirt, but much more difference with thicker clothes.

Look around and you will see that the surface of the Earth varies in color. In some places it is dark, in others light, and if you have flown above the cloud tops you will know that they shine very brightly indeed. Just as with our clothes, where the Earth is dark it absorbs more heat than it does where it is light. In other words, its albedo is higher in some places than it is in others. Scientists have measured the albedo of different surfaces, so they can be listed according to the proportion of light and heat they reflect. The figure is given as a percentage of the total radiation falling on them, sometimes written the conventional way, as 20 percent, for example, and sometimes as a decimal fraction, such as 0.2 (1.0 = 100%). Albedo values for some familiar surfaces are given in the table.

ALBEDO	
Surface	Albedo (%)
Fresh snow	75–95
Cumulus-type clouds	70–90
Stratus-type clouds	60–84
Sand (dry)	35–45
Melting or dirty snow, sea ice	30–40
Earth (average)	30
Desert	25–30
Concrete	17–27
Grass meadow	10–20
Plowed field (dry)	5–25
Asphalt	5–17
Green farm crops	3–15

Water has an albedo that changes according to the angle at which light strikes the surface. When the Sun is directly overhead and the surface is still, water absorbs about 98 percent of the light falling on it and looks black. When the Sun is just touching the horizon, the water reflects almost all the light. Go out in a boat when the Sun is low in the sky and you can be burned by the reflected light.

As the table shows, fresh snow has a high albedo. That is why you need to wear dark glasses if you are out on a sunny day soon after it has snowed. Snow blindness, caused by irritation of the eyes due to very bright light, can be painful.

At the edge of the snow

For snow to settle, the temperature at the ground surface must remain below freezing. Once it has settled, however, a layer of snow just a few inches deep will protect the ground from the chilling effect of the wind, so air just above the surface can be up to 50° F (28° C) colder than the ground beneath the snow.

The snow will also reflect solar radiation. Heat that is reflected cannot warm the ground, because it never reaches it, which means the snow does not allow the ground to warm—but nor does it prevent further gradual cooling. This is because where the surface of the Earth is exposed, beyond the edge of the snow, it radiates back into the sky almost all the solar radiation it absorbs, and in winter the ground radiates the heat it absorbed during the summer. The exposed ground is then cooler than the adjacent snow-covered ground, and heat is conducted from the warmer ground to the cooler ground, thus cooling the ground beneath the snow.

Positive feedback

Albedo can trigger temperature changes by positive feedback. *Feedback* occurs when the output from some part of a system affects the input. A thermostat works by feedback. When the temperature of the water in the tank or the central heating system rises above a threshold, the thermostat shuts down the heating device. Our bodies use feedback to maintain fairly constant internal conditions. When you are hungry you eat, and when you have eaten enough you no longer feel hungry, so you stop eating. If your body temperature rises beyond a threshold, you begin to sweat. These are all examples of *negative feedback*, so called because it reduces or stops the input after a certain point. It would be positive feedback if it made the input continue or even accelerate. Obviously, negative feedback is much commoner than positive feedback in the natural world, but positive feedback can sometimes happen.

As winter draws to a close, the intensity of the sunlight increases. This warms the ground, which warms the air in contact with it. Snow melts and precipitation falls through the warmer air as rain rather than as snow. Because even old snow reflects up to 40 percent of the radiation falling on it, a snow-covered surface warms more slowly than grass or bare soil, so the snow melts mainly from its edges, where it is in contact with warmer ground. The snow retreats, lingering longest in sheltered places that receive little sunshine and in hollows where cold air often collects.

This is the way spring usually arrives. Suppose, though, that the winter was especially severe, with much more snow than in most years. Now suppose that the cold winter happened at a time when other factors, such as the position of the Earth in its orbital and rotational cycles were reducing the amount of solar radiation reaching the planet (see the explanation of the Milankovitch cycles in the section "Louis Agassiz and the Great Ice Age" on page 43).

In high latitudes, where temperatures do not rise far above freezing even in summer, the snow might continue to reflect so much radiation that not all of the thick layer had time to melt before winter returned. The cold surface would chill the air immediately above it and the cold air would spill to the sides, beyond the edge of the snow. Consequently, the exposed ground surface adjacent to the snow would also remain cold. More snow would fall during the next winter, and the following spring the high albedo of the surface would again reflect too much radiation for all the snow to melt. By the end of the second summer, the layer of surviving snow would be thicker than at the end of the first summer and because of its chilling effect it would cover a somewhat larger area. Year after year, the high albedo would reflect so much incoming radiation that the air above the snow remained chilled, the snow-covered area continued to spread, and the depth of snow progressively increased until its weight was sufficient to compress the lowest layer into ice.

An ice sheet would then have formed, and as the years passed it would extend into lower latitudes, because once this positive feedback started its effect would be powerful. High albedo would lower the temperature, increasing the area of high-albedo snow, and causing further cooling, in a kind of vicious spiral. At this rate it might take no more than a few centuries for a full-scale ice age to become established, complete with vast ice sheets, pack ice, and valley glaciers. A century may seem like a long time, but compared to the duration of an established ice age, commonly around 100,000 years, it is very brief indeed. Change happening at this rate would be a snowblitz. Each year you would be able to measure the new area over which the ice had expanded.

Could it happen?

No one knows whether any ice age ever began so rapidly, and today most climatologists are more concerned about climatic warming than the risk of rapid cooling. Most ice ages seem to develop gradually. Nevertheless, there seems no reason why a snowblitz could not happen, even if it has not done so until now.

It might begin with greatly increased rainfall over the North Atlantic Ocean—possibly as a result of climatic warming. If enough rain fell, it might form a layer of freshwater floating on the denser salt water. This might alter the circulation of ocean currents, preventing warm water from the Gulf Stream from moving past northwestern Europe and into the Arctic Ocean. In winter, the freshwater layer would freeze more readily than seawater, because its freezing temperature is a little higher. The area covered by sea ice would expand, snow would settle on the ice, and this would increase the albedo. Extremely cold polar air masses that form in winter over North America would no longer be warmed by contact with the water as they crossed the ocean (see the section "Continental and maritime climates" on page 1). European winters would grow markedly colder and would last longer, because of the combined effects of increased albedo and reduced northward transport of warm water. An ice age might then develop in a matter of decades.

Positive feedback also works in the opposite way. That is what accelerates warming when an ice age ends. Once ice sheets start to retreat, the area of exposed ground increases. Ice sheets and glaciers scour away all the soil, so at first the surface consists only of bare rock. Rock has an albedo of about 22 percent, which means it absorbs 78 percent of the radiant heat falling on it. The rock becomes much warmer than the snow, which absorbs no more than about 60 percent even when it is dirty or melting, and the exposed rock melts the snow adjacent to it. As with the snowblitz, once the process had begun, positive feedback would act as a powerful driving force.

Climates are changing constantly and in the past they have been both warmer and cooler than they are today. They are changing still. Most change is gradual and can be detected only by examining records extending over many centuries, but there is no doubt that under certain circumstances positive feedback can drive a vicious spiral of rapid change.

SNOWBALL EARTH

During an ice age, ice sheets expand outward from the Arctic and Antarctic until they cover most of the land in latitudes higher than about 50° N and 50° S. The area that is covered by sea ice also increases. About 20,000 years ago, at the *last glacial maximum* when the ice sheets reached their greatest extent, the North Sea, Irish Sea, and English Channel did not exist. Ireland, Britain, and the European mainland were joined. It would have been possible to walk from North America to Asia, across the Bering Strait, or to Europe, over the sea ice to Iceland and then to the mainland.

At that time, ice sheets and frozen sea covered almost one-third of the Earth's surface. In places the sheets were more than 1.25 miles (2 km) thick. They contained so much water that the sea level was nearly 400 feet (122 m) lower than it is today. The world had not been so cold for 500 million years. Surely, this is as severe as it is possible for an ice age to be?

Ancient glacial deposits

That is what many scientists used to think, but in 1964 Brian Harland, a geologist at Cambridge University, in England, proposed an explanation for a puzzling observation. Glacial deposits, similar to those left behind by the Pleistocene ice ages (see the section "Louis Agassiz and the Great Ice Age" on pages 43), but very much older, can be found in many parts of the world. These deposits are 543 million to 1 billion years old. Harland suggested that during this period there had been an ice age that encompassed the entire planet.

Back in the 1960s, although many geologists believed that continents move, no one knew how the continents had been arranged on the surface of the Earth so long ago (see the sidebar "Continental drift and plate tectonics" on page 59). It was possible that they had been covered by ice as they moved close to the North or South Pole, and that the continents had subsequently drifted into the Tropics, carrying their glacial deposits with them. Harland thought this unlikely, however, because the glacial deposits were interspersed with layers of sediments that are typically deposited in the Tropics. It looked as though the continents had been covered by ice while they were close to the equator. In other words, the ice age had extended across both hemispheres and all the way to the equator.

Meanwhile, unknown to Harland, at the Leningrad Geophysical Observatory Mikhail Budyko was constructing climate models. Budyko is one of the most eminent and experienced climatologists in the world, and at the time he was studying the positive feedback effect of planetary albedo (see the section "Snowblitz" on page 52). His models showed that if the global climate were to cool, so that ice formed at lower and lower latitudes, the albedo would rise at an ever-faster rate. This is because the surface area for each degree of latitude increases with distance from the pole—it is a consequence of the Earth's spherical shape (see the diagram). Once the ice reached approximately latitude 30° N and 30° S, the models showed that the positive feedback due to reflection from the white surface would be so great that the sea would freeze right across the equator. Ice covering all the oceans would be an average 0.6 mile (1 km) thick. The entire Earth would resemble a snowball.

Continental drift and plate tectonics

Accurate maps of the world first became available in the 16th century, based on the projection devised by the Flemish cartographer Gerhard Kremer (1512–94), better known by his Latin name, Gerardus Mercator. As they studied the new maps, people noticed that Africa looked as though it might fit snugly against South America, and that North America, Greenland, and northern Europe also seemed to fit together like pieces of a jigsaw puzzle. For a long time this was thought of as nothing more than a curious coincidence. Then, early in the 20th century, the German meteorologist Alfred Lothar Wegener (1880–1930) proposed an explanation.

Wegener suggested that at one time all the continents had been joined. They then separated, drifted slowly to their present positions, and they are still moving. He called this "continental displacement" and published his idea in 1912, supporting it with many strands of evidence. He was drafted into the army on the outbreak of World War I, was wounded, and developed the idea further while in the hospital recovering from his injuries.

His idea received little scientific support at the time, because no one could think of any way continents could move. Interest increased in the 1940s. Geologists already knew that mineral grains in molten rocks align themselves with the Earth's magnetic field and retain that orientation as the rock solidifies. From time to time, however, the Earth's magnetic field reverses its polarity—north

becomes south and south becomes north. A ridge runs across the floor of each of the major oceans, and in the 1940s scientists found that the rocks on either side of the ridges form distinct bands, identifiable by reversals in their magnetic polarity. It seemed as though molten rock emerges from the ridges, pushes the seafloor away from the ridge, and then solidifies. In 1963 the American oceanographer Robert Sinclair Dietz (1914–95) called this process *seafloor spreading*.

In 1967, Cambridge geologist Dan McKenzie (born 1942) drew all the evidence together and proposed the theory of *plate tectonics*. Tectonics is a geological term that refers to rock structures and the forces producing them.

The theory of plate tectonics holds that the Earth's crust consists of separate pieces called *plates*. Below the crust, convection currents in the hot, dense, but slightly plastic rock of the mantle slowly move the crustal plates. That is how continents drift and how seafloors open and close. The boundaries between plates may be inactive—neither plate is moving—or active. Active boundaries are *divergent* if the plates are moving apart, *convergent* if they are moving toward each other, and comprise *transform faults* if the plates are moving past each other in opposite directions. At convergent margins between oceanic crust and continental crust, the oceanic crust is *subducted* beneath the less dense

(continues)

(continued)

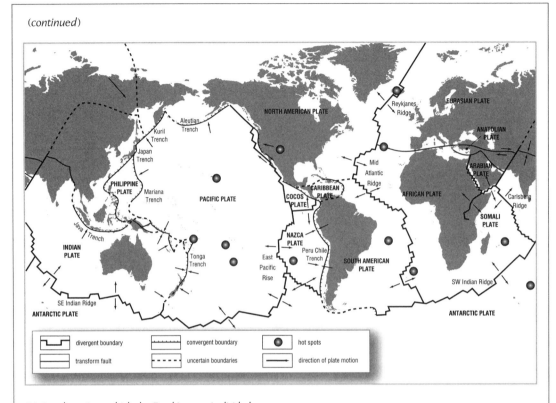

Major plates into which the Earth's crust is divided

continental crust and the continental plate may crumple, raising mountain ranges such as the Andes. Mountain ranges such as the Himalayas are raised when two continental plates collide and crumple. *Hot spots* are places of high volcanic activity. Some are at plate boundaries, but others are far away from them. The hot spots are caused by convection in the mantle. They remain stationary while the crustal plate moves over them.

The map shows the names and locations of the major plates and hot spots. It also shows the types of plate boundaries and the direction plates are moving.

Could it happen?

Climate scientists regarded this as an interesting exercise in computer modeling, but no one believed it had really happened. If the Earth had ever been as cold as that, life would have been impossible. Yet there was incontrovertible fossil evidence of life both before and after the supposed ice age. This objection weakened in the 1970s, with the discovery of large communities of organisms living on the ocean floor in the vicinity of *hydrothermal vents*—places where hot water, rich in minerals, rises from deep in the crust. Lichens and bacteria were also found to survive in the intense cold of the dry valleys of Antarctica.

There was a more serious objection, however. If ice ever covered the entire surface of the planet, calculations suggested the condition would be permanent. The surface would reflect up to 90 percent of the radiation falling on it. The remaining 10 percent would be insufficient to start a widespread thaw. The snowball would remain a snowball.

It was Joe Kirschvink, professor of geobiology at the California Institute of Technology, who coined the term "Snowball Earth" in the late 1980s. It was Kirschvink who proposed a mechanism, based on plate tectonics, for ending the ice age.

The thaw leading to "Greenhouse Earth"

As plates move in relation to one another, they generate intense volcanism along their margins. This activity would continue even if the surface were frozen. Volcanoes release carbon dioxide, which would find its way into the air. It would accumulate there, because the processes that remove the gas had shut down.

Carbon dioxide (CO_2) dissolves in cloud droplets (H_2O), forming carbonic acid (H_2CO_3), and is brought to the surface in rain. The acid rain

Latitude and surface area. Because the Earth is spherical, the surface area between two lines of latitude increases with distance from the poles, even though the distance between the lines of latitude remains constant.

reacts with minerals in surface rocks to form carbonates (CO_3). These are carried to the sea by rivers, where they react with calcium and magnesium in the water to form insoluble compounds that sink to the seafloor. Green plants and some bacteria also remove carbon dioxide by the process of photosynthesis. During the ice age, however, photosynthesis would cease entirely. The removal of carbon dioxide by rain would also cease. There would be no liquid water on the surface and therefore almost no evaporation, and the air would in any case be too cold to hold more than a tiny amount of moisture (see the sidebar "Why warm air can hold more moisture than cold air can" on page 18).

With no mechanism to remove it, the carbon dioxide would remain in the air and the concentration would gradually increase. Carbon dioxide is a *greenhouse gas.* That is to say, it absorbs infrared radiation. Although the ice reflected most of the radiation falling on the Earth, some was absorbed. When a body absorbs radiation, it grows warmer than its surroundings—in this case space—and radiates the heat away. Even during this total ice age, Earth absorbed and reradiated a small amount of heat. Carbon dioxide absorbed it, and very slowly the atmosphere grew warmer.

Ken Caldeira and Jim Kasting at Pennsylvania State University calculated that ending the ice age by this means would have required about 350 times the amount of carbon dioxide present in the atmosphere today. If the amount of volcanic activity was similar to today's, millions of years, or possibly tens of millions of years, would have passed before the ice began to break up at the equator.

Once the thaw had started, it would have continued. There was still no way to remove carbon dioxide from the air, so it would have continued to accumulate, and the temperature would have climbed higher and higher. Eventually it may have reached 122°F (50°C). All the ice melted and evaporation became intense. Huge clouds developed and it rained heavily and incessantly for many years. The rain removed the carbon dioxide from the air, the cloud tops reflected sunlight, and the temperature fell, finally stabilizing at a level which living organisms could tolerate. Snowball Earth had been replaced by "Greenhouse Earth," and at last that episode had also ended.

The cap dolostones

In many parts of the world, caps of *dolostone*—a sedimentary rock made from calcium-magnesium carbonate—cover the ancient glacial deposits. The "cap dolostones" usually lie beneath much thicker layers of clays and limestones. It appears that the dolostones were deposited very rapidly and then buried as the sea level rose.

Like most elements, carbon exists as more than one *isotope.* Isotopes are varieties of an element that are chemically identical, but have different atomic masses. All carbon atoms contain the same number of *protons*—the particles that determine the chemical properties of the element—but a varying number of *neutrons*. The number of neutrons alters the mass of the atom, but not its chemical properties. There are two stable isotopes of carbon: ^{12}C, accounting for 99 percent of all carbon, and ^{13}C, accounting for 1 percent. Biological processes use the lighter ^{12}C in preference to ^{13}C. Consequently, carbonate rocks made from the shells of marine organisms and therefore of biological origin contain less than the 1 percent ^{13}C found in the carbon dioxide released from volcanoes. Typically they are depleted by about 2.5 percent, so instead of containing 1 percent ^{13}C, they contain 0.999 percent—a minute, but highly significant difference. Changes in the proportion of ^{13}C in the carbonate rocks beneath the glacial deposits, in the cap dolostones, and in the rocks above them, suggests a large and rapid drop in biological activity, a period of low activity lasting about 10 million years, and then a slow recovery.

In 2000 Joe Kirschvink published evidence of an even earlier Snowball Earth episode, around 2.4 billion years ago. Kirschvink's evidence showed that the world's largest deposit of the metal manganese resulted from a series of chemical reactions that occurred as the Earth thawed from that ice age. The deposit he examined, the Kalahari Manganese Field, accounts for about 80 percent of all the manganese reserves in the world.

Snowball or "slushball"?

The evidence indicates that the "snowball Earth–greenhouse Earth" sequence occurred not once but at least twice, about 750 million years ago and 590 million years ago. Some scientists suggest it may have happened as many as four times during this period.

Why did it happen? No one really knows, but the most likely explanation centers, yet again, on plate tectonics. About 590 million years ago, during the time when these climate swings were happening, most of the continents lay in the Southern Hemisphere and there was very little land at the equator or in the northern Tropics. The map shows the location to which continental drift, driven by plate tectonics, had transported the continents. They clustered around the South Pole as a vast "supercontinent" broken by narrow straits, but largely isolated from the ocean currents transporting warm water from the equator. Their isolation would have allowed temperatures to fall, and once ice sheets formed and began spreading outward they could have reached the critical latitude where their growth accelerated.

Most geologists accept that these ancient ice ages happened, but not all of them agree that the ice reached the equator. Computer models made by Linda Sohl and Mark Chandler at the Goddard Institute for Space Studies suggest the ice may have reached latitude 10° N and 10° S,

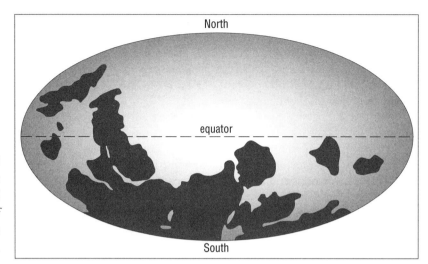

North

equator

South

A map of the world about 590 million years ago. Continental drift placed most of the continents in the Southern Hemisphere.

leaving about 30 percent of the ocean ice-free. This produces a "Slushball Earth" rather than a Snowball Earth. More importantly, it allows biological activity to continue.

Martin Kennedy, at the University of California, Riverside, believes life went on as normal during the ice ages. His research found the proportion of ^{13}C increased in the carbonate rocks deposited during the ice ages, rather than decreasing, and that the decrease in ^{13}C occurred after the ice had melted.

The debate now centers on the extent of the ice sheets and the argument is between supporters of the "snowball" and "slushball" versions. No one doubts, however, that these were the severest ice ages the world has ever known. During the coldest part of the Wisconsinian ice age, the ice sheets reached almost to latitude 40° N and 40° S in some places. This is a long way from latitude 30°, which Mikhail Budyko found to be critical. It is even further from 10°, the latitude the ice reached in the "slushball" scenario. So a repeat of this "deep freeze" seems unlikely. All the same, it shows that the Earth is capable of producing climates a great deal harsher than any that have occurred in the last few million years.

SNOW LINES

High mountains are often capped with snow all year round. The lower boundary of the permanent snow cover is called the *snow line*. Climb above the snow line and you should expect blizzards at any time of year, because mountains are windy places.

As you climb, the air temperature falls. A decrease in temperature with height is called a *lapse rate*. In dry air, the lapse rate—known as the *dry adiabatic lapse rate* (DALR)—is a fairly constant 5.5°F every 1,000 feet, or 10°C per kilometer (see the sidebars "Adiabatic cooling and warming" on page 000 and "Evaporation, condensation, and the formation of clouds" on page 000).

It follows that if the temperature at sea level is 59°F (15°C), which is the average temperature over the world as a whole, the temperature will always be lower than 32°F (0°C) above 5,000 feet (1,525 m). Even in summer, precipitation will fall as snow anywhere above this height, and the snow will never melt. This is approximately correct, but in the real world the situation is more complicated.

Dry air and moist air

Whether it is rain or snow, precipitation falls from air that is saturated with moisture, not from dry air. The lapse rate in saturated air—called the *saturated adiabatic lapse rate* (SALR)—is lower and more variable than the DALR. This is because the condensation of water vapor releases *latent heat*, and this warms the air (see the section "What happens when water freezes and ice melts" on page 99). The amount of latent heat that is released depends on the amount of condensation and that, in turn, depends on the quantity of water vapor present in the air. This varies with the temperature of the air, because warm air is able to hold more water vapor than cold air can (see the sidebar "Why warm air can hold more moisture than cold air can" on page 18). In other words, the SALR varies with air temperature. In very warm air it may be as low 2.2°F per 1,000 feet (4°C km⁻¹) and in very cold air it is close to the DALR, because very cold air is also fairly dry. Where the temperature at sea level is 59°F (15°C), the SALR is about 3°F per 1,000 feet (5.5°C km⁻¹), so in moist air the freezing temperature occurs at about 9,000 feet (2,745 m).

Although the sea-level temperature is usually given as 59°F (15°C), this is an average over the whole world. Obviously, the polar seas are much colder than this and tropical seas are much warmer. Indeed, sea-surface temperatures near the equator often rise above 80°F (27°C). Such warm air over the ocean is very moist, so its saturated adiabatic lapse rate may be around 2.5°F per 1,000 feet (4.5°C km⁻¹). With a starting temperature of

80°F (27°C) and this lapse rate, freezing temperature is reached at just over 19,000 feet (6,000 m). Off the coast of Maine, on the other hand, the sea-surface temperature may be at about 50°F (10°C), the saturated adiabatic lapse rate about 3°F per 1,000 feet (5.5°C km⁻¹). The freezing level will then be at 6,000 feet (1,800 m).

Average surface temperatures fall with increasing distance from the equator, and in very high latitudes they are below freezing throughout the year. The summer snow line in Greenland is at about 2,000 feet (610 m), but near the North and South Poles the freezing level is at the surface, so Arctic and Antarctic mountains are entirely snow-covered. It is a large difference.

Effect of the shape of a mountain

Much also depends on the shape and orientation of the mountain. As the diagram shows, one side of the mountain receives more direct sunshine than the other side. In the Northern Hemisphere this is usually the side that faces south or southwest, known as the *adret slope* (the opposite side, which faces north or northeast and is shaded, is called the *ubac slope*). This will make the snow line higher on the adret slope, because this slope is warmer. In middle latitudes, however, weather systems usually approach from the west. As the air reaches the mountain, it is forced to rise. This cools it and causes its water vapor to condense and rain or snow to fall. The western side of the mountain therefore receives more precipitation than the eastern side and the snow line is likely to be lower on the exposed side, especially in shaded places.

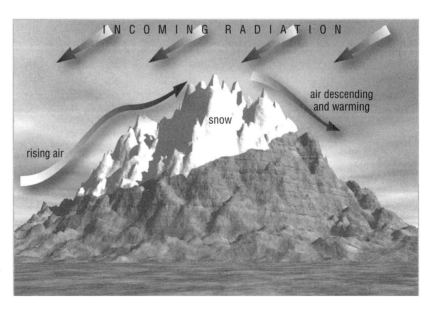

Snow line on two sides of a mountain

Actual lapse rates often differ from the standard dry or saturated adiabatic lapse rate. The local lapse rate is called the *environmental lapse rate* (ELR). The ELR is the rate at which the temperature decreases from the actual surface temperature, measured at a particular time and place, and the actual temperature measured at the same time at the tropopause above that place.

Mountain winds

When air is forced to rise over a mountain, it cools at the standard lapse rate—DALR or SALR—and this may be greater or less than the environmental lapse rate. If it is greater, by the time it reaches the summit the air may be cooler than the surrounding air. This will cause it to sink down the other side of the mountain, warming adiabatically as it does so and moving as a warm wind. Technically, a wind that moves down a mountainside is called a föhn wind. The best-known North American example is the chinook, which blows down the eastern side of the Rocky Mountains. It is sometimes called the "snow eater," because of the rate at which it melts snow. It has been known to raise the temperature by more than 40°F (22°C) in two minutes and a temperature rise of 1°F (0.55°C) a minute is quite usual. Föhn winds also tend to limit the amount of snow on the sheltered sides of mountains.

Except at the equator, the average surface temperature varies with the seasons. This means that the snow line also varies. It is higher in winter than it is in summer. In the Himalayas, for example, the summer snow line varies from about 13,000 feet (4,000 m) in the eastern part of the range to 16,250 feet (5,000 m) in the western part.

If the mountains are tall enough, their tops will be covered with snow throughout the year. Although the snow line descends in winter, there is a permanent snow line marking the lower margin of the snow that lies all year round. The permanent snow line is at about 18,000 feet (5,500 m) in the Andes and about 9,000 feet (2,750 m) in the Rockies.

Where snow is most likely

Real mountains are craggy, with many deep gulleys and high, projecting rock masses, so there are always shaded areas and some places are in perpetual shade. Snow lingers there, but even if there could be such a thing as a perfectly smooth, conical mountain, working out which parts are most likely to be covered with snow would still be difficult.

The diagram illustrates the problem. It represents a view of a perfectly conical mountain seen from directly above. From above, the mountain is

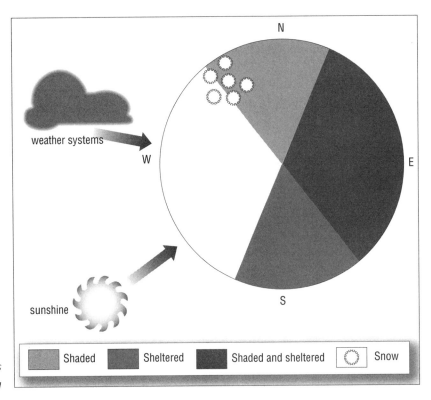

weather systems

W   E

sunshine

N

S

| Shaded | Sheltered | Shaded and sheltered | Snow |

Where mountain snow is most likely

circular. In middle latitudes of the Northern Hemisphere, the summer Sun is more or less to the southwest at noon. This is the time of day when the sunshine is most intense, so the side facing southwest is warmer than the northeastern half of the mountain, which is in shade. Weather systems approach mainly from the west, and so precipitation is heaviest on the western side—the side that is exposed to the weather and where approaching air is forced to rise. Combine these factors and, seen from above, the mountain can be divided into four unequal segments.

In the south and southeast, the mountain is in full sunlight and sheltered from the weather. Between northwest and southwest, it is fully exposed to the weather, but in full sunshine. Between northeast and southeast, it is both shaded and sheltered, so it is cool but also dry. This leaves the north and northwest section, which is shaded but partly exposed to the weather, and it is on this part of the mountain that snow may be expected.

In the end, there is no hard-and-fast rule to help you predict where the snow line will be. On average, the snow line is at about 16,000 feet (5,000 m) in the Tropics, at about 8,000 feet (2,400 m) at latitude 45° N and 45° S, and at a little over 5,000 feet (1,500 m) at 55° N and 55° S. On every continent there are mountains high enough to have snow lines. Even at the equator it is possible to experience a blizzard.

WHERE BLIZZARDS OCCUR

Airplanes sometimes crash, and so aircrews are taught how to survive until rescuers are able to reach them. They may need to find shelter and food in a harsh environment and so the training includes courses for winter survival and Arctic survival. Some years ago, a group of air force pilots undertaking a Canadian winter survival course, held in northern Alberta, emerged from their tents one morning to find the temperature was –50°F (–46°C). This, remember, was the winter, not the Arctic, survival course.

Manitoba, Saskatchewan, and Alberta, the Canadian prairie provinces, are very cold places in winter. Temperatures often fall below –20°F (–29°C) and sometimes they are a long way below. In Edmonton, Alberta, the temperature has been known to fall below freezing in every month of the year and in January and February it can reach –57°F (–49°C). Saskatoon, Saskatchewan, and Winnipeg, Manitoba, are only slightly warmer. The average January temperature in Saskatoon is –11°F (–24°C), but –55°F (–48°C) has been recorded and –48°F (–44°C) has been recorded in Winnipeg.

You might suppose from this that blizzards are fairly common in these bitterly cold places. Any precipitation must fall as snow, after all, and the prairies are certainly windy enough to drive such snow as does fall at a furious, blizzardlike speed. In fact, though, blizzards are rare, especially in the coldest months, because the air is too dry. On average, less than one inch (25 mm) of precipitation falls each month. In fact, despite being farther north, less snow falls in Canada than in the United States. In December, January, and February, for example, the average monthly precipitation in Winnipeg is 0.9 inch (23 mm). In Chicago it is 2.0 inches (50 mm). Chicago is warmer than Winnipeg, but average winter temperatures hover around freezing by day and fall well below freezing by night. Blizzards are more likely in Chicago than in Winnipeg, despite Chicago being 8° farther south and markedly warmer.

Cold climates are dry climates

Snow can fall heavily at sea level anywhere in latitudes higher than about 30°, but far from being confined to the Arctic, blizzards are less common in very high latitudes than they are in warmer regions. This is because snow cannot fall at all unless the air is saturated, and at temperatures below about 4°F (–16°C), air can hold barely enough water vapor to produce any precipitation at all.

When it is really cold, with temperatures a long way below freezing, the sky is usually clear, with barely a cloud to be seen. On days like these, people sometimes say "It's too cold for snow"—and they're right. It is not extremely cold air that brings blizzards, but relatively warm air. The sidebar "Why warm air can hold more moisture than cold air can," on page 18, explains why this is so. Snow is most likely when the air temperature is between 25°F (–4°C) and 39°F (4°C). At these temperatures the air holds enough moisture to produce precipitation, but the temperature below the cloud is low enough to prevent the snow from melting before it reaches the ground.

These conditions are most likely to occur at the beginning and end of winter, and that is when blizzards are most likely. There is often heavy snow around or shortly before Thanksgiving. In 1980, for example, there were snowstorms on November 17 and 18 along the whole of the eastern side of the United States from New Mexico northward, and there were severe winter storms around the Great Lakes on November 8, 1913, and November 10, 1975.

Spring blizzards

Spring blizzards often happen in March. There were especially severe storms in New England from March 11 to 14, 1888, and on March 9 and 10, 1978, in the midwest. Those storms brought an average 40 inches (1,016 mm) of snow to New England and part of New York State and caused more than 400 deaths. A blizzard swept through Colorado on March 18–20, 2003, dropping up to 7 feet (2 m) of snow in the mountains and bringing 60–70 inches (1.5–1.8 m) of snow to parts of Boulder and Jefferson Counties. More than 200 buildings collapsed in the Denver area.

One of the worst blizzards of modern times happened in 1993. It was so memorable it is often called simply "the blizzard of '93" or "the superstorm of March 1993." The conditions that produced it began on the morning of March 12 as a small area of low pressure over the Gulf of Mexico. Nothing might have come of it, but just as it was developing, a jet stream at 30,000 feet (9,150 m) was blowing southward from Canada, directly into the disturbance. The effect was to intensify the low, and pressure at its center continued to fall during the afternoon and evening of March 12.

By early the following morning the low had grown into a major storm located a little way south of the Louisiana coast and bringing snow, sleet, and rain to a large area of the southern United States. The storm brought thunderstorms, triggered tornadoes, and caused coastal flooding over the Florida panhandle. During the remainder of March 13 the storm continued moving north, reaching Chesapeake Bay by the evening, and intensifying all the way. By this time, the storm was bringing heavy snow and blizzards to the whole of the U.S. Atlantic coast, with heavy drifting and at times near-zero visibility. Still moving north, by March 14 the blizzards were affecting eastern Canada, but by then the storm was abating and by the end of that day it had died down.

That storm affected around 100 million people over the eastern one-third of the United States. It closed airports and brought traffic to a standstill. The damage it caused to property and the production and working time that were lost together cost billions of dollars, and 270 persons lost their lives.

Not all snowstorms happen in spring, of course. They can occur in winter. The 1996 blizzards over most of the eastern United States, and also in Britain, occurred in January, and in 1888, one of the harshest winters on record, Montana, the Dakotas, and Minnesota suffered the worst blizzards they had ever known from January 11 to 13. More recently, blizzards swept across France in early January 2003, and in early February they struck Britain.

The conditions that produce snowstorms

In winter, as the map shows, three types of air affect North America. Arctic air, covering most of Canada, is dry, and bitterly cold, dry air spills southward from the polar high-pressure region at its center. The Caribbean, Gulf of Mexico, and southeastern United States lie beneath mild, moist air moving westward from the Atlantic. Between these, the western coastal region and a broad band across the central United States are affected by air from the Pacific.

Associated with these air masses, the atmospheric pressure is usually low to the east of Greenland and high over the Arctic, central United States, and over the sea off California and over the southern Caribbean. The Pacific and Caribbean high-pressure areas are much farther south and exert less influence than they do in summer, and in winter air masses of different types are mixing to produce frontal systems in the belt of Pacific air. These systems move generally eastward across the continent (see the sidebar "Weather fronts" on page 14).

Typically, a weather system that brings blizzards to eastern North America starts as an area of low pressure off the coast of the Carolinas. It intensifies, causing the winds circulating around it to increase in strength, and then moves north, affecting the coastal belt from about Cape Hatteras to Nova Scotia (see the map on page 72). The winds flow counterclockwise, because of the Coriolis effect (see the sidebar on pages 74–75); the map on page 73 shows the consequences. The winds blow across the ocean, gathering moisture, and reach the East Coast as northeasterlies. As the low moves north, these winds cause flooding and erode beaches, but by the time they reach New England they also bring heavy snow and blizzards.

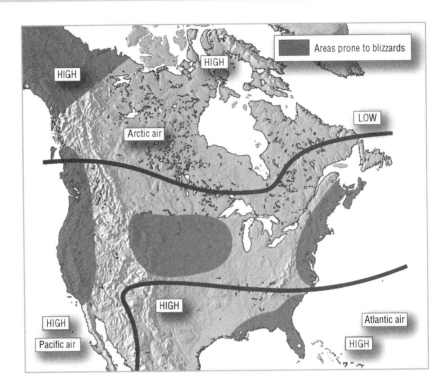

Winter air masses in North America

Farther south, cold, continental polar air occasionally pushes across Texas as far as the Gulf and Florida. That air can bring blizzards. More commonly, cold air advancing from the north meets warmer air from the Gulf. Cold air undercuts the warm air, lifting it and causing its moisture vapor to condense. The resulting rain turns to snow as it falls through the underlying layer of cold air, producing fierce storms, with blizzards, across the midwest.

Along the West Coast, storms developing in moist Pacific air produce blizzards as they reach the coast. Cold air is funneled through mountain passes and valleys as it crosses the Rocky Mountains, and wind speeds can reach 100 MPH (160 km/h). Alaska suffers from fierce storms carried by air moving eastward from the Bering Sea. Not only do these storms cause blizzards but their winds can also hurl huge blocks of sea ice onto the shore with enough force to damage any buildings they hit.

European blizzards

Western Europe receives most of its weather systems from the Atlantic. In winter these can bring deep areas of low pressure (depressions) with strong winds and heavy precipitation that falls as snow in the north. The deep

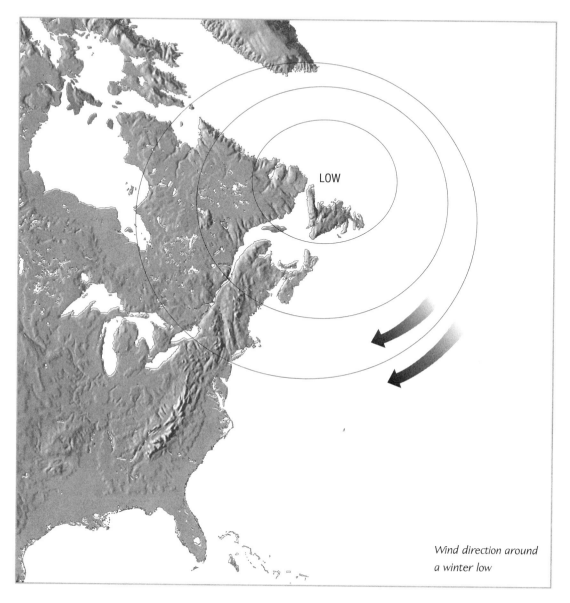

Wind direction around a winter low

interior of the continental landmass is very dry, however, and even in Siberia snowfall is light. In winter the relative humidity is often higher than 85 percent, but the air is so cold that very little water vapor is needed to saturate it. A relative humidity of 88 percent at an air temperature of –6°F (–21°C) is equivalent to a relative humidity of 6 percent at a temperature of 60°F (15.5°C).

For most of the time, Siberian winters are pleasant. Despite the cold, the sky is blue, the air calm, and the sunshine is bright enough to melt snow. Siberia does experience blizzards, of course. In the tundra regions of the north, the wind producing blizzards is called the *purga*. Further south,

The Coriolis effect

Any object moving toward or away from the equator and not firmly attached to the surface does not travel in a straight line. As the diagram illustrates, it is deflected to the right in the Northern Hemisphere and to the left in the Southern Hemisphere. Moving air and water tend to follow a clockwise path in the Northern Hemisphere and a counterclockwise path in the Southern Hemisphere.

The French physicist Gaspard Gustave de Coriolis (1792–1843) discovered the reason for this in 1835, and it is called the Coriolis effect. It happens because Earth is a rotating sphere, and as an object moves above the surface, Earth below is also moving. The effect used to be called the Coriolis "force" and it is still abbreviated as CorF, but it is not a force. It results simply from the fact that we observe motion in relation to fixed points on the surface.

Earth makes one complete turn on its axis every 24 hours. This means every point on the surface is constantly moving and returns to its original position (relative to the Sun) every 24 hours, but because Earth is a sphere, different points on the surface travel different distances to do so. If you find it difficult to imagine that New York and Bogotá—or

direction of Earth's rotation

N

initial direction
actual path

S

The Coriolis effect deflects moving bodies.

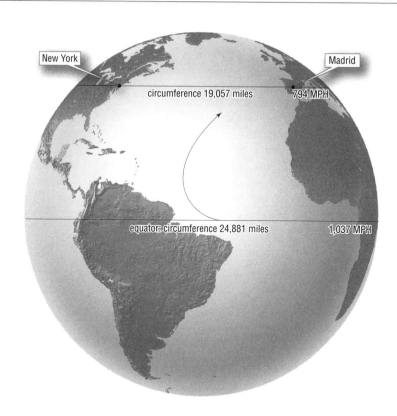

New York

Madrid

circumference 19,057 miles

794 MPH

equator: circumference 24,881 miles

1,037 MPH

The Coriolis effect

any other two places in different latitudes—are moving through space at different speeds, consider what would happen if this were not so: the world would tear itself apart.

Consider two points on the surface, one at the equator and the other at 40° N, which is the approximate latitude of New York and Madrid. The equator, latitude 0°, is about 24,881 miles (40,033 km) long. That is how far a point on the equator must travel in 24 hours, which means it moves at about 1,037 MPH (1,668 km/h). At 40° N, the circumference parallel to the equator is about 19,057 miles (30,663 km). The point there has less distance to travel and so it moves at about 794 MPH (1,277 km/h).

Suppose you planned to fly an aircraft to New York from the point on the equator due south of New York (and could ignore the winds). If you headed due north you would not reach New York. At the equator you are already traveling eastward at 1,037 MPH (1,668 km/h). As you fly north, the surface beneath you is also traveling east, but at a slower speed the farther you travel. If the journey from 0° to 40° N took you 6 hours, in that time you would also move about 6,000 miles (9,654 km) to the east, relative to the position of the surface beneath you, but the surface itself would also move, at New York by about 4,700 miles (7,562 km). Consequently, you would end not at New York, but (6,000–4,700 =) 1,300 miles (2,092 km) to the east of New York, way out over the Atlantic. The diagram illustrates this.

The size of the Coriolis effect is directly proportional to the speed at which the body moves and the sine of its latitude. The effect on a body moving at 100 MPH (160 km/h) is 10 times greater than that on one moving at 10 MPH (16 km/h). Sin 0° = 0 (the equator) and sin 90° = 1 (the poles), so the Coriolis effect is greatest at the poles and zero at the equator.

along the southern border of the belt of conifer forest known as the taiga and into Mongolia and Manchuria, it is called the *buran*.

The *buran* and *purga* blow from the northeast when continental polar air is drawn into the area behind a depression. They carry falling snow, lift lying snow, and quickly build to hurricane force (more than 75 MPH; 121 km/h). They are terrifying and very dangerous.

Vladimir Maximovich Zenzinov (1899–1953) was a Russian revolutionary who was sentenced to exile in Siberia three times and escaped twice. The second time he escaped disguised as the owner of a gold mine, traveling by sled drawn by caribou (reindeer) for almost 1,000 miles (1,600 km) to the seaport of Okhotsk (see map). From there he continued to Japan on a fishing schooner, and eventually back to Europe—and, soon after his return to St. Petersburg, to his third arrest and exile to an even more remote spot from which he did not escape. (He spent his five-year sentence writing about the people of this region.)

Yakutsk and Okhotsk. Siberia: Zenzinov's journey

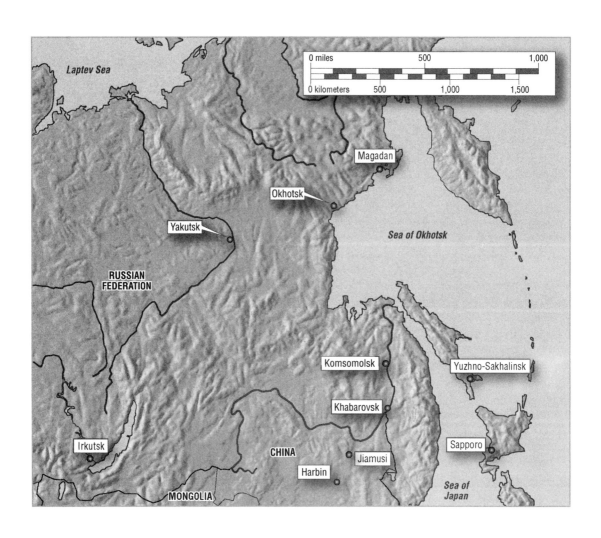

It was during his long trek across the northern wastes that on December 31, 1907, Zenzinov experienced a *purga*. He recounted that the storm began soon after midday as a light wind. By 1 P.M. twilight started to descend and the snow started to fall. The snow was so dense, he said, that he was unable to see the antlers of the deer pulling his sled, only their hindquarters. As the wind reached hurricane force, the snow sped past him with a rustling sound where it collided with the sled, but the wind constantly changed direction, striking him now in the face, then from the back, then from the left or right side. Had he faltered and fallen, the snow would have buried him in minutes.

Blizzards are commoner in some places than in others, but this should not lull you into a false sense of security, no matter where you live. They are possible wherever snow falls and strong winds blow, even on mountains in the Tropics. Britain has a mild climate, but every year a few hill walkers become disoriented and lost in blizzards in Scotland—and occasionally the rescuers do not arrive in time and someone dies.

Where people expect blizzards they are prepared for them and know what to do. It is where they are unexpected that they are likely to cause most harm. In February 1973, snowstorms and blizzards closed highways, disrupted communications, and caused chaos in Georgia and the Carolinas, mainly because people there had so little experience of such severe conditions. Nowhere can claim to be totally immune and it is wise to be prepared.

GALES AND WHY THEY HAPPEN

When it is snowing heavily, any wind stronger than 35 MPH (56 km/h) will turn a snowstorm into a blizzard. Even if the sky is cloudless, a wind of this force can lift freshly fallen snow from the ground if the snow is light and powdery. Once airborne, the snow will be driven by the wind just like falling snow. Again, the result is a blizzard.

A wind of 32–38 MPH (51–61 km/h) is known technically as a *moderate gale*. Winds stronger than this are called *fresh gale*, *strong gale*, *whole gale*, and *storm*. When the wind speed exceeds 75 MPH (121 km/h) the wind is a *hurricane*. We still classify wind strength according to a method worked out nearly two centuries ago by a British naval officer (see the box). He named each type of wind and gave it a *force number* between 0 and 12. On his scale a moderate gale is a Force 7 wind.

Commander Beaufort (as he was known at the time) described winds, but his scale does not explain why winds vary in strength or, indeed, why they happen at all. They are due to differences in air pressure.

How Torricelli weighed air and invented the barometer

Stand in a strong wind and you can feel its pressure. It pushes against you. Anything that can push you around must be a material substance, and a material substance has weight.

This is not as obvious as it seems to us today. The proof of it was discovered in the course of searching for the answer to an apparently unrelated question. In the early 17th century no one could understand why a suction pump will raise water to a height of about 33 feet (10 m), but no higher. Even using the most powerful engines available to drive it, no pump could raise water any higher than this.

People at that time believed that "nature abhors a vacuum." When a tight-fitting piston is drawn upward in a cylinder, one end of which is submerged in water, the piston will create a vacuum below itself. Nature would not permit this to happen, and so the water had to rise up the cylinder to prevent the vacuum occurring. But if this were so, why did the water not rise indefinitely?

Galileo (1564–1642) was also intrigued by the puzzle. He passed the problem on to his secretary and assistant Evangelista Torricelli (1608–47) in 1642, just a few months before he died.

Torricelli had a different idea, one that had nothing at all to do with vacuums and nature's opinion of them. Instead, he thought about what it would mean if air possessed weight. In that case, the weight of the entire atmosphere would press down on every surface exposed to it and it would press equally on all surfaces. What happened inside a suction pump, he

Wind force and Admiral Beaufort

In 1806 the Royal Navy issued a scale by which the commanders of its warships could estimate the strength of the wind by observing its effects. In its early versions (it was revised several times) no mention was made of the actual speed of the wind. Instead, the wind was defined in terms of the speed at which it would propel a man-of-war carrying a specified amount of sail. In a gentle breeze, for example, a ship under full sail and in smooth water would move at 3–4 knots (3.45–4.6 MPH; 5.5–7.4 km/h). Wind speeds were agreed in 1926 and finally added to the scale in 1939.

Its simplicity is the great advantage of the Beaufort scale. Once memorized, it allows people to judge the wind speed fairly accurately by observing its effects.

The scale was devised by Commander Francis Beaufort (1774–1857), later Admiral Sir Francis Beaufort, and it is still known as the Beaufort Scale. It was adopted internationally at the International Meteorological Conference, held in Brussels in 1874.

The Beaufort Scale classifies winds into 13 named "forces" (in 1955 meteorologists at the U.S. Weather Bureau added five more to describe hurricane-force winds). Wind speeds were originally given in knots, the unit that is still often used by ships and aircraft. In the scale given here, knots have been converted to miles per hour and rounded to the nearest whole number. (1 knot = 1 nautical mile per hour = 1.15 MPH = 1.85 km/h.)

Force 0. 1 MPH (1.6 km/h) or less. Calm. The air feels still and smoke rises vertically.
Force 1. 1–3 MPH (1.6–4.8 km/h). Light air. Wind vanes and flags do not move, but rising smoke drifts.

Force 2. 4–7 MPH (6.4–11.3 km/h). Light breeze. Drifting smoke indicates the wind direction.
Force 3. 8–12 MPH (12.9–19.3 km/h). Gentle breeze. Leaves rustle, small twigs move, and flags made from lightweight material stir gently.
Force 4. 13–18 MPH (20.9–29.0 km/h). Moderate breeze. Loose leaves and pieces of paper blow about.
Force 5. 19–24 MPH (30.6–38.6 km/h). Fresh breeze. Small trees that are in full leaf wave in the wind.
Force 6. 25–31 MPH (40.2–49.9 km/h). Strong breeze. It becomes difficult to use an open umbrella.
Force 7. 32–38 MPH (51.5–61.1 km/h). Moderate gale. The wind exerts strong pressure on people walking into it.
Force 8. 39–46 MPH (62.7–74.0 km/h). Fresh gale. Small twigs are torn from trees.
Force 9. 47–54 MPH (75.6–86.9 km/h). Strong gale. Chimneys blown down, slates and tiles torn from roofs.
Force 10. 55–63 MPH (88.5–101.4 km/h). Whole gale. Trees are broken or uprooted.
Force 11. 64–75 MPH (103.0–120.7 km/h). Storm. Trees are uprooted and blown some distance. Cars are overturned.
Force 12. More than 75 MPH (120.7 km/h). Hurricane. Devastation is widespread. Buildings are destroyed, many trees uprooted. In the original instruction: "Or that which no canvas could withstand."

suggested, was that the space above the rising piston contained no air and consequently the weight of the atmosphere was not pressing down on the water at the base of the cylinder. It was pressing down on the water surrounding the cylinder, however, and that pressure would push water some distance up the cylinder. The water would rise only a certain distance, because the pressure exerted by the weight of the atmosphere was insufficient to raise it any higher.

Now he needed an experiment to test his idea. The one he devised used a glass tube, sealed at one end, and a bath of liquid. He filled the tube with liquid all the way to the top and immersed it in the bath. Then he raised the tube to a vertical position with the closed end at the top, keeping the open end below the surface of the liquid throughout. If his theory were correct, the level of the liquid in the tube would fall to the height the pressure on the liquid in the bath could support.

That is what he did. He decided not to use water, because this would be impractical. It would require a tube more than 33 feet (10 m) long. This would be extremely heavy and difficult to maneuver when it was full of water. Instead he used mercury. This is very much denser than water and so the weight of the air would not raise it so high and the experimental apparatus could be much smaller: the tube could be 4 feet (1.2 m) long, rather than 33 feet (10 m). The drawing shows how it worked.

The experiment was successful. Torricelli found that the mercury in the tube fell to a height of about 30 inches (762 mm) above the level of the mercury in the bath. There was no piston and no pump. The column of mercury was supported only by the air pressure outside the tube, proving that air has weight. No other explanation was possible.

Torricelli left his apparatus standing where it was, but then something unexpected happened. He observed over the succeeding days that the level of mercury in the tube varied. Some days it was a little higher and on other days it was a little lower. How could that be? He concluded that the only possible reason was that the weight of the air changed. Sometimes it was heavier, pushing the mercury a little higher, and sometimes it was lighter, and the mercury fell slightly. His experimental apparatus was registering changes in the pressure exerted by the surrounding air. Torricelli had invented the instrument we know as the barometer.

Why air pressure varies

Imagine a circle drawn on the ground. Above that circle there is a column of air reaching all the way to the top of the atmosphere. The weight of all that air is pushing downward on the ground within the circle and the force exerted by that weight is measured as air pressure.

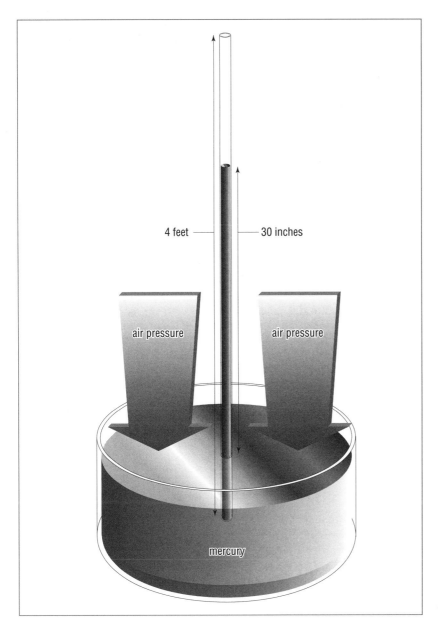

4 feet — — 30 inches

air pressure   air pressure

mercury

Torricelli's barometer

Now suppose there are two imaginary circles, both the same size but one in a very warm place and the other in a very cold place. Contact with the ground will warm the air, so one column of air will be warm and the other cold. When molecules absorb heat, that energy makes them move faster and farther away from one another. This means the column of warm air contains fewer air molecules than the column of cold air. If one column contains fewer molecules than the other, it must weigh less, because its molecules are what make air (or anything else) a material substance at all, so it will exert less pressure on the surface. The air pressure inside one circle will be lower than that inside the other. In the real world, it is local differences in air pressure that produce weather.

Inflate a balloon and air pressure inside stretches the rubber. Once inflated, the air pressure is greater inside the balloon than it is outside. Release the balloon, or burst it, and the air will escape. It will flow from the region of high pressure inside to the region of low pressure outside.

Air moves out of areas of high pressure into areas of low pressure, and the force with which it does so is proportional to the difference between the high and low pressures. You can think of this difference as a slope, or gradient, down which the air flows. It is known as a *pressure gradient*. If there is a large pressure difference and the centers of high and low pressure are close together, the pressure gradient will be steep. If they are far apart, or the difference in pressure is small, the pressure gradient will be shallow. The force moving the air is called the *pressure-gradient force*, or PGF.

While it remains inside the balloon, the air is confined by the balloon itself, and without the balloon the pressure difference would not arise. Simply blowing into the air has no effect on air pressure. You might wonder, therefore, how pressure differences are able to develop in the atmosphere, where there are no balloons to help. You might suppose air would move around freely, equalizing pressures before gradients could form, in which case wind would be impossible.

Air does not move in straight lines

Gradients form because air does not flow in straight lines. Instead of moving directly from a center of high pressure to a center of low pressure it follows an almost circular path at right angles to the pressure gradient. In 1857 the Dutch meteorologist Christoph Buys Ballot found that in the Northern Hemisphere air flows counterclockwise around centers of low pressure and clockwise around centers of high pressure. This became known as Buys Ballot's law (see the box on page 83). The law is a consequence of the combined effect of the pressure-gradient force (PGF) and the Coriolis effect, or CorF (see the sidebar on page 74).

Wind consists of air set in motion by a pressure gradient and flowing approximately at right angles to it. The strength of the wind depends on the steepness of the pressure gradient. You can work this out by looking at a weather map that shows the isobars. The closer together the isobars are, the steeper the gradient and, therefore, the stronger the wind. Isobars are very like the contours on an ordinary map. Closely packed contours indicate a steep slope (gradient) and closely packed isobars indicate a steep pressure gradient.

Calculating the actual wind force is more complicated. This also depends on the density of the moving air, which in turn depends on its temperature, and relating all the relevant factors involves some advanced mathematics. All the same, when you see a weather map with isobars closely packed together you can be sure it means strong winds.

When you see such a weather map in winter, when the surface air temperature is close to freezing, the next thing to look for in the forecast is

Christoph Buys Ballot and his law

In 1857 the Dutch meteorologist Christoph Buys Ballot (1817–90) published a summary of his observations on the relationship between atmospheric pressure and wind. He had concluded that in the Northern Hemisphere, winds flow counterclockwise around areas of low pressure and clockwise around areas of high pressure. In the Southern Hemisphere these directions are reversed.

Unknown to Buys Ballot, a few months earlier the American meteorologist William Ferrel (1817–91) had applied the laws of physics and calculated that this would be the case. As soon as he learned of this, Buys Ballot acknowledged Ferrel's prior claim to the discovery, but nevertheless the phenomenon is now known as Buys Ballot's law. This states that in the Northern Hemisphere, if you stand with your back to the wind the area of low pressure is to your left and the area of high pressure to your right. In the Southern Hemisphere, if you stand with your back to the wind the area of low pressure is to your right and the area of high pressure to your left. (The law does not apply very close to the equator.) The diagram illustrates this.

The law is a consequence of the combined effect of the *pressure-gradient force* (PGF) and the *Coriolis effect*, sometimes incorrectly (because no force is involved) called the *Coriolis force*, and always abbreviated as CorF. Air flows from an area of high pressure to one of low pressure, like water flowing downhill. Just as the speed of flowing water depends on the steepness of the slope (the gradient), so the speed of flowing air depends on the difference in pressure between high and low—the pressure gradient. Gravity is the force that makes water flow downhill. The force making air flow across a pressure gradient is the pressure-gradient force.

(continues)

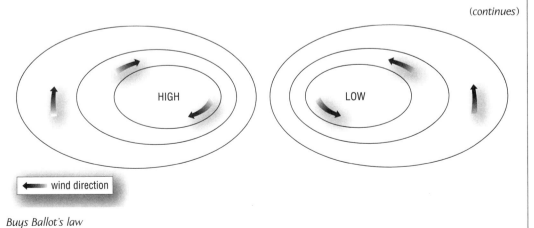

wind direction

Buys Ballot's law

(continued)

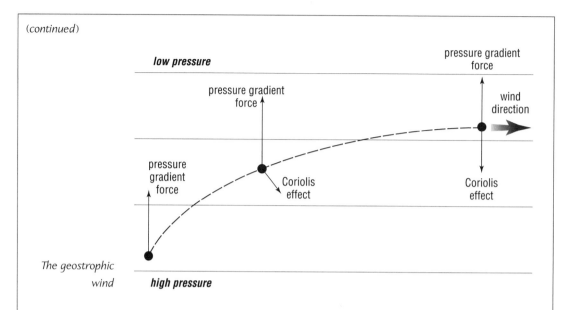

As the air flows at right angles to the pressure gradient, the CorF, acting at right angles to the direction of flow, swings it to the right in the Northern Hemisphere and to the left in the Southern Hemisphere. As it starts to swing to the right, the CorF decreases, until the CorF and PGF produce a resultant force that accelerates the moving air. CorF is proportional to the speed of the moving air, so it increases, swinging the air still more to the right. This continues until the air flows parallel to the isobars (at right angles to the pressure gradient). At this point, the PGF and CorF are acting in opposite directions, but with equal magnitude, so they are in balance.

If the PGF were the stronger force, the air would swing to the left and accelerate. This would increase the CorF, swinging it back to the right again. If the CorF were the stronger, the air would swing further to the right, the PGF acting in the opposite direction would slow it, the CorF would decrease, and the air would swing to the left again. The eventual result is to make the air flow parallel to the isobars (pressure gradient) rather than across them. (See the diagram.)

Near the ground, friction with the surface and objects on it slows the air. This reduces the magnitude of the CorF (which is proportional to wind speed), altering the balance in favor of the PGF and deflecting the air so it flows at an angle to the isobars, rather than parallel to them. Over land, where the surface is uneven and therefore friction is greatest, the wind usually blows across the isobars at an angle of about 45°. Over the ocean it crosses at about 30°.

Clear of the surface, the air does flow parallel to the isobars. This is called the *geostrophic wind.*

precipitation. If weather fronts (see the sidebar "Weather fronts" on page 14) are shown on the map, precipitation is likely (but not inevitable, because some fronts are weak) and it will fall as snow. Driven by winds greater than Force 7, heavy snow will turn into a blizzard. Even if no snowfall is forecast, the packed isobars may mean recent falls will be lifted by the wind. Either way the result will be a blizzard.

HAIL, SLEET, SNOW

Snow is frozen water, but not all frozen water falling from clouds is snow. Ice can also fall as hail, it can form on surfaces as frost, and even the word *snow* is somewhat vague. There are many kinds of snow (see "Snowflakes and types of snow" on page 110).

Whether water falls from a cloud as fog, rain, drizzle, sleet, snow, or hail depends partly on what is happening inside the cloud, but also on what happens to the falling water after it leaves the cloud.

Not all of the water that falls from clouds reaches the ground. Wait for a day, in any season of the year, when there are light showers. These fall from puffy white or gray cumulus clouds. Look at the clouds in the distance and beneath some of them you may see what appears to be a kind of gray veil with clear air below it. The veil has the same appearance as a distant shower, but showers reach all the way to the ground and this veil extends only part of the way. It is called *virga*, and it is exactly what it looks like: a shower that fails to reach the ground, because its water droplets evaporate before they can do so.

Rising air cools adiabatically (see "Adiabatic cooling and warming" on page 2) and the lower its temperature, the less water vapor it can hold. The sidebar "Why warm air can hold more moisture than cold air can" on page 18 explains why this is so. Beyond a certain height, therefore, the air will become saturated and water vapor will start to condense into liquid droplets. This is how clouds form (see the sidebar on page 86), the type of cloud varying according to the vigor with which the air rises.

Below the cloud, the relative humidity of the air is less than 100 percent (it must be, because otherwise cloud would fill it). This air is not saturated. Inside the cloud, the air is saturated. We know that the division between the two layers of air is quite sharp, because clouds have clearly defined bases, although if you fly just beneath clouds you can see that they are rather wispier than they look from the ground. When water falls from the base of a cloud it enters unsaturated air and so it starts to evaporate. The sidebar explains what "humidity" means and how it is measured.

Mass, drag, and terminal velocity

What happens next depends on the water. When a droplet of water falls through the air, its weight pulls it downward, but the air resists its movement. Try to wave a sheet of paper through the air quickly and the paper will curve back, because of the resistance offered by the air. The falling droplet's speed increases until the downward force of its weight balances the resistance of the air, acting as an upward force (called *drag*). After that the droplet no longer accelerates. It has attained its *terminal velocity*.

Not all droplets reach the same terminal velocity. This is because the weight of an object is proportional to its volume, but drag acts on its surface area, and the greater the volume, the smaller the ratio of its volume to its surface area. Suppose, for example, a spherical water droplet has a radius of 4 (the units do not matter). Its volume (given by the equation $4/3\pi r^3$) is 268 and its surface area ($4\pi r^2$) is 201. To work out how much surface area there is for each unit of volume, divide the surface area by the volume ($201 \div 268$) and the answer is 0.75. Now imagine a droplet half as big, with a radius of 2. Its volume will be 33.5, its surface area 50.3, and for each unit of its volume it will have 1.5 units of surface area ($50.3 \div 33.5$). The bigger the droplet, the more it weighs in proportion to its surface area and, therefore, the greater its terminal velocity will be. Drizzle feels gentle, because it falls slowly, with a terminal velocity of around 2.5 feet per

Evaporation, condensation, and the formation of clouds

When air rises it cools adiabatically. If it is dry, at first it will cool at the *dry adiabatic lapse rate* of 5.5°F every 1,000 feet (10°C per km). Moving air may be forced to rise if it crosses high ground, such as a mountain or mountain range (1 in the illustration), or meets a mass of cooler, denser air at a front (3). Locally, air may also rise by convection where the ground is warmed unevenly (2).

There will be a height, called the *condensation level*, at which the air temperature falls to its dew point. As the air rises above this level, the water vapor it contains will start to condense. Condensation releases latent heat, warming the air, and if the air continues to rise once the relative humidity of the air reaches 100 percent, it will cool at the *saturated adiabatic lapse rate* of about 3°F per 1,000 feet (6°C per km).

Water vapor condenses onto minute particles called *cloud condensation nuclei* (CCN). If the air contains CCN consisting of minute particles of a substance that readily dissolves in water (*hygroscopic nuclei*), water vapor will condense at a relative humidity as low as 78 percent. Salt crystals and sulfate particles are common examples. If the air contains insoluble particles, such as dust, the vapor will condense at about 100 percent relative humidity. If there are no CCN at all, the relative humidity may exceed 100 percent and the air will be supersaturated, although the relative humidity in clouds rarely exceeds 101 percent.

Cloud condensation nuclei range in size from 0.001 μm to more than 10 μm diameter, but water will condense on to the smallest particles only if the air is strongly supersaturated, and the largest particles are so heavy they do not remain airborne very long. Condensation is most efficient on CCN averaging 0.2 μm diameter (1 μm = one-millionth of a meter = 0.00004 inches).

At first, water droplets vary in size according to the size of the nuclei onto which they condensed. After that, the droplets grow, but they also lose water by evaporation, because they are warmed by the latent heat of condensation. Some freeze, grow into snowflakes, then melt as they fall into a lower, warmer region of the cloud. Others grow as large droplets collide and merge with smaller ones.

second (0.76 m s^{-1}). Rain, with much bigger drops, falls at 13 to more than 30 feet per second (4–9 m s^{-1}).

Up to a point, ice behaves in the same way as liquid water. Although it is slightly less dense than very cold water, this makes no difference to its weight-to-drag ratio, because both ice and liquid water are about 1,000 times denser than air. What does make a difference is its shape.

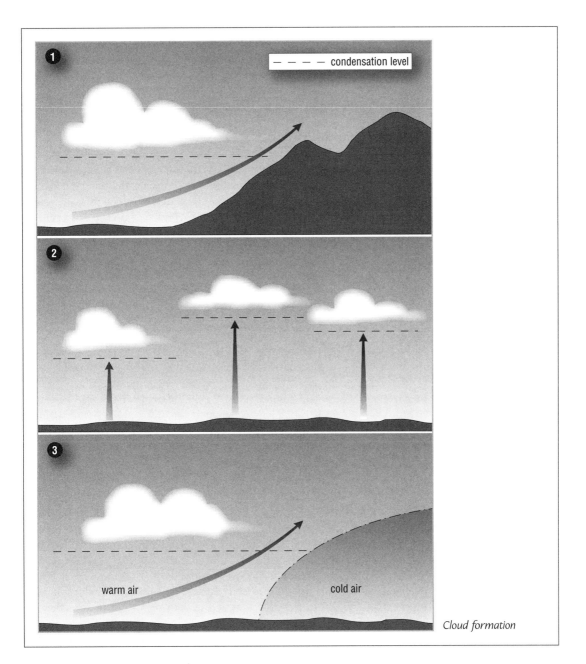

— — — — condensation level

warm air   cold air

Cloud formation

Humidity

The amount of water vapor air can hold varies according to the temperature. Warm air can hold more than cold air. The amount of water vapor present in the air is called the *humidity* of the air. This is measured in several ways.

The *absolute humidity* is the mass of water vapor present in a given volume of air, measured in grams per cubic meter (1 g m^{-3} = 0.046 ounces per cubic yard). Changes in the temperature and pressure alter the volume of air, however, and this changes the amount of water vapor in a given volume without actually adding or removing any moisture. The concept of absolute humidity takes no account of this and so it is not very useful and is seldom used.

Mixing ratio is more useful. This is a measure of the amount of water vapor in a unit volume of dry air—air with the water vapor removed. *Specific humidity* is similar to mixing ratio, but measures the amount of water vapor in a unit volume of air including the moisture. Both are reported in grams per cubic meter. Since the amount of water vapor is always very small, seldom accounting for more than 7 percent of the mass of the air, specific humidity and mixing ratio are almost the same thing.

The most familiar term is *relative humidity*. This is the measurement you read from hygrometers, either directly or after referring to tables—and it is the one you hear in weather forecasts. Relative humidity (RH) is the amount of water vapor in the air expressed as a percentage of the amount needed to saturate the air at that temperature. When the air is saturated the RH is 100 percent (the "percent" is often omitted).

Why drops of water are spherical

Liquid water tends to form spherical droplets. It does so because of *surface tension*. As the drawing shows, water molecules attract one another—the positive charge on the hydrogen end of one water molecule attracts the negative charge on the oxygen end of a neighboring molecule. Within a body of liquid, each molecule is attracted equally in all directions. The forces acting on it are balanced, and so the molecule is free to move in any direction. At the surface, however, there is a layer of molecules with no water molecules attracting them from above. These are held by the attraction of molecules to the side and below. The forces are unbalanced and so the molecules are held very firmly by the attraction of molecules beside and below them. This tension is so strong that it behaves like a skin covering the water. Some insects can walk across it, and it will bear the weight of small, solid objects such as paper clips, provided these are laid on the surface very gently.

Only liquids experience surface tension. Ice is solid and its shape is determined by the way it forms. It may form approximately spherical blocks, like hail, but it can also assume the delicate shapes of snowflakes.

If the water is in contact with nothing except air, surface tension will pull it into a spherical shape. A sphere has a smaller surface area in relation

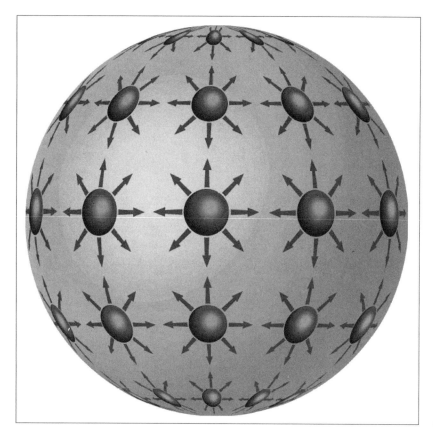

Surface tension

to its volume than any other shape. A cube with a total surface area of 24 square inches (155 cm^2) encloses a volume of 8 cubic inches (131 cm^3), for example, but a sphere enclosing the same volume has a surface area of only 19.35 square inches (125 cm^2). A sphere is the most efficient shape for enclosing a liquid and this means it requires the least energy to maintain. Given the freedom to assume any shape, liquids adopt the most economical one—a sphere.

Why some fall faster than others

Increase the surface area of a falling object and the drag also increases, as shown in the diagram. Increase the surface area in relation to the volume, and therefore the weight, and its terminal velocity will decrease. In other words, a spherical hailstone will fall at the same speed as a water droplet of the same weight, but ice with any shape other than spherical will fall more slowly.

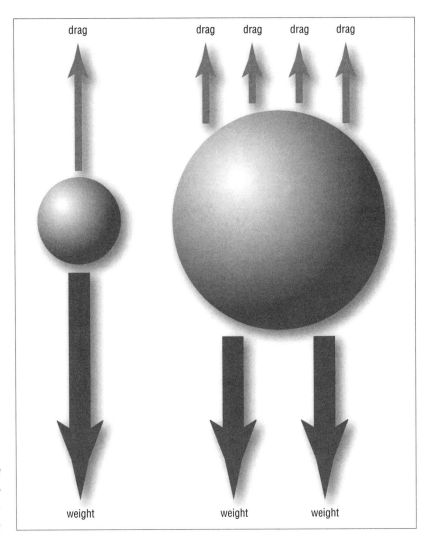

Drag and weight. Small droplet: low weight, low drag. Large droplet: high weight, high drag

There are two consequences of this. The first is that snowflakes drift down very gently. Depending on their size and precise shape, they fall at about 1 or 2 feet per second (0.3–0.6 m s^{-1}). The second consequence is that once hailstones grow larger than an average raindrop, they fall faster. Hailstones reach terminal velocities of 25 feet per second (7.6 m s^{-1}) or more, and giant hailstones, nearly one inch (2.5 cm) in diameter, fall at around 65 feet per second (20 m s^{-1}). That is fast enough to injure anyone that they hit, and to damage farm crops and the roofs of buildings.

Big droplets fall faster than small droplets, but this does not apply to the smallest droplets of all. These weigh so little that their movement is entirely governed by the stronger motion of the air around them. This is why cloud droplets remain inside their clouds until they have collided with other droplets, coalesced with them, and grown to a size large enough for them to start falling.

Once it leaves its cloud, a water droplet enters unsaturated air and starts to evaporate. This makes it grow smaller, altering its volume-to-surface area ratio and slowing its fall. The more slowly it falls, the longer it remains in the air, and so the more of it that will evaporate. The rate of evaporation sets a limit to the distance a water droplet of any particular size can fall before it evaporates altogether. If it is to reach the ground from a height of 1,000 feet (300 m) or so, a water droplet must leave the cloud with a radius no smaller than about 100 μm (about 0.004 inch) and, even so, the air below the cloud must be close to saturation. Droplets of this size reach the ground as drizzle.

Cloud droplets are no more than 20 μm (0.0008 inch) in diameter, one-tenth the size of drizzle droplets. Some of them do fall from their cloud, but they travel only an inch or two (25–50 mm) before they evaporate. They make the bottom of the cloud wispy when seen at close quarters, but sharp when seen from a distance.

Rain, sleet, or snow?

Ice crystals will form inside a cloud if the air temperature is below freezing. It often happens that the upper part of a cloud is below freezing, but the lower part is not. Ice forms near the top, but the crystals melt as they fall, and precipitation falls as rain. Even if precipitation leaves a cloud as ice crystals, these will melt if they have to fall very far through air at above freezing temperature. To fall as snow, the temperature must usually be no higher than freezing below about 1,000 feet (300 m).

If the temperature in the lower part of the cloud is close to freezing, precipitation will leave it as very cold water droplets. These will remain liquid if the temperature is above freezing in the air beneath the cloud, but if this air is just below freezing temperature, some or all of the droplets will freeze. They may fall as tiny crystals, much the same size as drizzle droplets. These will not stick to objects. Usually, they bounce when they strike a hard surface. In North America this is known as *sleet*. In Britain "sleet" is a mixture of snow and rain falling together.

Bigger snowflakes need cloud temperatures that are below freezing throughout. This allows ice crystals to combine without melting, and snowflakes form best in cloud temperatures of 32°F (0°C) down to 23°F (–5°C). Then they must fall through air beneath the cloud that is also below freezing temperature, although it may be warmer than the air inside the cloud.

The size of snowflakes depends largely on the movement of the air. If the air moves vigorously, the flakes are broken apart before they can grow very large, but in very calm air flakes can reach an inch (25 mm) or more across. These are the flakes that cling to surfaces. If you walk through falling snow of this kind, before long your coat and hat are covered in it. It is the shape of its crystals that make it cling so firmly (see "Snowflakes and types of snow" on pages 110–115).

Snow may also fall as tiny pellets. These are white, often roughly spherical or conical in shape, and most are no more than one-tenth of an inch (2.5 mm) across. Many are smaller. Their white color is due to the fact that they are composed of individual ice crystals loosely joined together with air spaces between them, rather like tiny, folded-up snowflakes. This structure also makes them soft. Being so small, they fall slowly, but even so they are often smashed when they strike hard ground. These pellets are called *soft hail*, or *graupel* (from the German word for sleet). Soft hail forms in clouds that contain little liquid water. Water vapor is deposited as ice directly onto them. If, as they fall, they enter a region where the temperature is above freezing and water is abundant, water may freeze onto them as a layer of clear ice. Ice pellets may also fall if raindrops freeze or snowflakes melt and then freeze again.

Hail

True hail is different. It forms in storms that are moving across the surface, steered by a strong wind at high level.

A hailstone begins as a rain droplet. Ordinarily it would be heavy enough to fall from the cloud, but instead it is carried aloft by strong upcurrents. High in the cloud, the water freezes and the raindrop becomes a small sphere of ice. Near the top of the cloud it is swept forward by the high-level wind. Then it starts to fall. As it falls, it passes through tiny droplets of water that have been chilled to below freezing temperature. These supercooled liquid droplets freeze instantly when the hailstone touches them, forming a layer of white rime ice. As it falls further, the hailstone enters a part of the cloud where the water content is higher, but there are still many supercooled droplets. These also freeze on contact, but spread as they do so, forming a layer of clear ice. By this time, the advancing storm has caught up with the falling hailstone. It enters the upcurrents and is carried aloft again. This happens repeatedly, producing a layered structure as the hailstone falls through the cloud, only to be carried back to the top once more. If you could slice a big hailstone in half, you would see that it is made up of layers, like an onion. The layers are alternately white and clear, each pair of layers made up from white rime ice covered by a layer of clear ice.

Its outer layer of clear ice gives a hailstone its strength. When it hits the ground it does not shatter, it bounces. Its size depends on the number of times it has made its *accretion circuit*, of being carried to the top of the cloud, dropped, and carried aloft again, acquiring another pair of layers with each round trip. Most hailstones are quite small, seldom growing to more than about $1/4$ of an inch (6 mm) across, but in really huge, violent clouds they can become much larger.

Water vapor can change directly into ice, and ice directly into vapor, without passing through a liquid phase. This is called *deposition* when water vapor changes to ice and *sublimation* when ice vaporizes. You must have seen it happen. Hoarfrost is caused by deposition, and when patches of snow shrink or disappear even though the temperature is well below freezing, the ice crystals have sublimed into dry air.

Tiny ice crystals can even fall from a cloudless sky if the air is cold enough and contains freezing nuclei. Water vapor changes directly into ice, rather than condensing into liquid droplets. The resulting crystals sometimes glitter in the sunlight and are known as *diamond dust*.

Some consequences of supercooling are attractive and harmless. Freezing fog and freezing rain are less pleasant.

FREEZING RAIN AND FREEZING FOG

As air cools, its capacity for holding water vapor decreases and, therefore, its relative humidity increases (see the sidebar "Why warm air can hold more moisture than cold air can" on page 18). When the relative humidity reaches 100 percent, the air is saturated. Ordinarily, water vapor will start to condense into liquid droplets as the air approaches saturation.

In order to condense, however, tiny solid particles must be present to which water molecules can attach themselves (see the sidebar "Evaporation, condensation, and the formation of clouds" on page 86). Dust, smoke, salt, and sulfur dioxide are among the substances with particles onto which water vapor will condense. These are called *condensation nuclei* and most air contains plenty of them. Over land, there are 300–400 of them in every cubic inch of air (18–24 cm^{-3}) and over the oceans, far from any source of dust, there are about 60 in every cubic inch (4 cm^{-3}).

In really clean air, water vapor is more reluctant to condense. The air becomes supersaturated and under laboratory conditions its relative humidity can be increased to more than 300 percent before droplets form spontaneously. Natural air is never this clean, but air is often supersaturated by 1 or 2 percent.

Freezing nuclei

Just as condensation nuclei must be present before water vapor will condense out of saturated air, so freezing nuclei must be present before water droplets will freeze at low temperature. Freezing nuclei are much rarer than condensation nuclei, and the colder the air, the fewer of them there are. Air seldom contains more than 0.06 of them per cubic inch (0.004 cm^{-3}) and at around –20°F (–29°C) there may be fewer than 0.0006 per cubic inch (approximately one nucleus in every 1,700 cubic inches of air or 27,863 cm^3). Fine soil particles are common freezing nuclei, and volcanic dust and chemical compounds released by plants may also contribute, but once ice crystals have started forming they encourage water to freeze onto them. Minute ice crystals are the best freezing nuclei of all.

Even in the presence of freezing nuclei, however, airborne water droplets do not turn into ice the moment the temperature falls below 32°F (0°C). At 15°F (–9°C) a cloud still consists almost entirely of water droplets. As the temperature falls to below –4°F (–20°C), ice crystals begin to outnumber the water droplets, but it is not until the temperature falls below −20°F (−29°C) that clouds consist wholly of ice crystals, and even then there are exceptions. In the absence of freezing nuclei, water droplets can be cooled to −40°F (−40°C) before they will freeze spontaneously.

Supercooling

Water that has been chilled below freezing temperature is said to be *super-cooled*, and supercooled cloud droplets are very common. Temperatures are below freezing in the upper regions of most big clouds, even in summer. In saturated air, in which water vapor is condensing, if the temperature at ground level is 80°F (27°C), air will be at freezing temperature (32°F, 0°C) at 16,000 feet (4,880 m). In winter, when the ground-level temperature is, say, 30°F (−1°C), it will be 20°F (−7°C) at about 3,000 feet (900 m). Even in summer, much of the rain that falls in middle latitudes is snow that has melted during its descent.

At just below 32°F (0°C), water lying on the ground will start to freeze. Ice will appear around the edges of ponds and over puddles. Cloud droplets at this temperature are still liquid and most of them will remain so at much lower temperatures. They are still able to form raindrops, so it is quite possible for rain to be composed of water at below-freezing temperature. For most of the year, supercooled raindrops will fall through warmer air beneath the cloud, so by the time they reach the ground they will have warmed to above freezing, although the rain may still feel cold on your face and hands.

Rain that freezes on contact

In winter, supercooled rain can cause problems. The air temperature beneath the cloud is usually higher than that inside the cloud, but in winter it may nevertheless be a degree or two below freezing. The supercooled raindrops are warmed as they fall, but not to a temperature above freezing. They fall as *freezing rain*—rain that is below freezing temperature when it reaches the ground.

Any solid object will act as a freezing nucleus for these droplets and the rain will freeze on contact with it. Freezing is almost instantaneous, but it affects only the water in direct contact with the surface. As each raindrop strikes, the first part of the drop freezes and the supercooled water behind it spills to the sides, freezing as it reaches the surface. As the diagram illustrates, each drop spreads and freezes into a thin film of ice. Consequently, a rain shower coats everything onto which it falls with a layer of clear ice. Freezing rain turns roads and sidewalks into skating rinks and makes walking and driving hazardous.

When the ground-level temperature is low enough, the raindrops do not need to be supercooled to produce freezing rain. It sometimes happens that a layer of warm air lies above a layer of cooler air. This situation can arise, for example, when cold air pushes beneath warmer air at a cold front (see the sidebar "Weather fronts" on page 14). Temperature usually decreases with height, so this is called a *temperature inversion*. Rain may fall from a cloud in the warm air above the inversion layer. The rain will be a degree or two above freezing temperature, but if the air beneath it is cooler, a few degrees below freezing, the ground and objects near the ground will be at the same temperature as the air. The falling raindrops will cool as they fall through the cold air beneath the inversion, and as they strike they will be further chilled by contact with the surface and will freeze onto it. Again, a layer of clear ice will form very quickly.

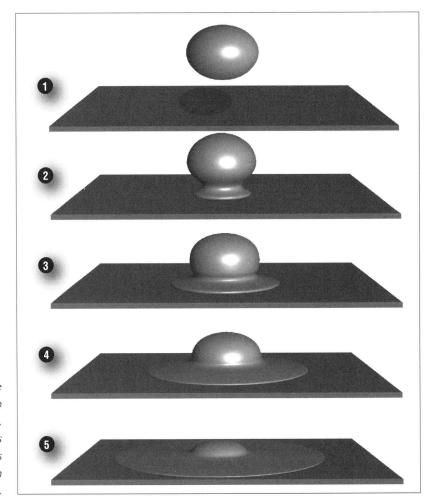

Freezing rain. As the supercooled raindrop strikes the surface, it spreads, freezing as it does so, until it has deposited a thin layer of ice.

Freezing rain is distinguished only by the fact that it freezes on contact with a surface. The rain itself can be of any type. It may be a shower, with large drops, or more prolonged drizzle. In either case it coats everything with clear ice, the thickness of the ice depending only on the amount of rain that falls.

Fog and frost

Water vapor condenses when air is cooled, but there are several ways to cool air and some of them cause condensation at ground level. This produces fog, composed of minute droplets identical to those in cloud. Indeed, sometimes fog is cloud. If moist air rises as it crosses high ground, adiabatic cooling may make cloud form before the air reaches the top. Hill walkers often find themselves in fog that is really cloud.

Warm, moist air may also drift over cold ground. The horizontal movement of heat is called *advection*. As the air is chilled by contact with the ground beneath it, its water vapor may condense to form *advection fog*.

The third common cause of fog is radiation, and it is called *radiation fog*. During the day the ground is warmed by the Sun and at night it radiates away the heat it received by day, so it cools rapidly. If the air above it is clear, but close to saturation, the ground may cool sufficiently to cause low-level condensation in the early hours of the morning, and by dawn there will be fog.

The temperature at which air reaches saturation, so water vapor condenses, is called its *dew point*. Obviously, this varies according to the amount of water vapor present in the air (see the sidebar "Humidity" on page 88), so the drier the air, the lower its dew-point temperature.

It can happen that the dew-point temperature is below freezing. In this case, water vapor will not condense into liquid droplets, but will be deposited directly as ice crystals. At night, heat radiated from the surface may lower the temperature to below the dew-point temperature of the air in contact with it. Water vapor will then condense as dew, but if the dew-point temperature is below freezing and the ground cools sufficiently, deposition will produce ice crystals on all exposed surfaces. In the morning you will see them as hoarfrost. It is the ice that transforms gardens into a sparkling white wonderland—and that drivers must scrape from their windshields before they can set off on their travels.

Suppose, though, that the air is rather moister than this, so its dew-point temperature is above freezing. As it is chilled from below, fog will form. If the ground, and objects on the ground, are much colder than freezing, the fog will freeze onto all exposed surfaces. This produces rime ice. Air trapped among the ice crystals makes it white and because it forms from the freezing of individual, tiny droplets of liquid, it has an uneven texture, but it is thicker and more solid than hoarfrost.

Freezing fog

Freezing will be especially rapid if the fog consists of supercooled droplets, which it may be if the air is chilled in stages. First, the air is cooled to below its dew-point temperature, so liquid droplets form. Then it is cooled further, to below 32°F (0°C), and the droplets become supercooled. They will now freeze instantly onto any surface that is at a temperature below freezing.

This is called *freezing fog* and, although it is not so dangerous as freezing rain, it can cause serious difficulties, especially for drivers. After it has stood in the open for a short time, the exterior of a car is at the same temperature as the air. As it travels, the airflow over the car carries away any heat from inside the vehicle that may be warming the outer skin. You may be warm inside the car, with the heater on, but the outside of the car is cold. If you drive through freezing fog, the droplets will freeze instantly on contact with the windshield and the defogger will be of no help. It warms only the inside of the glass to evaporate condensation from air inside the car. With ordinary fog, the wipers will clear droplets from the windshield, but in freezing fog they merely spread them into an uneven, semi-opaque layer of white ice. Meanwhile, as the driver struggles to see the road ahead through this film of ice, droplets may also be freezing onto the road surface, so the road is also acquiring a coating of ice.

When freezing rain or freezing fog are forecast, motoring organizations and the police advise drivers to stay at home. You should attempt only essential journeys in such conditions.

WHAT HAPPENS WHEN WATER FREEZES AND ICE MELTS

Water is one of the commonest substances on our planet. It is also by far the most remarkable: if water did not possess some extremely peculiar properties our weather would be very different.

At the range of temperatures found over the surface of our planet and in the lower atmosphere, water exists as a gas, liquid, and solid, often as all three in the same area. When you see a partly frozen pond, ice and liquid water are clearly visible side by side, and the air contains invisible water vapor.

This is its first peculiarity. With most substances, the smaller the molecules from which they are made, the lower their freezing and boiling temperatures. Water molecules, comprising one atom of oxygen and two of hydrogen, are quite small. Judging by their size, water should freeze at about –148°F (–100°C) and boil at about –112°F (–80°C). If it did, there would be no liquid water or ice anywhere on Earth. All of the water would exist as vapor. There would be no oceans, lakes, rivers, glaciers, or ice sheets. Precipitation would be impossible and the entire surface of the Earth would be one vast desert, where nothing at all could live.

Again, the density of most substances increases as they are cooled, because their molecules pack together more closely, and this steady increase in density continues until they turn into solids. Water does increase in density as it cools, but the change is only slight, and freshwater reaches its maximum density while still a liquid. Ice is less dense than liquid water. That is why it floats. If this were not so, ice forming over lakes and ponds, not to mention the oceans, would sink to the bottom, which would be highly inconvenient for bottom-dwelling aquatic life. What is more, once the ice lay on the ocean bed it is difficult to see how the warmth of the Sun shining on the surface of the sea could ever penetrate deeply enough to melt it. The oceans and large lakes would exist as ice covered by a layer of liquid water.

Structure of the molecule

Both of these properties are due to the structure of the water molecule itself. A molecule is composed of atoms, in the case of water, two atoms of hydrogen joined to one of oxygen, usually written as H_2O. An atom comprises a nucleus containing *protons*, each with a positive electric charge, surrounded by a cloud of *electrons*, each with a negative electric charge precisely equal to the positive charge on a proton. The charges usually balance, so the atom as a whole possesses no overall charge (but if an atom loses or gains electrons it will acquire a charge, in which case it is said to have been *ionized*).

When atoms join together to form molecules, those of many elements do so by sharing one or more electrons. This type of linkage is called a *covalent bond* and it is what holds the water molecule together. A hydrogen atom possesses one electron, but the oxygen atom has a vacancy for two electrons, so both of the hydrogen atoms in the water molecule share their electrons with the oxygen atom, as shown in the diagram.

Like charges repel each other, and repulsion between those electrons in the oxygen atom that are not shared with hydrogen pushes the two hydrogen atoms into positions separated by an angle of 104.5°, as shown in the diagram showing the structure of the water molecule. The effect of this is to leave a small negative electric charge on the oxygen side of the molecule and a small positive charge on the hydrogen side. The two charges balance, so the molecule as a whole has no charge, but it is slightly positive on one side and slightly negative on the other. Molecules of this kind are called *polar*.

Polar molecules attract each other by the attraction of opposites. In the case of water, a bond forms between the hydrogen end of one molecule and the oxygen end of the next, as the illustration shows. It is called a *hydrogen bond* and is fairly weak (compared with other types of chemical bonding), but it is what gives water the high surface tension that

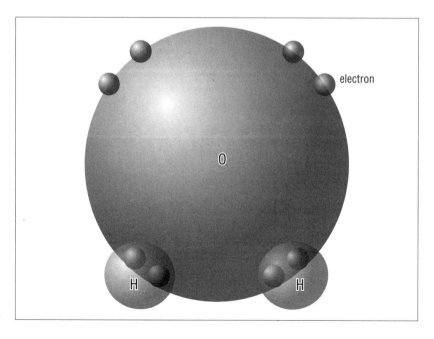

The water molecule

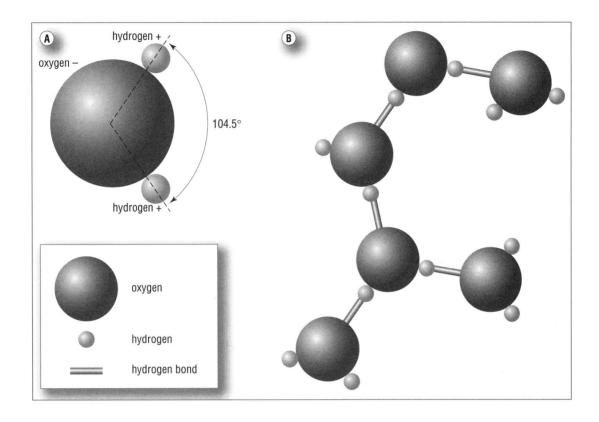

The structure of water

makes it form drops—because molecules at the surface are securely bonded to those on either side and below. (For an explanation of surface tension see "Hail, sleet, snow" on page 85.) Mercury is the only substance that is liquid at room temperature and that has a higher surface tension than water.

What happens when water is heated

While it is a liquid, the molecules of water are joined into groups by hydrogen bonds. When any substance is heated it expands. So does water, but it expands less than most liquids. Heating makes molecules absorb energy. This makes them move faster, so they take up more space, which is what causes the expansion. Water molecules also vibrate faster when they are heated, but within their groups the hydrogen bonds are like strings tethering them and restricting their expansion. Heat water enough, however, and the molecules vibrate so violently that they break their hydrogen bonds and escape. Free of their bonds, they can leave the liquid altogether and enter the air as separate molecules. All exposed surfaces of liquid water lose molecules this way, but the warmer the water the faster they lose them.

Energy is needed to break the hydrogen bonds. When water is heated, its temperature rises, but extra heat is required to break the hydrogen bonds and change liquid water into water vapor, a gas. This extra energy is absorbed by the molecules without changing the temperature of the water and the same amount of heat energy is released when the bonds form again. For pure water at 32°F (0°C), 600 calories of energy must be absorbed to change one gram (1 g = 0.035 oz) from liquid to gas (evaporation or vaporization). It is called *latent heat*, and the latent heat of water is higher than that of any other substance. (The scientific unit is the joule (J), and the latent heat of vaporization is 2,501 J g^{-1}.) The Scottish chemist Joseph Black was the first scientist to observe this, although he was not the first to publish a description of the phenomenon (see the sidebar).

The discovery of latent heat

Joseph Black (1728–99) was a Scottish chemist and physician. He ran a successful medical practice, but was also a lecturer in chemistry at the University of Glasgow and professor of medicine at the University of Edinburgh. In 1766 he was appointed professor of chemistry at Edinburgh University. He was a busy man.

His researches made major contributions to the development of chemistry, but in about 1760 he turned his attention to a different problem: heat and temperature. In 1761 Black heated ice slowly, closely observing its temperature. He found that the ice melted, but that its temperature did not change as it did so. He concluded that the ice must have absorbed heat while it was melting, so that water contained more heat than ice, but that the absorbed heat did not affect the temperature.

This meant that the *amount* of heat a substance contains is not the same thing as the *intensity* of that heat. When we measure the temperature of a substance, the thermometer registers the *intensity* of the heat, but gives no indication whatever of the *amount*. This amount, which we cannot measure directly, Black called *latent heat*—"latent" means "hidden."

Black did not rest there. The following year, 1762, he observed what happens when water boils. Again, he found that the water absorbs heat with no change in its temperature, and therefore that water vapor contains latent heat.

He observed the reverse of both changes, by condensing steam and freezing water. In both cases he found that the latent heat was released. As water freezes or water vapor condenses the temperature of the surrounding medium rises.

Black published no description of his discovery. The first published account was written by the Swiss geologist, meteorologist, and physicist Jean André Deluc (1727–1817), who discovered latent heat in 1761 independently of Black. Black did describe latent heat in his lectures, however, and he explained it personally to a young, impoverished engineer called James Watt (1736–1819). Watt realized the significance of the large amount of latent heat contained in water vapor—and he put that understanding to very good use. Watt's engines transformed manufacturing and contributed greatly to the industrial revolution.

When water molecules absorb latent heat, the temperature of the water does not increase. The latent heat they absorb is supplied by their surroundings, no heat is returned, and consequently the surroundings lose heat. In other words, evaporation cools the air. We benefit from this property of water when sweat evaporates from our skin, cooling it.

Condensation converts water vapor, a gas, into liquid, where molecules are linked by hydrogen bonds. The formation of those bonds deprives the molecules of some of their energy, which is released as latent heat. The bond represents the energy holding molecules together, so the amount released when they form is precisely the same as the amount that is absorbed by the molecules when they break.

The absorption and release of latent heat have a very important influence on the way clouds form in unstable air. Warm air rises by convection, its water vapor condenses, and the release of the latent heat of condensation warms the air again, making it rise higher (see the sidebar "Evaporation, condensation, and the formation of clouds" on page 86). More vapor condenses and the air goes on rising until it reaches a level at which its density is the same as that of the surrounding air. This process leads to the formation of heaped cumulus clouds or, if the air is very unstable and moist enough, cumulonimbus storm clouds (see "Heavy snowstorms and what causes them" on page 134).

Melting, freezing, and the change between gas and solid

Latent heat is also absorbed when ice melts and is released when water freezes. In this case, hydrogen bonds exist in both the liquid and the solid, but as water freezes, more hydrogen bonds form. The original hydrogen bonds remain. All that happens is that additional bonds form when water freezes and dissolve when ice melts. Because fewer bonds are involved, less latent heat is released in freezing than is released when water vapor condenses. The freezing of one gram of water releases 80 calories ($334 J g^{-1}$). That is why the air often feels a little warmer when ice is forming, and it is the absorption of the same amount of latent heat to melt ice that makes the temperature drop during the thaw.

Water can also change directly between the solid and gaseous phases (between ice and water vapor) without passing through a liquid phase. The change from ice to water vapor is called *sublimation* and the change from water vapor to ice is *deposition* (but "sublimation" is sometimes used for both processes).

Sublimation and deposition also absorb and release latent heat. Not surprisingly, since the energy of latent heat is used in the making and

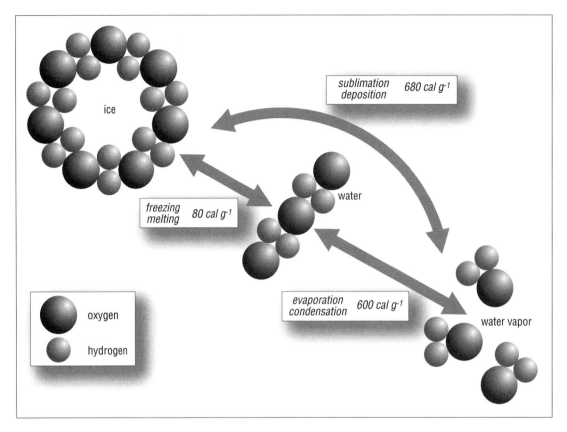

Latent heat of water

breaking of hydrogen bonds, the amount of latent heat involved in sublimation is the sum of those required for condensation–vaporization and freezing–thawing. It is 680 calories for each gram (2,835 J g^{-1}).

The hydrogen bonds in ice pull the molecules into a very complex but ordered structure in which each molecule is connected to four others. As the diagram shows, the resulting structure is fairly open. When the ice melts, some of the hydrogen bonds break, and the water molecules separate into groups once more. These small groups are able to slide freely past one another and they fill the spaces that existed in the crystal structure of the ice. Once the ice has melted, the same number of water molecules occupies a smaller space. That is why water expands as it freezes, contracts as it thaws, and why pure water is at its most dense just above freezing, at 39°F (4°C).

At sea-level pressure, at 50°F (10°C) one cubic foot of pure water weighs 62.2 pounds (0.799 kg m^{-3}). At 39°F (4°C) water weighs 62.3 pounds per cubic foot (0.800 kg m^{-3}), and as ice at 32°F (0°C) it weighs only 57.1 pounds per cubic foot (0.733 kg m^{-3}). As the temperature rises above 39°F (0°C) ordinary expansion occurs. That is why ice floats, rather than sinking to the bottom.

The universal solvent

We use water for washing and to dilute drinks, because many common substances will dissolve in it. It is one of the most powerful of all solvents. A substance that dissolved any other substance it encountered would be a "universal solvent." There is no such substance, which is as well, because it would dissolve any container and anything onto which it spilled. Water comes close, however.

Its solvent properties mean that natural water is never pure. Rainwater carries substances that dissolved into it while it was in the cloud and during its fall to the surface. Even over the middle of a large ocean, thousands of miles from the nearest land and even further from any factory, rain contains carbon dioxide and sulfur dioxide that have dissolved from the air and it may also contain nitrogen oxides, produced when the energy of lightning oxidizes atmospheric nitrogen.

Substances dissolve in water partly because of its polar molecules, which attract areas of opposite charge on their molecules. The presence of such impurities alters some of the properties of water, a fact we exploit when we scatter salt on roads to melt ice.

Salt is sodium chloride, $NaCl$, in which the ionic bond forms when a sodium atom donates one electron to a chlorine atom. This leaves the sodium atom short of one electron, giving it a positive charge (written as Na^+), and the chlorine atom with a negative charge due to its extra electron (written as Cl^-). It is the attraction of opposite charges that holds the molecule together.

In water, the sodium and chlorine separate, the sodium being attracted to the oxygen end of a water molecule (O^-) and the chlorine to the hydrogen end (H^+). The sodium and chlorine are attached to and completely surrounded by water, but one consequence is that the freezing temperature is reduced. Water containing 35 parts of salt to 1,000 parts of water freezes at 28.56°F (–1.19°C). This is the average salinity of seawater, usually expressed as 35 per mil (‰); and seawater is densest at 32°F (0°C). If the temperature is barely below freezing, the addition of salt will be enough to melt any ice forming on a road surface.

WILSON BENTLEY, THE MAN WHO PHOTOGRAPHED SNOWFLAKES

People have been fascinated by the beauty of snow and ice for thousands of years. In fact, the English word *crystal* is from the Greek word *krustallos*, which means ice.

This fascination was not confined to the West, of course, and although anyone examining snowflakes closely might have realized that their crystals are hexagonal (six-sided), the first written record of this discovery is not European, but Chinese. Some time between 140 and 131 B.C.E., in a work called *Moral discourses illustrating the Han text of the "Book of Songs,"* a scholar called Han Ying wrote that "Flowers of snow are always six-pointed." This fact about snowflakes was well known in China from that time, but many centuries passed before any mention of it appeared in European writings.

Olaf Mansson, or to give him his Latinized name Olaus Magnus (1490–1557), the Archbishop of Sweden, is believed to have been the first. In 1555 he published a book on natural history called *Historia de gentibus septentrionalibus*, in which he described snow crystals and included drawings of them. His book became popular throughout Europe and there were many editions and translations. The first English translation appeared in 1658, entitled *History of the Goths, Swedes and Vandals*.

A little later, in 1591, an English mathematician, Thomas Harriot (1560–1621), noted the same observation. He mentioned it in correspondence with Johannes Kepler, but did not publish it. Johannes Kepler (1571–1630) also wrote a description of snowflakes in *A New Year's Gift, or On the Six-cornered Snowflake*, published in 1611.

More detailed studies had to wait for the invention of the microscope. Once that instrument was obtainable, snowflakes were popular as objects for examination. Antoni van Leeuwenhoek (1632–1723), the most famous 17th-century microscopist, studied them. One of these early microscopists was the English physicist Robert Hooke (1635–1703). He became fascinated by the instrument, and improved it. His *Micrographia*, published in 1665, contained his own detailed drawings of snowflakes, seen through the microscope, and descriptions of their crystal structure.

In the following centuries, snowflakes were of interest mainly for their beauty. This changed in 1931, when art and science combined in the work of Wilson A. Bentley.

The snowflake man

Wilson Alwyn Bentley was born on February 9, 1865, on his family's farm in the village of Jericho, in northern Vermont. After his father died, Wilson and his brother managed the farm together. They were successful and the farm prospered. Wilson lived on the farm for the whole of his life and combined his scientific work with farmwork.

Wilson studied at home until he was 14 years old, taught by his mother, who had been a schoolteacher. She owned a small microscope, which she used as a teaching aid. Wilson was fascinated by what he saw with it, and was especially interested in snowflakes, dewdrops, frost patterns, and hailstones. He drew the shapes the microscope revealed, but this proved unsatisfactory. Eventually he managed to buy a bellows camera and a microscope objective to connect it to the microscope. This allowed him to photograph microscope specimens. All of his photographs were taken with this camera. It was the only one he ever owned.

Every winter, Bentley photographed snowflakes. Eventually he had a collection of more than 5,000 photographs. He discovered that the shape and size of snowflakes are determined by the temperatures and air currents inside the cloud. This made it possible to deduce the conditions inside a cloud from the types of snowflakes falling from it.

In summer he turned his attention to raindrops, and devised a method that is still used today for measuring their size. He sprinkled a layer of sifted flour into a wide dish, forming a layer about 1 inch (25 mm) deep, then stood this outside in the rain. When a raindrop fell into the flour it formed a ball of dough approximately its own size. Bentley was able to remove the dough balls and measure them. Between 1898 and 1904, he measured more than 300 raindrops. From their sizes, he was able to deduce the way they had formed.

In 1898 he wrote his first magazine article. It was for *Popular Scientific Monthly* and was followed by many popular articles and scientific papers. He reported most of his more serious discoveries in the *Monthly Weather Review*.

He was awarded the first research grant ever made by the American Meteorological Society in 1924. The amount was small, but its significance great. The grant meant that his work over several decades had been recognized and was appreciated by the scientific community.

Snow Crystals, written in collaboration with William J. Humphreys, is the title of the only book he ever published. Humphreys, the chief physicist at the U.S. Weather Bureau, persuaded Bentley to go through his collection and select the best pictures for publication. Bentley chose nearly 2,500 and Humphreys contributed an introduction describing the photographic technique. *Snow Crystals* was published in 1931 by the McGraw-Hill Book Company. (It is still in print: see "Bibliography and further reading" at the end of this book.)

Wilson Bentley kept detailed meteorological records throughout all the years he was photographing, measuring, and studying the weather around his home. He made his last record on December 7, 1931. He fell ill soon after that and died on the farm on December 23.

Bentley's observations were so carefully made and his photographs of such high quality that they attracted the interest of scientists. Bentley was not quite alone. A Polish scientist, A. B. Dobrowolska, was also studying ice crystals and wrote many articles about them, but it was Bentley's pictures that really fired imaginations. Today there are field guides to snow crystals.

The classic scientific book on the subject is by Ukichiro Nakaya, of the University of Hokkaido, Japan, a leading world authority on snow. Nakaya's book, *Snow Crystals: Natural and Artificial*, was published in 1954. Professor Nakaya was inspired by Wilson Bentley, but went further by making artificial snowflakes in his laboratory.

Studying snowflakes

Studying snowflakes is not easy. They are very fragile and easily damaged and, of course, they melt within seconds unless they are kept below 32°F (0°C). Shining a strong light on them in order to see them more clearly can be enough to destroy them.

There is a solution to the problem, however. A weak solution of a polyvinyl plastic in a common solvent (ethylene dichloride) will capture snowflakes and other ice crystals. The solution is chilled to a degree or two below freezing and a thin coat of it is painted onto a surface, such as glass or board, which has also been chilled. The coated plate is placed outdoors while it is snowing, left there until it has collected several snowflakes, then placed somewhere cold indoors for about 10 minutes, while the solvent evaporates. After that it can be warmed gently to room temperature. The snowflakes melt, their water evaporates through the very thin plastic film covering them, and a perfect impression of them is left behind, permanently marking the plate.

Classification

No two snowflakes are identical, but if you examine a large number of them you will find there are several distinct types. This has allowed scientists to work out a way of classifying them, and in 1951 an international system of classification was adopted for snowflakes, hailstones, and other forms of ice that fall as precipitation.

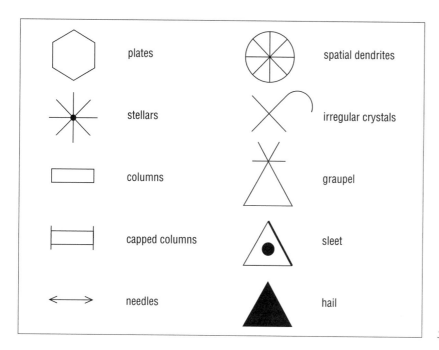

Symbols for ice crystals

The classification divides ice crystals into seven types, shown in the illustration. *Plates* are six-sided flakes. *Stellars* are six-pointed flakes. *Columns* are rectangular crystals, sometimes joined together. *Capped columns* are like columns, but with a bar at each end; when two or more join together the bars remain. *Needles* are fine, splinterlike crystals, which may also be joined together. *Spatial dendrites* are crystals with many fine branches, like fern fronds. *Irregular crystals* are clumped together chaotically, so they have no regular shape.

A further three symbols are added to describe forms of ice precipitation. These are for *graupel*, *sleet*, and *hail*. Each of the types can be divided further into subtypes. Having a standard classification allows scientists to refer to ice crystals by names everyone understands.

Ukichiro Nakaya developed this basic classification into one that grouped ice crystals in seven major ways to form 41 types of snowflakes. He published this classification for snowflakes in 1936, and in 1966 the Nakaya scheme was expanded to describe 80 distinct snowflake types.

Scientists now know a great deal about what happens when water freezes and how microscopically small crystals link together into big snowflakes. The stimulus for the research leading to these discoveries owes much to the magnificent photographs taken in the early years of the 20th century by Wilson A. Bentley.

SNOWFLAKES AND TYPES OF SNOW

Snow comes in many varieties. Sometimes huge snowflakes drift slowly downward, each one different from all the others. Catch one and, for the few moments before it melts and vanishes, you can wonder at its delicate beauty. At other times the flakes are small and hard. Examine these under a magnifying glass and they may look like tiny rods or needles, perhaps joined at their ends to make crosses or with straight arms radiating from a central point. The possibilities are bewildering.

As a group of water molecules locks into the shape of an ice crystal, several forces influence the way the pattern develops. The most important of these are surface tension and the latent heat that is released by freezing. Surface tension pulls molecules toward one another and tends to smooth the surface. When you make ice cubes in a freezer, or when a pond freezes over, the surface of the ice is smooth. This is because it froze first at the surface, from the outside inward. The latent heat escaped into the air and the sides of the container, leaving surface tension as the dominant physical force. (See "Hail, sleet, snow," page 85, for an explanation of surface tension and "What happens when water freezes and ice melts," page 99, for an explanation of latent heat.)

How ice crystals grow

Snowflakes do not form in this way. They freeze onto a freezing nucleus, from the inside outward, and the latent heat has to travel outward from the center before reaching the air. This tends to destabilize the crystal. Molecules further from the center are warmed just enough to loosen their hydrogen bonds a little, so they move slightly away from the crystal surface. They cannot escape altogether, however, because they remain held by surface tension.

Now projecting from the crystal, these tiny ice splinters are in a good position to gather fresh water molecules as the crystal falls downward through the cloud. A mixed cloud, made from water droplets, but with ice crystals forming, contains many droplets of supercooled water. Water evaporates from the surface of supercooled liquid droplets and the resulting water vapor is deposited on ice crystals. Consequently, the ice crystals grow at the expense of the supercooled droplets.

Ice is deposited from water vapor onto the projections, releasing the latent heat of deposition (680 cal g^{-1}, 2,835 J g^{-1}), surface tension and the destabilizing influence of diffusing latent heat always working against one another. As the projection grows larger, it sweeps more and more water molecules from the air through which it is traveling. The projections are the growing tips, like the growing tips of a plant.

As the snowflake grows bigger, the balance of forces affecting it shifts. The diffusion of latent heat becomes more important, and the influence of surface tension diminishes. Really large flakes form when smaller flakes touch and attach themselves to each other. By the time it reaches the ground, a snowflake may comprise only two individual crystals locked together, but a really big snowflake consists of up to 200 crystals.

Why most snowflakes have six points, but each one is unique

Surface tension affects individual molecules and influences the shape of the first part of the crystal to form. With water molecules, the shape of the crystal is such that projections are most likely to develop in six directions. Most snowflakes, but by no means all, have six sides or six branches.

The hexagonal (six-sided) shape arises from the shape of the water molecule. Oxygen atoms are very much larger than hydrogen atoms, and the bonds linking oxygen and hydrogen in the molecule are much shorter than the bonds linking the hydrogen of one molecule to the oxygen of another. As water crystallizes, each molecule bonds to four others, as shown in the illustration. Three of its neighbors are in the same plane and the fourth is either above or below. This arrangement pulls the molecules into stacks of hexagonal rings. Less energy is required to add another hexagon to the side of a growing crystal than is needed to add one above or below. Consequently, snowflakes grow by adding more hexagonal crystals to their sides, thus repeating the structure until the snowflake has become a hexagonal plate.

Once a projection from a crystal reaches a certain size, its edges become unstable and it starts producing smaller growing tips of its own. All around the flake, the projections experience the same environment and the same forces act on them in the same way, so they respond in the same way. They all grow at more or less the same rate. This results in an almost perfectly symmetrical flake. It is the symmetry of its delicately branching form that makes a snowflake so beautiful. Hoarfrost on plants and windowpanes grows in the same way, freezing from the inside out, and it also produces delicate, intricate patterns.

The symmetry can be lost. If the snowflake is a wide enough plate to remain level as it falls, usually spinning slowly, it will remain symmetrical. If it is tilted on its side, so it falls on its edge, the snowflake will grow more on one side than on the other. By the time it leaves the cloud it will be asymmetrical.

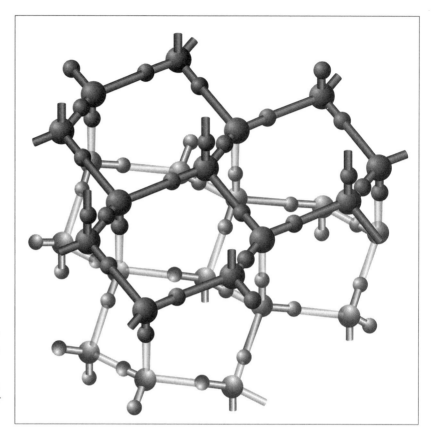

The hexagonal ice crystal. Each molecule is linked to four others. The molecules arrange themselves as stacks of hexagonal rings.

Most snowflakes are symmetrical, but each one is also different from all the other snowflakes around it. This is because every flake follows its own path as it falls. Snowflakes fall slowly through air that is moving. They may be caught in upcurrents or deflected to one side or the other. Some remain airborne for longer than others. These movements carry them into regions where the temperature is a fraction of a degree higher or lower, there is a little more or less moisture, or a variation in the number and type of solid particles, which affects the rate at which water condenses and freezes. Each flake responds to the conditions it experiences, but no two flakes are exposed to quite the same conditions.

Temperature affects the shape

Snowflakes that originate near the top of a big cloud are usually columnar in shape. They form in a temperature of around –30°F (–34°C). Flakes forming in the temperature range 18–23°F (–8°C to –5°C) are also columns. Those that form in a temperature of 3–10°F (–16°C to –12°C) are star-shaped. If the snowflakes are large plates, they formed at either 10–18°F (–12°C to –8°C) or 27–32°F (–3°C to 0°C). Examining the shape of a snowflake provides clues about the conditions in which it formed.

Big snowflakes fall to the ground when the temperature is fairly mild. If the temperature inside the cloud is between 32°F (0°C) and 23°F (–5°C), a very thin film of water coats the surface of each ice crystal. When two crystals touch, this film freezes, binding the crystals together. Air beneath a cloud is usually warmer than the air inside it, so when they leave their cloud, big flakes often fall through air that is barely below freezing and may be above it. If the air temperature is higher than about 30°F (–1°C), the snow may reach the ground but then melts quickly. It will not settle.

Availability of atmospheric moisture

Obviously, water must be present for ice crystals to form at all, and the more water there is, the larger the snowflakes are likely to be. The availability of moisture is also linked to temperature, because the warmer air is, the more water vapor it can hold. The water molecules from which ice crystals are made must be carried by the air as vapor. Air at around freezing temperature can hold nearly six times more water vapor than air at 0°F (–18°C). (See the sidebar "Why warm air can hold more moisture than cold air can" on page 99.) This is another reason why big snowflakes form at mild temperatures—more moisture is available to them.

Snowflakes can grow big where the temperature is mild, but only if the cloud itself is tall enough for temperatures near the top to be much lower. Ice crystals will not form at all at temperatures higher than about –40°F (–40°C) unless freezing nuclei are present. Most freezing nuclei initiate the formation of crystals between 10°F (–12°C) and –13°F (–25°C). Any precipitation will fall as rain if the temperature is higher than this throughout the cloud. If the raindrops are supercooled and the temperature beneath the cloud is below freezing, it will be freezing rain (see "Freezing rain and freezing fog," page 94). When it snows with big, gentle flakes, you may be sure the temperature in the lower part of the cloud is only a little below freezing and that the cloud is tall, extending upward to a height where the air is very much colder.

Inside the cloud

What starts as a fall of big flakes may reach the ground as graupel, or soft hail. This tells you more about the cloud that produced it. Graupel is not true hail (see "Hail, sleet, snow," page 85), but a mixture of snow and ice.

The process leading to it begins with the formation of ice crystals at a very low temperature near the top of a tall cloud. As they fall, the crystals clump together into big flakes. This means that the temperature is mild in the middle layers of the cloud and the air there is moist. At a still lower level, the flakes encounter liquid droplets supercooled to just below freezing temperature, so the cloud is mixed, containing both ice crystals and water droplets. The droplets freeze onto the falling flakes, coating them with ice so they are like minute snowballs, and these are what reach the ground.

At really low temperatures, the air can hold very little water vapor. When people say "it's too cold for snow," this is what they mean. Cold air is also dry air. Air dries as its water vapor condenses or crystallizes, and the last of the vapor that is "squeezed" from the cooling air may form ice crystals. Like crystals in warmer air, these gather more water molecules as they fall, but moisture is already very scarce in the cold air, and so they have few encounters. They grow slowly and at low temperatures have no surface film of water that would allow them to clump, so they remain as tiny, compact splinters. If there is a wind to drive them, they are dense enough to sting when they hit your face. Examine them under a strong magnifying glass and you will see that some are like columns or needles and others have very irregular shapes.

The smallest ice crystals of all form at temperatures below –20°F (–29°C). These crystals still require freezing nuclei, but when the temperature falls lower than –40°F (–40°C) water will freeze without nuclei. Such low temperatures are common at high altitudes. Near the tropopause, at about 33,000 feet (10 km) over middle latitudes in winter, the temperature is about –70°F (–57°C). Air that is this cold is too dry for there to be many ice crystals, but they are quite abundant a little lower, in air that has been lifted along a weather front with colder, denser air. Despite their altitude you can see them clearly. Indeed, they are very common as thin, wispy clouds of the cirrus type. Sometimes winds sweep them into long, thin strands, curled at the ends, called *mares' tails*.

There are many parts of the world where winter temperatures regularly fall to below –20°F (–29°C). They do so in polar regions, of course, but also in many parts of North America, Europe, and Asia. Occasionally, relatively moist air may move into a very cold region; when this happens, water may crystallize, just as it does in cirrus-type clouds. In effect, these clouds form at low level and ice crystals fall from them. Crystals also fall from high-altitude clouds, but these sublime into vapor when they reach warmer air. Those that fall from low-level clouds may reach the ground before they have time to sublime. They fall as light snow composed of crystals the size of sugar grains.

Once fallen, snow changes

After it has fallen, snow begins to change. Even in the coldest weather, bright sunshine often melts the topmost layer, which freezes again at night, so a thin crust of clear ice lies on top of the snow.

Where the snow is deep, a different type of change may take place at the base. Some of the crystals comprising the first snowflakes to have fallen sublime and the resulting vapor immediately freezes again, but into much larger crystals, called *hoar*. This process then extends upward into the overlying snow. Hoar crystals are dense, but packed more loosely than the original snow and they flow readily. They weaken the snow and are a major cause of avalanches (see "Avalanches," page 116).

We use the single word *snow* to describe a number of distinct ways in which ice crystals form, grow, and subsequently change. This is because, despite the fact that many of us see at least some snow every winter, we are more familiar with liquid water, for which we have more names. We talk of "showers," "torrential rain," "persistent rain," "cloudbursts," "drizzle," "mist," and "fog," all of which are types of liquid precipitation. Not surprisingly, people living in regions where water is frozen for most of the time have fewer words for types of rain and more for the many different types of snow.

AVALANCHES

A mountain in winter appears to be covered in snow. Seen from afar, the snow looks fairly even. Rocks break through the surface in some places, in others the fields of smooth snow are interrupted by groups of trees, but the snowfields themselves look safe and inviting. Skiers visit them, climbers cross them, snowmobilers race across them, and vacationers take the ski lift to see the mountain at close quarters, admire the view, and play in the snow.

Countless thousands of people visit the mountain snowfields every year—and every year thousands of them experience directly what happens when the safe, smooth snow starts to move. They are caught in an avalanche. Every year about 150 people die in avalanches over the world as a whole.

The force of moving snow

Once snow starts to move down a slope it is likely to accelerate. The faster it moves, the more kinetic energy the mass of snow possesses (see the sidebar). It slams into snow lying further down the slope with enough force to dislodge it. The dislodged snow joins the sliding mass and the energy of the avalanche grows.

Even a small avalanche is dangerous. Objects in its path experience an impact of 0.1–0.5 ton per square foot (900–4,500 kg m^{-2}) of exposed surface. If a timber chalet 30 feet (9 m) long and 12 feet (3.7 m) high stood directly in the path of this avalanche it would be hit by a force of 36–180 tons (30–150 tonnes). The chalet would be demolished—and that is not all. The remains of the chalet—pieces of timber of all sizes, roof shingles, glass, furniture, and everything else the building contained—would be

Kinetic energy

Kinetic energy (KE), which is the energy of motion, is equal to the mass of a moving body multiplied by the square of its velocity (or speed). Expressed algebraically, KE = $\frac{1}{2}mv^2$, where m is the mass and v is the velocity.

This formula gives a result in joules if m is in kilograms and v is in meters per second. If you need to calculate the force in pounds exerted by a mass measured in pounds moving in miles per hour, the formula must be modified slightly to: KE = $mv^2 \div 2g$, where v is converted to feet per second (ft per second = MPH × 5280 ÷ 3,600) and g is 32 (the acceleration due to gravity in feet per second).

swept down the slope with the snow. After it has traveled some distance, an avalanche no longer consists only of snow. Hidden in the mass of snow there are all of the more solid objects it has gathered along the way.

Obviously, a big avalanche has much more force. It can transport up to 300,000 cubic yards (8,500 m³) of snow and its impact can be as much as 9 tons per square foot (88 tonnes m⁻²). It would strike the chalet with a force of 3,240 tons (2,930 tonnes). That is enough to demolish a solidly constructed building and uproot full-grown trees—and all of this material would continue downhill as part of the avalanche.

How an avalanche begins

Any snow lying on a mountainside may shift, but avalanches are more likely in some places than in others. If the slope is very steep, snow cannot accumulate as a thick layer. Its own weight will cause the snow to slide away harmlessly, in small amounts. Nor will snow accumulate on shallower slopes if the underlying surface is very smooth. Avalanches seldom start on grassy slopes, for example. The snow slides off slippery surfaces, such as grass.

Level areas are also safe, provided they are near the summit of the mountain. Snow can lie as a very thick layer on a slope that is almost horizontal. It will remain stable, but an avalanche descending from a higher level might dislodge it. That is why level areas are safe only if there is little snow on the slopes above them.

The most dangerous places are where the slope is about 30° to 40°. This is not so steep as to prevent snow from accumulating, nor so shallow as to ensure that the snow layer is stable. The drawing shows the parts of a mountain that are safe and the slope that is especially dangerous. Snow sometimes slides off shallower slopes, however. Wet snow that is well lubricated at the base may start moving on a gradient of 10–25°, and very light, powdery snow may slide off a 22° slope.

While it lies still on the mountainside, a snow layer looks stable. You can walk, toboggan, or ski across it and it gives no sign of moving. If it is to move, something must happen to destabilize it. There are three ways this can happen.

Sudden warming can produce instability. This does not happen directly. Snow is a good insulating material and even though the warmth of the sunshine melts the snow at the top of the layer, the warmth will not reach the lower layers. The danger comes not from the layer itself, but from thinner snow at a higher level on the mountain. If this snow melts, it will send a stream of water down the mountainside. The water may penetrate beneath the snow lying further down the mountain and partly dissolve the snow that is in contact with the surface. This detaches the snow from the surface and lubricates it. There will be no visible sign of what has happened, but the snow has now become unstable.

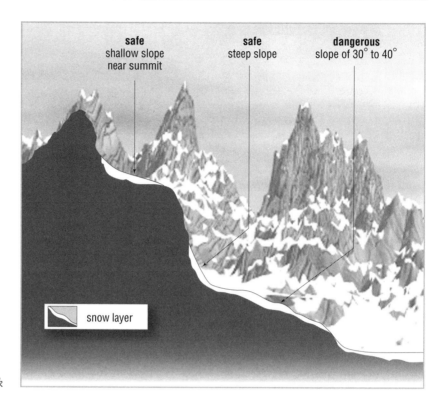

Slope and avalanche risk

    The snow itself can change. If some of the snow at the base of the layer sublimes and the water vapor is immediately deposited once more as ice, part of the layer will have been transformed from tightly-packed snow to hoar (see "Snowflakes and types of snow," page 110). The bonds between snow grains are much weaker in hoar than in other types of snow, so the entire layer has lost some of its cohesion. It may feel crunchy when you cross it, but otherwise the snow gives no indication that it is now unstable.

    Snow will also be destabilized if its weight increases to beyond a certain threshold. When snow (or anything else) lies on a slope, it is subject to two forces: gravity and friction. Friction tends to prevent movement in the layer that is in direct contact with the solid surface. Gravity works against friction, tending to pull the snow down the slope. The two opposing forces produce a *shearing stress* between the snow and the mountainside. For the snow to slide, gravity must overcome friction. The resultant force, called a *shearing force*, will move the snow. Cohesion within the snow layer will then ensure that the entire depth of snow starts moving together. Gravity acts on the *mass* of the snow. It will increase if the mass of snow increases. Consequently, a heavy fall of snow onto a layer of snow that fell earlier may add enough mass to destabilize the snow.

People at the foot of the mountain will know if there has been a heavy fall of snow, because it will have fallen where they are as well as on the mountainside. Seeing the snow on the ground, they may decide it would be unwise to go onto the mountain because of the increased risk of avalanches. Unfortunately, however, the absence of a snowstorm in the valley does not mean that snow layers near the summit have not thickened. There is another way snow can arrive.

Air approaching the mountain from the far side will be forced to rise as it crosses. This will chill the air, causing cloud to form and, because of the low temperature, any precipitation will fall as snow. It will fall on the windward side of the mountain, of course, and people on the other (lee) side will be unaware of it. They will not be able to see the summit, because it is shrouded in cloud, so they will not know what is happening there. As the air crosses the summit, the irregularity of the surface produces eddies that swirl over the top and down onto the lee side—carrying snow with them. As the diagram shows, these eddies can deposit a substantial amount of snow, but only on snowfields at a high elevation. The weather may be fine lower down on the lee side, with clear skies and good visibility. Yet, unknown to the skiers and climbers, the snow above them has become unstable.

Lee side snow. The wind drives snow into the windward face and carries it over the summit. On the lee side, the wind loses energy as it forms eddies. It loses much of its snow, depositing it as a thick layer. This can happen even when it is not snowing on the lee side of the mountain.

wind direction

Types of avalanches

There are degrees of instability, but when a snow layer becomes highly unstable, the smallest vibration may set it in motion. A gunshot might be enough, or the rush of a passing skier, the shout of someone hailing a distant friend, or the sudden loud snap of a breaking branch.

Snow suddenly starts to move. If the snow is dry and powdery it may be that just a few snow grains are disturbed. They roll and bounce a little way, dislodging a few more. Then, like the cartoon snowball that grows into a monster as it rolls down the hillside, the disturbance grows. More and more snow joins the rush.

This is called a *point-release* avalanche, because it begins at a particular point. Farther down, the avalanche widens, so it has the shape of an upturned V by the time it reaches a level area that is large enough to halt it. A point-release avalanche affects only the surface of the snow layer. Most of the layer remains in position. The avalanche looks spectacular, because it advances as a great, tumbling cloud of snow, but the mass of moving snow is fairly small. Point-release avalanches are not very dangerous in themselves, but they can further destabilize the underlying snow, preparing the way for a much worse *slab avalanche*.

Slab avalanches are the dangerous ones. They are rectangular and happen when an entire layer of snow moves together, descending as a single slab. This is the way thawing snow often falls from a roof. It begins when the snow melts near the ridge, releasing water that destabilizes the snow lower down. This snow starts to slide, but is checked by the large mass of snow below it and piles up against it. The shearing stress, between the snow and the roof, builds up until gravity wins over friction and the entire slab moves in one piece. This happens suddenly, without warning, and with a loud whoosh the snow falls to the ground.

This is what happens in a slab avalanche, but on a mountainside the slab may be up to half a mile (800 m) wide. The slab may remain intact as it slides, producing a *hard slab* avalanche. Or it may break into several smaller slabs, as a *soft slab* avalanche.

Snow and wind

Once it is in motion the snow accelerates rapidly. Wet snow clings together and flows like mud, a wall of material rolling forward, pushed by the weight of snow behind. Avalanches of wet snow seldom reach speeds of more than about 55 MPH (88 km/h).

Light, dry, powdery snow moves faster. The grains are loosely packed, so there are relatively large air spaces between them. This reduces the friction between the grains. Avalanches of this kind of snow often rush down mountainsides at 80–100 MPH (130–160 km/h) and they can be faster. Speeds up to 190 MPH (305 km/h) are not unknown.

A large mass of moving snow pushes air ahead of itself. This generates an *avalanche wind* that precedes the snow. A big slab avalanche can produce a wind of 185 MPH (297 km/h)—equivalent to a category 5 hurricane. A wind of this strength will uproot trees and cause serious structural damage to buildings, so that by the time the snow arrives they are already weakened.

The avalanche cuts a path for itself, called the *avalanche track*. Later, when all the snow has gone, the track often remains. It resembles a chute, usually with a pile of debris—mainly boulders and broken trees—at the bottom. If the avalanche passed through a forest, there will be a strip down the slope that has been cleared of trees. This marks the track.

Snow is likely to become unstable on particular parts of a mountain, so avalanches tend to start in the same, limited number of places. They also tend to follow the same tracks. Avalanche tracks are best avoided, because the snow may use them again and once it is on the move there is very little time to get out of its way.

The foot of the avalanche track, where the snow finally comes to a standstill, is the *runout zone*. It is extensive and on fairly level ground. The runout zone is where the avalanche exhausts itself. The snow and its cargo of debris spread and tumble across it, but then they come to rest.

Safety

Most popular winter resorts are closely monitored and the authorities take steps to avoid avalanches. In some places you may see strong fences built across a slope. The fences are there to hold back snow that might otherwise slide. Where snow is accumulating and may become unsafe, a controlled explosion may be used to trigger a small avalanche, thereby preventing a bigger avalanche later. Warnings are issued and slopes may be closed to the public when weather conditions make avalanches likely.

These services are not provided away from the resorts, and even where they are provided you should be aware of your surroundings at all times. Avoid small hollows and bowls and stay away from recognizable avalanche tracks. Try to estimate the angle of the slope you are on and the slope above you. You can measure the slope with a *clinometer*—a type of pocket compass that also measures gradients. If you must cross a steep slope that is thickly covered with snow, do so very carefully to avoid triggering an avalanche yourself. Beware of slopes where you can see isolated trees, bushes, or rocks projecting above the snow. There could be weaknesses in the snow running as faults from one object to another and making the snow unstable. Watch out for cracks in the snow surface and listen for noises from underneath it. These are indications that the layer is becoming unstable. If you see or hear them, move off the slope. In North

America, avalanches most often occur on slopes facing between north and east. This is where the snow is coldest and deepest and also where its internal cohesion is often weak.

If you are caught in an avalanche, let go of anything you are carrying and try to remove your backpack to make your body lighter. Use swimming movements to try to stay close to the surface. When you stop moving, try to stick an arm or leg above the snow to help rescuers find you. Once the snow has come to a standstill it will probably set very hard. You will not be able to dig yourself out unless at least the upper part of your body is already above the surface.

If you are completely immersed in the snow, use your arms and hands to push the snow away from your face and make a small space. Keep this space open—it contains the air you need to breathe while you wait to be rescued. Before the snow has time to set, take a deep breath to push the snow away from your chest. Then breathe as steadily as you can and try not to panic.

Shout only if you hear rescuers nearby. If you can hear them there is a chance they will hear you. Otherwise conserve your energy, because your voice will carry only a very short distance no matter how loudly you scream.

Do not venture onto mountain snow unless you are at a resort with emergency services or you have trained for the conditions. While at a resort, always follow the safety advice you are given. Do not stray from the recommended areas and slopes.

Avalanches are extremely dangerous. They kill people every winter. Take sensible precautions, however, and you can avoid being caught by one.

COLD AIR AND WARM WATER

At Brighton, on the south coast of England, there is a curious tradition. Every New Year's Day, people bathe in the sea. Admittedly, they do not stay long in the water. For most of them, a fast run into the sea and a fast run back to the beach is quite enough, but tradition holds that they must immerse themselves completely and duck their heads below the water, so they are wet all over. The event is usually filmed for the TV news and shows the participants shivering and laughing. Unless they are good actors, they actually enjoy it.

The custom is not confined to Brighton—and by no means are the English bathers the world's hardiest. Muscovites also take the midwinter plunge and they have to break the ice to gain access to the water, and then return to the shore before it has time to freeze again. Moscow is much colder than Brighton and the bathers believe the brief exposure to intense cold is good for their health.

Provided they remain in the water for only a very brief time, the ordeal may be less severe than it looks. Out of the water, the air temperature at Brighton on New Year's Day is, at best, only a degree or two above freezing, and there is usually a wind to make it feel even colder (see page 160 for the effect of wind chill). In Moscow, the average daytime temperature in January is 15°F (–9°C). The sea temperature around Britain on New Year's Day is usually about 50°F (10°C). Bathers in Moscow cannot immerse themselves in the sea, of course, but the thick layer of ice covering the water provides good insulation. The water below the ice is warmer than the air above it.

During their run down the beach the bathers will feel very cold, but the water itself will feel distinctly warmer. Those who watch the Brighton event on TV admire the courage of the bathers, or mock their silliness, on the basis of a false comparison. They know the coast in summer, when the air is warm and the sea feels very cold. In midsummer the sea is several degrees colder than the air over land and usually much colder than the ground surface, but in winter the situation is reversed. Russian viewers may also be misled. They know that lakes and rivers are places to cool off on hot summer days, but may not be aware that in winter the waters are sheltered from the bitterly cold air.

Specific heat capacity

Water must absorb much more heat than must land before it becomes noticeably warmer and, once having absorbed heat, it is slower than land to lose it.

In fact, it takes about five times more heat to raise the temperature of water by a given amount than is required to warm the same weight of dry sand.

The amount of heat that must be absorbed in order to warm a particular substance is known as the *specific heat capacity* of that substance. Specific heat capacity varies from one substance to another, and the specific heat capacity of water is much higher than that of any other commonplace substance. The table below gives the specific heat capacities of water, ice, sand, and a few familiar rocks. Specific heat capacity also varies slightly with temperature, so when a value for specific heat capacity is given, it is necessary to specify the temperature at which the value is correct. The units used are joules per kilogram per kelvin ($J kg^{-1} K^{-1}$) or calories per gram per degree Celsius (cal $g^{-1} °C^{-1}$).

The high heat capacity of water is another consequence of the hydrogen bonds linking its molecules (see "What happens when water freezes and ice melts," on page 99). What we feel as warmth on our skin is the energy with which molecules strike it. Warm a substance, and its molecules move faster, so they strike our skin harder. Our skin sensors detect the impacts and our brain interprets them as heat. Water molecules also move faster when they are warmed, but their hydrogen bonds restrict that movement. Much more heat energy is needed to accelerate them than would be needed if they were free to move independently of one another.

Radiation and blackbodies

When a body—such as a lake, ocean, or continent—is warmed by radiation, it absorbs that warmth and its temperature rises. As soon as its temperature

SPECIFIC HEAT CAPACITIES OF COMMON SUBSTANCES

Substance	Temperature		c	
	°C	°F	J kg^{-1} K^{-1}	cal g^{-1} °C^{-1}
fresh water	15	59	4,187	1.00
sea water	17	62.6	3,936	0.94
ice	−21– −1	−5.8–30.2	2,009–2,094	0.48–0.50
dry air	20	68	1,006	0.2403
basalt	20–100	68–212	837–1,005	0.20–0.24
granite	20–100	68–212	795–837	0.19–0.20
white marble	18	64.4	879–921	0.21–0.22
quartz	0	32	712	0.17
sand	20–100	68–212	837	0.20

Specific heat capacity and blackbodies

When a substance is heated, it absorbs heat energy and its temperature rises. The amount of heat it must absorb in order to raise its temperature by one degree varies from one substance to another, however. The ratio of the heat applied to a substance to the extent of the rise in its temperature is called the *specific heat capacity* for that substance. It is measured in calories per gram per degree Celsius (cal g^{-1} $°C^{-1}$) or in the scientific units of joules per kilogram per kelvin (J kg^{-1} K^{-1}; $1K = 1°C = 1.8°F$). Specific heat capacity varies slightly according to the temperature, so when quoting the specific heat capacity of a substance it is customary to specify the temperature or temperature range to which this refers.

Pure water has a specific heat capacity of 1 cal g^{-1} $°C^{-1}$ (4,180 J kg^{-1} K^{-1}) at 59°F (15°C). This means that at 59°F (15°C) one gram of water must absorb one calorie of heat in order for its temperature to rise by one degree Celsius (or 0.56 cal to raise its temperature by 1°F). Seawater at 17°C (62.6°F) has a specific heat capacity of 0.94 cal g^{-1} $°C^{-1}$ (3,930 J kg^{-1} K^{-1}).

The desert surface consists of granite rock and sand. At temperatures between 68°F (20°C) and 212°F (100°C), the specific heat capacity of granite is 0.19–0.20 cal g^{-1} $°C^{-1}$ (800–837 J kg^{-1} K^{-1}). Within the same temperature range, the specific heat capacity of sand is 0.20 cal g^{-1} $°C^{-1}$ (837 J kg^{-1} K^{-1}). These values are typical for most types of rock.

Water has a specific heat capacity about five times that of rock. This means water must absorb five times more heat than rock to produce a similar rise in temperature. It is why water warms up so much more slowly than sand and rock. Visit the beach on a really hot day in summer and by lunchtime the sand will be so hot you have to run across it to avoid hurting your bare feet, but when you splash into the water, it is refreshingly cool. The reason for this is the difference in the specific heat capacities of water and sand.

In the desert, the rock and sand, with a low specific heat capacity, heats up rapidly. By the middle of the day it is extremely hot. Specific heat capacity works both ways, though. Substances that heat quickly also cool down again quickly. The molecular configuration that confers a rapid response to absorbed heat also ensures the heat cannot be long retained once the external supply shuts down.

The ground radiates its heat into the sky. If there were clouds, they would absorb much of this heat and re-radiate it, effectively trapping heat and keeping the air warm. But the desert sky is cloudless and the desert behaves much like a blackbody. A blackbody is any object that absorbs all the radiation falling on it, then re-radiates the whole of the absorbed energy, but at a longer wavelength. There is no such thing as a perfect blackbody (some energy is inevitably lost), but the Sun and Earth come close. The wavelength of the radiation from a blackbody is inversely proportional to the temperature: the higher the temperature, the shorter the wavelength.

During the day, the desert rock and sand absorb heat from the Sun. Their temperature rises and they re-radiate their energy into the sky, but at the same time they continue to absorb solar radiation. The balance between the energy they absorb and the energy they radiate allows the surface temperature to rise to a peak in the early afternoon, after which it remains steady. Then, as the Sun sinks toward the horizon, the balance starts to shift. Radiation from the surface remains constant, but less solar energy is absorbed. The surface starts to cool, but slowly. Once the Sun sinks below the horizon and darkness falls, there is no more sunshine for the desert to absorb, but neither is there anything to halt its blackbody radiation, which continues. The surface temperature then plummets. Desert nights are cold. Sometimes they are very cold indeed.

is higher than the temperature of its surroundings, the body starts to radiate away the heat it absorbed, at a wavelength that is inversely proportional to its temperature—the higher the temperature, the shorter is the wavelength. This is called *blackbody radiation* and it is related to specific heat capacity (see the sidebar).

Conductivity, albedo, and transparency

Sea and land respond to solar radiation differently, and there is a further difference. Heat the surface of a substance, and the heat is conducted beneath the surface. Eventually, the whole volume warms. How quickly it warms depends on its conductivity. This varies widely between substances. Metals, for example, are good conductors of heat. Air is a very poor conductor, and dry soil contains air between its particles, the amount varying according to the size of the particles. Sand is made from big particles and the spaces between them, called pores, are also big. Clay is made from very small particles and has less air-filled pore space.

When the ground is heated by the Sun, the uppermost layer may warm quickly, but the temperature a foot or so below the surface may hardly change at all. If you have visited a sandy beach on a very hot day you will know that the sand can be too hot to walk on comfortably, but dig just below the surface and you find cool sand. This variation of temperature with depth has been measured. On a hot, sunny day, the surface of sand reached 104°F (40°C), but 2 inches (5 cm) below the surface the temperature was only 68°F (20°C), and at a depth of 6 inches (15 cm) it was 45°F (7°C).

Sand conducts heat poorly because of the amount of air it contains. At the same time as its temperature was being taken, so was the temperature of clay. At the surface the clay reached 70°F (21°C), cooler than the sand because heat was being conducted downward, away from the surface, much more efficiently through its small, closely spaced particles. At a depth of 2 inches (5 cm), the temperature was 57°F (14°C) and at 6 inches (15 cm), 39°F (4°C).

If the soil is moist, however, heat is conducted deeper, because water is a better conductor of heat than air. Moist soil will therefore absorb more heat than dry soil. If the soil is very moist it will absorb even more, because then the high specific heat capacity of water becomes important.

Not all the solar radiation that reaches the surface is absorbed. Some is reflected. How much is reflected varies from one surface to another and is measured as the albedo of that surface (see the table on page 54). Sand, for example, has an albedo of 35–45. The albedo of water varies with the height of the Sun above the horizon. When the Sun is high, in the middle part of the day, water can have an albedo of about 2 percent, which means it absorbs 98 percent of the solar energy reaching it. Early and late in the day, when the Sun is low, much more light is reflected and the albedo rises to 35 with the Sun 10° above the horizon. When the Sun is crossing the horizon, the albedo reaches more than 99.

Water is transparent, which means sunlight and heat that are not reflected penetrate below the surface. If the water is very clear, radiation can penetrate to about 30 feet (9 m). In fact, the heat is usually carried much deeper, because water is seldom still. Waves and currents mix the water, carrying warm surface water far below the surface. In summer, the North Sea warms to a depth of about 130 feet (40 m), which is typical for seas in middle latitudes.

Influence of oceans

These effects combine to magnify the different responses of land and sea to solar radiation. It is not simply that the sea warms and cools more slowly than the land, it does so *much* more slowly. This fact has major implications for our climates. In the first place, it allows us to distinguish distinct continental and maritime types of climate (see "Continental and maritime climates," page 1). In winter, however, it can produce blizzards.

Picture what happens to a mass of air as it crosses a large continent. By late fall, the land has lost the warmth it accumulated through the summer. It is cold, and it chills the air passing over it. Cold air is also dry air (see "Why warm air can hold more moisture than cold air can," on page 18), so by the time it reaches the far coast, the air mass is cold and dry. Then it crosses the ocean. The water is warmer than the air, so the air warms a little. This increases its capacity to hold moisture, and water evaporates into it. By the time it reaches the far side of the ocean it has become relatively mild, moist, maritime air. Now it encounters land again, and is chilled once more. As it moves inland, its temperature falling, it starts losing its moisture, and in winter it is likely to lose it in the form of snow, possibly driven by strong winds. In other words, there are blizzards.

Were it not for the high heat capacity of water, there would be little difference in temperatures over land and sea, and in high latitudes much of the sea would freeze over in winter. Its heat capacity is one more remarkable property of water. It gives maritime regions milder winters than they would have otherwise, but it also delivers fierce snowstorms.

SNOWSTORMS, DRIFTING, AND BLIZZARDS

When people say "Six inches of snow fell last night," what do they mean? We often talk about the amount of snow that falls as though this were a precise figure that we could determine simply by looking out of the window. Step outdoors, however, and you may or may not see six inches (15 cm) of snow. More probably you will find some places where the snow lies three inches (7.5 cm) deep, others where it is more than a foot (30 cm) deep, and some places where there is no snow at all. So how can we arrive at a figure of six inches?

Snow is not like rain. Being liquid, rain flows and it cannot be compressed. Squeeze water as hard as you like, and its volume does not change. On open ground, away from shelter, one inch (25 mm) of rain is the same everywhere. Snow does not flow. It accumulates where it lands and the wind carries it to particular places, so more accumulates in some places than in others. Nor is all snow the same. Wet snow, falling as big flakes, takes up more space than dry, powdery snow. Snow can be compressed, because of the air spaces between grains.

Perhaps, then, we should be more specific. When we talk of "six inches of snow," perhaps we should state what kind of snow we mean, where this six-inch (15-cm) depth is to be found, and whether it is typical for the area.

There is really only one way to deal with the problem and that is to be careful in choosing where to measure the depth of snow and then to convert snowfall into its rainfall equivalent. This is what meteorologists do and the result tells them something more useful than the amount of snow. It tells them how much water fell. They collect the snow, melt it, and report snowfall as its rainfall equivalent. This varies with temperature.

CONVERTING SNOWFALL TO RAINFALL EQUIVALENT

Snow to water ratios

Temperature		Ratio
°F	°C	
35	1.7	7:1
29–34	–1.7–1.1	10:1
20–28	–6.7––2.2	15:1
10–19	–12.2––7.2	20:1
0–9	–17.8––12.8	30:1
less than 0	less than –17.8	40:1

The table shows the ratio of snowfall to rainfall at a range of temperatures. At 29–34° F (–1.7–1° C), for example, the depth of a layer of freshly fallen snow is equivalent to one-tenth of that depth of water.

Wind and the city

One of the worst blizzards of modern times struck the area around Buffalo, New York, in late January 1977. Buffalo lies in the snowbelt east of the Great Lakes (see "The lake effect," on page 142) and several feet of snow falls there in most winters, but the 1977 blizzard was much worse. Moist winds from Canada, blowing for five days at 70 MPH (113 km/h), deposited 4 feet (1.2 m) of snow on top of 3 feet (0.9 m) that had fallen earlier in the winter. In places the drifts were 30 feet (9 m) deep.

Drifting is caused by the wind. It is not the force of the wind that matters, so much as the amount of snow the wind carries, although the two are sometimes related. If the wind is strong enough it will lift snow from the ground, adding the raised snow to the load that is falling. This is what happened in Buffalo. The gale picked up snow lying on the frozen surface of Lake Erie and drove it into the city.

Except on the open plains and over the sea, the wind near ground level rarely blows from the same direction for very long, and both its direction and strength vary from place to place. Hills, trees, buildings, and obstructions of every kind deflect it, and this effect is strongest in cities, especially cities where buildings are of different heights.

Obstructions and friction with the ground combine to slow the wind. Climb a few hundred feet above ground level and wind speeds usually increase, often by a large amount. So cities tend to be a little less windy than the countryside surrounding them. On one occasion, for example, when the wind speed at Heathrow Airport, on the western outskirts of London, was measured as 6.4 MPH (10 km/h), the wind in central London was blowing at 4.7 MPH (7.6 km/h). That was in the middle of the day, however, and at night the situation reversed, with the wind blowing harder in the city center than on the outskirts.

Urban climate

This difference between conditions in the city and the countryside is due to the fact that the ground surface cools at night, but in a large city vehicles and buildings release a great deal of heat, especially in winter. This forms a *heat island*, with the city warmer than the surrounding countryside.

Warm air rises over the city and meets cooler air above the buildings. The resulting mixing makes the airflow turbulent, and turbulence brings air from above the city down to street level. This air is still moving at its original speed, so the wind that is blowing high enough above the buildings not to be much slowed by them is brought to ground level, but it slows as it buffets and eddies around buildings, reducing the wind speed near ground level. The stronger the wind, the greater the difference between city and rural wind speeds. The diagram shows how wind can eddy around tall buildings.

This is a general effect and the details can vary. A long, straight city street lined with tall buildings on both sides is like a canyon. If a wind is blowing approximately parallel to the street, the buildings can funnel the wind along, just as happens in a natural canyon. This accelerates the wind, because the same volume of air must travel the same distance in the same time, but along a constricted path.

Wind behaves in a much more complicated fashion if it is blowing in any direction other than parallel to the streets. When the wind strikes the face of a building, some of the flow is deflected upward and some downward. At roof level, air deflected upward meets the main flow again and rejoins it, but on the downwind (lee) face of the building air is being drawn away by the wind and the pressure is slightly reduced. This draws some air down the side of the building as an eddy. At ground level, some of the air deflected down the face of the building flows back into the street, where it may meet

Wind around buildings

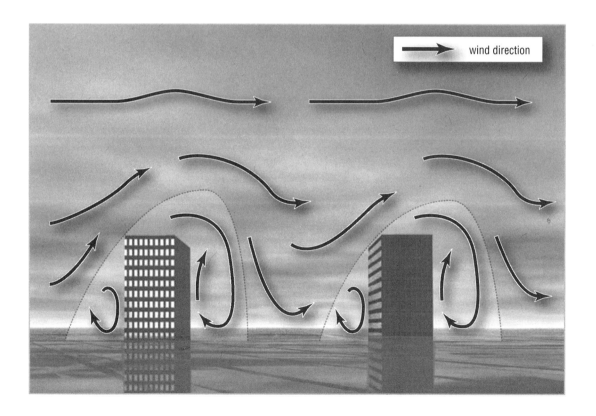

wind direction

air approaching from the building across the street. Where the two airflows collide they often spiral around one another, forming a street-level vortex. When you see bits of paper and dust whirling in a circle, it is because they are caught in an eddy vortex of this kind. The rest of the air moving down the face of the building spills to the sides, forming more eddies.

Snowdrifts

Overall, the effect of all this obstruction and turbulence is to slow down the wind, and the stronger the wind, the more it is slowed by its passage through the city. This reduction in speed affects the way snow falls. If snow is carried by a wind blowing directly onto the face of a building, some of its snow will stick to the walls, but this is a minor effect. If the wind literally blew snow onto walls it would cover them with a thick, fairly even layer. Snow might then fall under its own weight, slithering down the wall the way it will slither off a sloping roof. That is not what happens, of course. The snow collects at the foot of the wall, but not because it has fallen down the side of the building. As the drawing shows, the foot of the wall is where the snow fell in the first place.

Slowing the wind reduces its energy, and the amount of any material the wind can carry depends on how much energy it possesses. In this the wind is very like a river. A fast-flowing river carries silt, sand, and small stones. After heavy rain, river water is often brown because of the large quantity of soil it is carrying. As the river slows, its energy is reduced and the heavier particles, such as stones, sink to the bottom. The river is no longer able to carry them, and more and more of its load sinks as its energy continues to fall, the heaviest particles settling to the bottom first. Similarly, as the wind loses energy it, too, starts to drop the load of material it has been carrying.

Snowdrifts will develop wherever a snow-laden wind loses energy. It loses energy by being deflected when it strikes the face of a building. Predictably, therefore, the wind will drop some of its load of snow, which will fall at the base of the building. That is why snow tends to pile up against the sides of houses, so you may have to dig your way out of the door after a heavy overnight fall.

There is usually a narrow gap, where the snow is thinner, between the wall and the snowdrift. When the wind strikes the wall, it is deflected into a curved path, down the wall face and then away from the wall, and consequently it drops most of its snow a short distance from the wall. If the wall is low, some of the wind will cross over the top and eddy down the lee side. This will also produce a relatively thin layer of snow against the foot of the wall and a deeper snowdrift a short distance downwind.

Roads can be blocked by snow. In effect, a drift fills the road, sometimes to the height of the land on either side so that the road disappears.

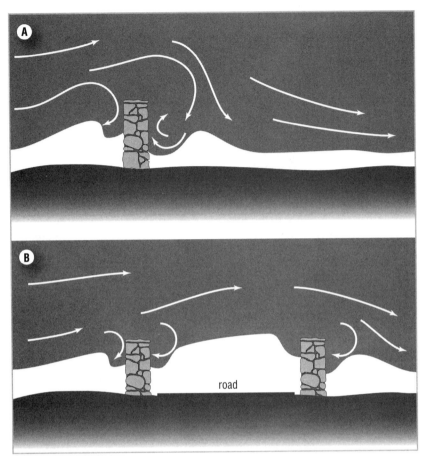

Snowdrift. A wall (A) produces two snowdrifts, one on each side, with a space between the wall and the drift. High banks lining a road (B) also produce two drifts. In this case the downwind drift behind one bank overlaps the upwind drift in front of the other bank, so the road quickly fills with snow.

Tall poles often line roads in places prone to heavy snowfalls to help travelers and snowplow drivers to locate the line of the road. Where the road surface is at the same level as the ground to either side, the entire area may be covered evenly. Where the road runs through a cutting, below the level of the land on either side, wind eddies with little energy will drop more snow onto the road than falls elsewhere, forming a drift starting on the lee side of the road. Sunken roads are likely to be in shade most of the time, so when the thaw arrives their drifts can persist for weeks longer than the snow that fell on more exposed ground.

Blizzards, driven by fiercely strong winds, can produce deep drifts, but so can even the gentlest breeze. The less energy the wind has to start with, the more easily that energy may be diminished. In still air, snow falls vertically downward and every exposed surface is covered equally. Drifts can form under these conditions, but they are uncommon. Usually there is some air movement and the snow falls at an angle to the vertical. Where it meets obstructions, the light wind loses the little energy that it has, and snow accumulates.

Drifts are dangerous

Drifts are a major inconvenience and clearing them from blocked roads can be a slow, costly operation. They are also extremely dangerous, because it is difficult, and in unfamiliar terrain impossible, to estimate their depth or even to see them. A person who falls into one may have great difficulty escaping.

The 1856–57 winter was very severe. In Richardson County, Nebraska, a storm in early December drove 20 cattle into a valley and then snowdrifts blocked them in, so they were unable to escape. It was February before their owner found them. Some had survived by feeding on tree branches. Those storms filled ravines 30 feet (9 m) deep.

A blizzard that started on Easter Sunday, April 13, 1873, in Howard County, Nebraska, lasted several days. By the time it ended, houses and stables had been buried in snowdrifts. When the storm began, one woman was at home with her two daughters, Lizzie and Emma. The mother was unwell and went to bed, while the daughters tended the fire. The wind was so fierce and the snow so fine that snow blew into the house. Then an especially strong gust blew in the door with a great, whirling cloud of snow, and scattered burning coals from the fire around the living room. While the girls were putting out the fire another gust carried away the roof and snow started to fill the room. They climbed into bed beside their mother, but at dawn they decided to seek help from a neighbor who lived a mile away. They had to climb over the wall of the house, because the snow completely blocked the doorway. The storm was still raging.

They were hopelessly lost as soon as they were out of sight of the house. All day they wandered through the continuing storm and when night fell they scooped a hole in the snow and lay there hugging each other for warmth. By Tuesday morning, Lizzie, the elder girl, was dead. Emma pressed on through all of that day and the following night. It was Wednesday before the storm abated, the Sun shone, and the visibility improved a little. That is when she found the neighbor's house. Emma survived, but her mother perished.

In February 1799 a woman called Elizabeth Woodcock was walking home from a market in Cambridge, England, to the village of Impington, a distance of 3 miles (4.8 km). She fell into a snowdrift and was trapped there for eight days. By the time rescuers arrived, she had heard the nearby church bells ring twice for the Sunday morning service. Fortunately she was still alive and made a full recovery. Not everyone is so lucky.

HEAVY SNOWSTORMS AND WHAT CAUSES THEM

In February 2003 large parts of the northeastern United States were paralyzed by the heaviest snowstorms in years. Roads were blocked, and in some places completely buried and hidden. Airports closed in New York, Philadelphia, Baltimore, and Washington while snowplows cleared the runways. Amtrak had to cancel one-quarter of its services in the Northeast. More than two feet (60 cm) of snow fell on Washington, D.C., bringing the city almost to a standstill. There was only one train every two hours on the Washington subway. Even the Smithsonian Institution and the zoo were forced to close, as well as stores, cafés, and museums. In Maryland on February 18, snow was accumulating at a rate of 4 inches (10 cm) an hour in one of the worst snowstorms in the state's recorded history. Four feet (1.2 m) of snow fell in parts of the Appalachian Mountains in western Maryland. Not even the president could escape. Returning to the capital from Camp David, his 14-vehicle motorcade crawled behind snowplows and the journey took 2.5 hours. Then the storms moved into New England, where they dropped 2 feet (60 cm) of snow. Travel chaos was bad enough, but the storms also cost at least 37 lives. At least four people died in their cars from carbon monoxide poisoning, probably because they were running the engines to keep warm and snow blocked the exhaust pipe.

Severe storms, of the kind that bring torrential rain in summer and heavy snow in winter, form in very unstable air. As well as rain or snow, they often produce hail, thunder and lightning, and strong winds. In extreme cases they can trigger tornadoes, although these rarely happen in winter.

Near coasts, winter is a time of *squalls*, which are violent but isolated storms. They develop when skies are clear. At night, the land cools, radiating into the sky the warmth it absorbed during the day. If the sky is cloudy, the clouds absorb the heat radiated from below, warming the air and the ground beneath, so in winter clear nights are colder than cloudy nights. In winter the sea is warmer than the land (see "Cold air and warm water," on page 123) and it continues to warm the air in contact with it by night as well as by day. The result is that after a clear night, very cold air will lie over the land and there will be a layer of much warmer, moist air over the sea. If the warm air then crosses the coast, it will rise above the cold, denser air and become unstable. That is what produces huge cumulonimbus storm clouds.

On a much larger scale, violent storms sometimes develop ahead of an advancing cold front (see the sidebar "Weather fronts" on page 14) along a *squall line*—a series of storms along a line that may extend for up to 600 miles (965 km). There are several ways a squall line can develop. If the cold air behind the front is moving fast and sinking at the same time (a front where this happens is known as a *kata-front*), it can push strongly beneath the warm air ahead of it. Alternatively, heavy rain may cool the air around it by dragging cold air down from a higher level in the cloud. This will make the cool air sink and push under adjacent warmer air within the same air mass, where it is not raining, creating a false front.

In addition, very large thunderstorms can "reproduce." An individual storm seldom lasts for more than an hour or two before it breaks down and dissipates. The storm sustains itself by drawing in warm air. This rises, its water vapor condenses releasing latent heat that warms the air, and the air continues to rise as a vigorous upcurrent. Precipitation falling from high in the cloud drags down cold air, and as it enters the warmer air in the lower part of the cloud some of the water evaporates, absorbing latent heat and chilling the surrounding air. This forms a cold downcurrent. Ordinarily, the downcurrent descends into the upcurrent. It cools the rising air, slowing the upcurrent and eventually suppressing it. That is when the storm ends and the cloud begins to dissipate. At the same time, the strong downcurrents flowing out of the base of the cloud at a *gust front* may push under adjacent warm air, pushing it upward and making it unstable. The lifted air then produces a new storm cloud ahead and to the right of the dying one.

Stability and lapse rates

Whatever the mechanism, all storms require an area of low pressure containing moist, unstable air (see the sidebar) and a disturbance to set the unstable air in motion. Once these requirements are met, storm clouds will grow rapidly and the storm itself will follow.

Whether air is stable or unstable is a matter of lapse rates. Air temperature decreases with height. At the surface, the average temperature over the world as a whole is 59°F (15°C). At the tropopause, the boundary at about 36,000 feet (11 km) above which temperature remains constant with further increases in height, it is –74°F (–59°C). Subtracting one temperature from the other shows that air temperature decreases by 133°F (74°C) between sea level and 36,000 feet (11 km), or by 3.7°F for every 1,000 feet (6.7°C km^{-1}). This is the average lapse rate, but local lapse rates vary widely. The actual local lapse rate is called the *environmental lapse rate*. In winter, for example, the surface temperature may be, say, 30°F (–1°C), in which case the environmental lapse rate will be 2.9°F per 1,000 feet (5.3°C km^{-1}).

Suppose that dry air is forced to rise, perhaps to cross a mountain. As it rises it will expand and cool at the dry adiabatic lapse rate, or DALR (see the sidebar "Adiabatic cooling and warming" on page 2) of 5.5°F per 1,000 feet (10°C km^{-1}). This rate of cooling is constant, regardless of the initial temperature of the rising air. As it rises, the air cools faster than the

Air pressure, highs, and lows

When air is warmed, it expands and becomes less dense. When air is chilled, it contracts and becomes more dense.

Air expands by pushing away the air around it. It rises because it is less dense than the air immediately above it. Denser air flows in beneath it, lifting it upward, and this air in turn is warmed by contact with the surface, so it also expands and rises. If you imagine a column of air extending all the way from the surface to the top of the atmosphere, warming from below causes air to be pushed out of the column, so it contains less air (fewer molecules of air) than it did when it was cooler. Because there is less air in the column, the pressure its weight exerts at the surface is reduced. The result is an area of low surface pressure, often called simply a *low*.

In chilled air the opposite happens. The air molecules move closer together, so the air contracts, becomes denser, and sinks. The amount of air in the column increases, its weight increases, and the surface atmospheric pressure also increases. This produces an area of high pressure, or simply a *high*.

At sea level, the atmosphere exerts sufficient pressure to raise a column of mercury about 30 inches (760 mm) in a tube from which the air has been removed. Meteorologists call this pressure one *bar* and used to measure atmospheric pressure in *millibars* (1,000 millibars (mb) = 1 bar = 10^6 dynes cm^{-2} = 14.5 lb in^{-2}). Millibars are still the units quoted in newspaper and TV weather forecasts, but the international scientific unit has changed. Scientists now measure atmospheric pressure in pascals (Pa): 1 bar = 0.1 MPa (megapascals or millions of pascals); 1 mb = 100 Pa.

Air pressure decreases with height, because there is less weight of air above to exert pressure. Pressure measured at different places on the surface is corrected to sea-level pressure, to remove differences due only to altitude. Lines are then drawn, linking places where the pressure is the same. These lines, called *isobars*, allow meteorologists to study the distribution of pressure.

Like water flowing downhill, air flows from high to low pressure. Its speed, which we feel as wind strength, depends on the difference in pressure between the two regions. This is called the *pressure gradient*. On a weather map it is calculated from the distance between isobars, just as the distance between contours on an ordinary map allows the steepness of hills to be measured. As the diagram shows, the steeper the gradient, the closer together the isobars are, and the stronger the wind.

Moving air is subject to the Coriolis effect, which swings it to the right in the Northern Hemisphere and to the left in the Southern Hemisphere, with the result that clear of the surface, winds flow parallel to the isobars rather than across them. The wind is also affected by friction with the surface. This is greater over land than it is over the sea. The result is that surface winds do not flow parallel to the isobars. They cross them at about 30° over the oceans and at about 45° over land, in the direction of the center of low pressure.

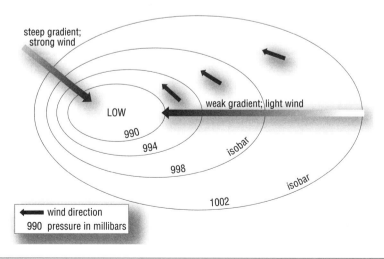

Pressure gradient and wind speed

average lapse rate. Imagine that the surface air temperature is 30°F (–1°C) and the rising air starts at 31°F (–0.5°C). By the time it reaches 1,000 feet (300 m), the temperature of the rising air will be 25.5°F (–3.6°C) and that of the surrounding air 27.1°F (–2.7°C). The rising air is cooler, and therefore denser, than the air around it. As soon as it has cleared the mountaintop, it will sink and warm adiabatically until it reaches air at its own temperature. This air is said to be *stable*.

If the rising air is moist, however, it may soon cool to its dew point temperature, at which water vapor starts to condense. Condensation releases latent heat, warming the air, and so further cooling will be at the saturated adiabatic lapse rate (SALR). This varies according to the relative humidity of the air, but averages 3°F per 1,000 feet (6°C km⁻¹). The height at which condensation commences is called the *lifting condensation level*. Imagine it is at 200 feet (61 m), where the rising air will have cooled from 31°F (–0.5°C) to 29.9°F (–1.2°C). Its rate of cooling then slows, and at 1,000 feet (300 m) its temperature is 27.8°F (–2.3°C). This is warmer than the surrounding air, at 27.1° F (–2.7°C), and so the air will go on rising. Air that continues to rise once it has been lifted is said to be *conditionally unstable*, because the initial lifting was a necessary condition for it to become unstable.

Now see what happens when the difference in starting temperatures is greater. If the rising air starts at 40°F (4.4°C) and reaches its lifting condensation level at 500 feet (150 m), after which it continues to cool at the SALR, the air will still be warmer than the surrounding air at 30,000 feet (9 km). It will rise all the way to and then through the tropopause, because it will still be warmer than air in the lower stratosphere. Such air would be very unstable indeed and would certainly produce huge storms, although air is not often this unstable. It reaches a height at which it has lost so much of its moisture that condensation ceases and its further cooling is at the higher DALR.

Conditions inside the cloud

Inside the cloud, conditions are very violent. Its base is at the lifting condensation level of 500 feet (150 m). Minute water droplets are carried upward in the rising air. Above about 14,000 feet (4,270 m), where the temperature is around –3°F (–19°C), the droplets freeze into ice crystals, but continue to rise. Cold air sinks from the top of the cloud, so there are upcurrents and downcurrents with speeds that often reach 20 MPH (32 km/h) and can exceed 60 MPH (96 km/h), but the most violent storms occur when wind above the cloud carries away the rising air. This draws more air from below and intensifies the upcurrents. Rising air swept away from the top of the cloud often forms a distinctive anvil shape, visible because of the ice crystals in it. If you see a big, dark cloud with a white anvil at the top, you can expect a violent storm.

At the center of a storm the air pressure is low, sometimes very low. Air drawn into the low will spiral around it, generating winds with speeds that are proportional to the pressure gradient (see "Gales and why they happen," on page 78). Rain falling from the cloud will be driven by a strong wind with even stronger gusts ahead of it, where air is being drawn into the upcurrents, and behind, where the cold downcurrents flow out of the cloud. If the precipitation falls as snow, blizzards are very likely.

Water droplets and ice crystals are rising, ice crystals are descending, and there are many collisions. Graupel and hailstones grow in this mixture of water and ice, and so do snowflakes (see "Snowflakes and types of snow," on page 110).

Lightning

Something else also happens. The storm cloud acquires an electric charge, so it is electrically positive at the top and mainly negative near its base. How this situation develops is uncertain, but the sidebar outlines the likely processes.

Charge separation

In a cumulonimbus storm cloud, positive charge usually accumulates near the top of the cloud and negative charge near the bottom. There is also a small area of positive charge, of uncertain origin, at the base of the cloud.

Scientists are uncertain just how this separation of charge occurs, but probably several processes are involved. Some separation may be due to the fact that the ionosphere, in the upper atmosphere (above about 37 miles; 60 km), is positively charged and in fine weather the surface of the Earth is negatively charged, with a steady, gentle downward flow of current. This means it is possible that a positive charge is induced on the underside of cloud droplets (by the negative charge below) and a negative charge on their upper surfaces. If the droplets then collide in such a way as to split them, the charges may separate. It is also possible that falling cloud particles may capture negative ions.

The most important mechanism is believed to occur when water (H_2O) freezes to form hail pellets. A hailstone forms when a supercooled water droplet freezes. This happens from the outside inward. Hydrogen ions (H^+) then move towards the colder region, so the hailstone contains a preponderance of H^+ in its icy outer shell and of hydroxyl (OH^-) in its liquid interior. As freezing progresses, the interior of the hailstone expands, bursting the outer shell. This releases tiny splinters of ice carrying a positive charge (because of the H^+). Being so small and light, these splinters are carried to the top of the cloud by updrafts. The heavier hailstone centers, with their negative charge (OH^-), sink to a lower level.

Air is a good insulator, but eventually the electrical field produced by this charge separation can amount to more than 300,000 volts per foot (984,000 V m^{-1}) and the insulation is overcome. The result is a spark of lightning. If it flashes inside the cloud or between one cloud and another, we see it as an overall white light, called sheet lightning.

Forked lightning is a spark between the negative base of the cloud and a local area of positive charge on the ground, traveling along an irregular path where the air offers least resistance. The stroke begins with a *stepped leader*. This leaves a track about 8 inches (20 cm) wide in which air molecules have been ionized—stripped of electrons—so the air along the track is electrically charged. Before it reaches the ground, the stepped leader triggers a *return stroke*. The return stroke travels upward along the same ionized path. It is extremely bright and this is the flash we see. The stepped leader and return stroke neutralize the charge near the base of the cloud, but then a new flash begins at a higher level, with a *dart leader* and its return stroke traveling along the existing path. A single lightning flash comprises three or four separate strokes.

A lightning flash rarely lasts longer than about 0.2 second, but in this time it releases so much energy that the air through which the spark travels is heated, by up to 54,000°F (30,000°C) in less than one second. This makes the air expand so fast that it explodes, sending out the shock waves we hear as thunder. These travel at the speed of sound, which is much slower than the speed of light, so if the storm is some distance away we see the lightning before we hear the thunder. At a distance of one mile from the storm, we see the lightning approximately 5 seconds before we hear the thunder (3 seconds km^{-1}).

Thunder often keeps on rumbling for several seconds. This is because a lightning flash may be more than one mile (1.6 km) long and its irregular shape means some parts of it are closer than others to an observer some distance away. Sound from the nearest part of the lightning stroke reaches the observer first and sound from more distant parts follows. As they travel, the sound waves are damped by the air and refracted upward by the decrease in air temperature with height. Higher frequencies—the high-pitched notes—are lost first, so thunder has a deep sound. It can seldom be heard at all from a storm that is more than about 6 miles (10 km) away, because over this distance all the sound waves are lost.

Precipitation

Precipitation is certain beneath such a fearsome cloud, and it will be heavy. In the upper part of the cloud, most of the water is frozen and ice crystals clump together into snowflakes. Whether these survive all the way to the ground depends on the temperatures they experience as they fall. The lower the freezing level, which is the height at which the temperature falls

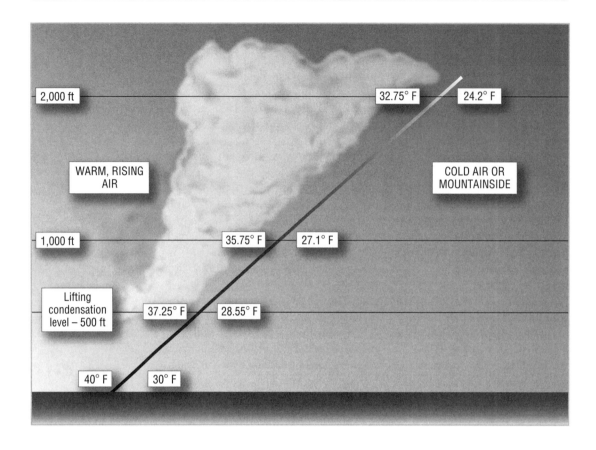

2,000 ft | WARM, RISING AIR | 32.75° F | 24.2° F | COLD AIR OR MOUNTAINSIDE

1,000 ft | 35.75° F | 27.1° F

Lifting condensation level – 500 ft | 37.25° F | 28.55° F

40° F | 30° F

to 32°F (0°C), the more likely it is to fall as snow. Snow is unlikely if the freezing level is above 1,000 feet (300 m).

In our imagined cloud, the freezing level is just above 2,000 feet (600 m), so it seems that snowflakes and ice crystals will have a long way to fall through air at higher than freezing temperatures. If the freezing level is to be at 1,000 feet (300 m) and the lifting condensation level is at 500 feet (150 m), the surface temperature of the air must be 36.25°F (2.36°C), rather than our supposed 40°F (4°C)—still above freezing.

It sounds as though this cloud will deliver rain, but perhaps it will not. Passage over mountains (called *orographic lifting*) is only one mechanism that can force air to rise. Cold air undercutting warmer air at a front will also cause lifting and can trigger instability in the same way. In fact, this is how most storms begin.

The warm air starts with a surface temperature of 40°F (4.4°C). The base of the cloud, at 500 feet (150 m), is at 37.25°F (2.9°C) and at 1,000 feet (300 m) the temperature is 35.75°F (2°C). Snow and ice will not melt very rapidly at these temperatures. Remember, though, that the air has been forced to rise up the slope of a mountainside or front. Cloud starts to form at 500 feet (150 m), where the air is cold enough for water vapor to condense, but the visible cloud base follows the slope, as the illustration shows. Precipitation does not follow the slope, of course. It falls vertically (and is then driven by the wind). If it is a mountainside that forms the slope, then that is where the precipitation will fall. If the slope is frontal, precipitation will fall through the frontal zone into the air beneath.

Even at 500 feet (150 m), where the temperature inside the cloud is 37.25°F (2.9°C), the cold air beside it is 28.55°F (–1.9°C). Precipitation falling from any higher level will leave the cloud at a temperature barely above freezing and enter much colder air extending all the way to the ground. Consequently it will fall as snow.

Snow will not fall if it forms above about 1,000 feet (300 m) and the air below it is warm. Even in the middle of summer, the clouds that produce showers and storms in middle latitudes are full of snow, but it all melts before reaching the ground and falls as rain. Obviously, the air must be cold before snow will fall. Less obviously, the air producing the snow must be relatively warm.

When it does fall heavily, even in places that expect winter snow, it can cause serious disruption. As the experience of February 2003 shows, transport can be brought to a standstill, businesses forced to close, and, worst of all, lives can be lost.

THE LAKE EFFECT

On Christmas Eve, 2001, a storm struck western New York State. By the time it ended, on New Year's Day, it had dropped 81.6 inches (2 m) of snow on Buffalo. It was an epic storm. Not surprisingly, it caused widespread disruption. The people of Buffalo are accustomed to winter snow, however. This was not the first such storm to hit them. In December 1937 a storm dropped 4 feet (1.2 m) of snow on the city in a single day.

On December 1 and 2, 2002, it was the turn of Ashville, New York. It received 26 inches (66 cm) of snow from a single storm. The 2002–03 winter was much colder than usual across most of the Northern Hemisphere and the winter storms were especially severe. From January 10 through 12, snow fell at the rate of 4–5 inches (10–12.5 cm) an hour over western New York State, and 24 inches (61 cm) fell on Perrysburg, in Cattaraugus County, south of Buffalo. A few days later, another storm delivered more than 24 inches (61 cm) in less than 9 hours at Oswego and 40 inches (1 m) fell at West Leyden. Oswego is no stranger to heavy snow. During a 1966 storm that lasted from January 27 to 31, 8.5 feet (2.59 m) of snow fell there.

There was another severe winter in 1976–77. In January, Hooker, New York, received 12.4 feet (3.78 m), and in the course of that winter, almost 39 feet (11.86 m) of snow fell on Hooker. That is more than enough to bury a two-story house.

Parts of northern Michigan have received about 33 feet (10 m) of snow in a single winter and the average snowfall over the state is more than 16 feet (5 m). Snowfall is not spread evenly, of course, with so much falling every day to make up the total. Much of it arrives during severe storms, often as blizzards.

When air crosses water

All of these places lie to the east of one or more of the Great Lakes, and the heavy snowfall they experience affects the whole of the United States and Canada from eastern Minnesota and Manitoba in the west to Pennsylvania, New York, eastern Ontario, and Quebec in the east. The moisture that falls as snow comes from the lakes themselves. Over the years, this region has averaged much higher snowfalls than places in the same latitude but farther away from the lakes. It comprises a snowbelt extending downwind for about 50 miles (80 km) from the nearest lakeshore.

As autumn advances, the Great Lakes cool very slowly, remaining free of ice well into the winter (see the sidebar "Specific heat capacity and blackbodies" on page 125). In some winters the lakes do not freeze over at all. Their surface water remains above freezing temperature throughout.

Air masses cross North America mainly from west to east. As the land radiates away the warmth it absorbed during the summer, the continental air becomes very cold. From time to time, Arctic air spills southward over the continent, lowering the temperature even more (see "Cold waves," on page 149). As it crosses the lakes, this extremely cold air comes into contact with water that is relatively warm. This raises the temperature of the lowest layer of air and, as the air grows warmer, water evaporates into it.

A layer of warm, moist air is now lying beneath a large mass of very cold air. The cold, denser air subsides beneath it, pushing it upward, and as the warm air rises it cools and its water vapor condenses. The air has become unstable (see "Heavy snowstorms and what causes them," on page 134) and as it rises, cloud starts to form in it. The cloud is most commonly stratus, stratocumulus, or large cumulus, depending on the amount of moisture the air holds, and it starts to develop about halfway across the lake. The cloud travels eastward with the general air movement.

Then the air reaches the cold, continental landmass again. Contact with the land slows the air. As air continues to arrive from over the lake and air accumulates on the lee shore, the resulting convergence forces air to rise. The cloud thickens and precipitation starts falling—as snow, of course, because of the very low temperature in the subsiding air. The diagram shows what happens.

The lake effect

cold air

cold air

cold air

mild, moist air

Where the snow falls, and how much

Just where the snow falls depends on the direction and speed of the winds that drive the clouds. These are variable. A deviation of a degree or two in the track it follows makes a difference of 1–2 miles (1.6–3.2 km) by the time a storm has traveled about 50 miles (80 km). The speed of the wind determines how far the snowstorms will travel. The stronger the winds are, the farther they will carry the snow. They tend to travel farthest in late autumn and early winter.

The amount of snow is also very variable. It is heaviest when the contrast between the temperatures of the cold air and water is greatest. The warmer the water and colder the air, the more evaporation there will be, and if the air is very cold, so will the surrounding land be, triggering rapid condensation and precipitation. These conditions most often occur in December and January. The snowfall amount also depends on the *fetch*—the distance the air travels across the water. The longer the air remains in contact with the water, the more time there is for water to evaporate into it.

If the lakes freeze over, the supply of moisture is cut off and the snowbelt effect ends.

Not only the Great Lakes

There are other expanses of water—seas as well as lakes—that generate smaller snowbelts, and some of these are in North America. Cape Cod, Massachusetts experiences heavy snowstorms, but is beyond the limit of the Great Lakes snowbelt. A high-pressure region centered over Quebec for most of the winter generates Cape Cod's snow. Air circulates clockwise around centers of high pressure (in the Northern Hemisphere). In this case, the circulation draws Arctic air southward over the Atlantic and then toward the North American coast. As it approaches from the northeast, the air crosses the warm water of the Gulf Stream. The air temperature rises near the ocean surface, water evaporates, and the unstable air rises as it nears the coast, triggering cloud formation and snow.

The Gulf Stream flows approximately parallel to the entire length of the United States Atlantic coast, so a similar lake effect, due to the sea, of course, also happens elsewhere along the coast. Easterly winds that cross the Gulf Stream and are then funneled along Long Island Sound bring heavy snow to New York and New Jersey. Winds from the southeast that blow inland along Chesapeake Bay bring snow to Baltimore. This is "lake-effect" snow, even though it is the ocean rather than a lake that causes it.

The Great Salt Lake in Utah also has a snowbelt to its south. The Great Salt Lake remains ice-free through the winter because it is so salty. When cold air is drawn southward across it, there are heavy snowstorms inland from the lee shore.

The Gulf Stream heads eastward across the ocean before reaching Canada. Consequently the warm water of the Gulf Stream produces no lake-effect snow in Canada. Canada does have two large expanses of water, however, and these generate lake-effect snowstorms. Hudson Bay and the Gulf of St. Lawrence feed snow-laden air to the mainland. Hudson Bay usually freezes over in January, ending the lake effect. The St. Lawrence remains open through the winter, however.

Lake effects in Europe and Asia

No other continent has a snowbelt comparable to that of northeastern North America, because in no other continent is there an area of water comparable to the Great Lakes in just the right location to produce one. Lake Baikal, in Siberia, is the eighth-largest lake in the world and it influences the climate of the region around it, making it warmer in winter and cooler in summer, but in fall it causes fog rather than snow, and by the middle of December it has frozen completely.

This does not mean there are no European or Asian snowbelts. Every autumn, as temperatures fall over Siberia, cold, dense air subsides to produce a large area of high pressure. Air flows outward from the high and some of the air crosses Lake Ladoga, in western Russia, and is then funneled westward through the Gulf of Finland and across the Baltic Sea, as shown on the map. Over the Gulf and the Baltic, the cold, dry air comes into contact with much warmer (though still very cold) water. It acquires moisture and reaches the eastern coast of Sweden as moist, relatively warm air that starts cooling as soon as it crosses the coast, depositing snow over the southeastern part of the country. This is lake-effect snow.

Siberian air also flows eastward away from the winter high-pressure center. This air crosses the arid highlands of Mongolia and the Gobi Desert, then brings cold, dry weather to northern China. Harbin, China, for example, has an average annual rainfall of 21.8 inches (553 mm), but only 1 inch (25 mm) falls between the end of October and beginning of March. The air crosses the coast, as shown on the map, and in the north it gathers moisture from the Sea of Japan and arrives as relatively warm, moist air at the western coasts of Honshu and Hokkaido, Japan. The warm Kuroshio Current flows through the Sea of Japan and adds to the warming. The average January temperature in Vladivostok, Russia, is 7.3°F (−13.7°C) and at Niigata, Japan, directly opposite on the other side of the Sea of Japan, it is 34.5°F (1.4°C). As the air crosses the Japanese coast, it is forced to rise over the high hills along the western side of both islands, and it deposits its moisture as lake-effect snow.

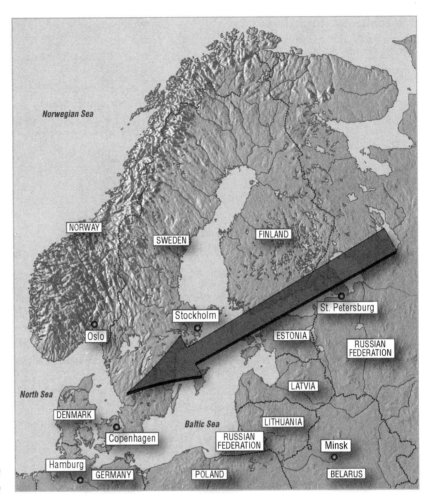

Lake effect in eastern Sweden

Farther south, Siberian air crosses the Yellow Sea, acquiring moisture that it deposits over western parts of the Korean Peninsula. The effect there is smaller, because the air travels a shorter distance over water than it does in crossing the Sea of Japan.

Advantages as well as disadvantages

Deep snow may block roads, bring down power and telephone lines, and close schools and businesses, but these are difficulties that can be overcome. If everyone knows that snow is likely, preparations can be made to minimize the inconvenience. Then people can take other steps to maximize the advantages.

Snow is a great tourist attraction and some of the best winter resorts in eastern North America lie in the snowbelt. The hills lying to the east of Lake Ontario receive more than 17 feet (5 m) of snow every winter, making this the snowiest place east of the Rocky Mountains.

The North American lake effect is not confined to winter, however. Air moving eastward over the Great Lakes in summer, brings rain to lands that otherwise would be much drier. The effect is small, but it is enough to allow farmers to grow potatoes, other vegetables, and fruit, and it encourages the growth of pastures that are nutritious enough to sustain dairy farming. Bangor, Maine, and Minneapolis, Minnesota, are at latitudes 44.80° N and 44.88° N, respectively. Bangor has an average annual rainfall (falling as snow in winter, of course) of about 40 inches (1,016 mm), while Minneapolis receives 27.6 inches (701 mm).

It is not only the rain that favors horticulture. The lake effect delays the start of spring, because of the time it takes for the snow to melt and because the lakes warm slowly, so the snowbelt region continues for some time to experience temperatures that are below the minimum for plant growth. This is not the disadvantage that it seems, because it means that

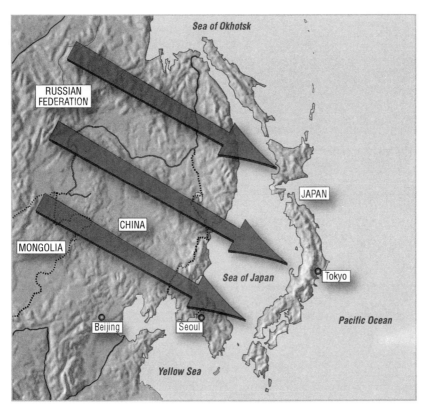

Lake effect in Korea and Japan

plant growth does not begin until after the last of the winter frosts has passed. Crops are much less likely to suffer frost damage.

The lake effect also moderates summer temperatures. The average summer (June, July, and August) temperature in Bangor is 66°F (19°C) and in Minneapolis it is 71°F (22°C)—in both cases measured at the airport. The difference is small, but also misleading, because Minneapolis is at an elevation of 833 feet (254 m) and Bangor is at 183 feet (56 m). Correct for the difference in elevation of the two cities at the average lapse rate of 3.6°F per 1,000 feet (6.5°C km^{-1}), and the true difference in average summer temperatures is 8.3°F (4.6°C). There is no significant difference in the corrected average winter temperatures for the two cities—this is a summer effect only.

Scandinavia and eastern Asia do not enjoy a summer lake effect. As temperatures rise over Central Asia, the Siberian high that dominates the continent's weather in winter weakens and is then replaced by generally low pressure. Air reaches Europe, including Sweden, from the west. Japan experiences the Asian summer monsoon, with rain carried on southwesterly and southerly winds that blow along the line of the islands rather than across them. The summer winds are generally light, but they bring heavy rain.

COLD WAVES

Over most of Europe, from Britain as far south as northern Italy, January 1987 brought a spell of bitterly cold weather. In some places, temperatures were the lowest of the 20th century. Icy easterly winds from Siberia blew across the continent and there were heavy falls of snow.

While Europeans shivered, however, Americans were enjoying an unusually mild winter. The warm conditions lasted until April, but then the weather turned very cold in the central and southern states. Winds from the north, called *northers*, brought a blast of cold air down the eastern side of the Rocky Mountains, all the way from the Canadian Arctic. This was uncomfortable, but it brought a blessing. The low temperatures prevented development of the conditions that generate tornadoes—warm spring sunshine and high humidity, producing unstable air. Ordinarily, there are more than 100 tornadoes in April, the month when they are most likely, but only 20 were recorded in April 1987. As a result, there were fewer tornadoes in 1987 than there are in most years.

These spells of very cold weather are called *cold waves*. They are the opposite of heat waves. Cold waves arrive suddenly and the temperature falls rapidly. In the northern, northeastern, and central parts of the United States, a cold wave is defined as a fall in temperature of at least 20°F (11°C) to no higher than 0°F (–18°C) within 24 hours. In California, Florida, and the Gulf Coast states, the temperature must fall by 16°F (9°C) to no more than 32°F (0°C) within 24 hours.

The term *cold wave* is not defined so precisely elsewhere in the world, but the phenomenon is not confined to North America. It happens throughout the middle latitudes and can have a variety of causes.

The Great Cold Wave of February 1899

North American cold waves draw Arctic air southward and occasionally this bitterly cold air can extend across most of the continent. During two cold waves, together lasting from January 29 to February 13, 1899, temperatures fell to below 0°F (–18°C) as far south as the Florida panhandle. On February 13 the temperature reached –2°F (–19°C) in Tallahassee. The cold air also covered Texas, where on February 11, –8°F (–22°C) was recorded at Fort Worth, –4°F (–20°C) at Temple, and an all-time low of –23°F (–30°C) at Tulia—not equaled until the winter of 1933. Ice flowed down the Mississippi River on February 17. It passed New Orleans and entered the Gulf of Mexico, and in some places the Mississippi ice was 1 inch (2.5 cm) thick.

The "Great Cold Wave of February 1899" was one of the worst on record, but only because of its geographic extent. At Albany, New York, temperatures remained below 0°F (–18°C) from January 20 to February 3, and from February 9 to 18, 1979. Montana endures up to 12 cold waves every winter. On January 20, 1954, the temperature at Rogers Pass, 40 miles (64 km) northwest of Helena, was –70°F (–57°C). That is the lowest temperature ever recorded in the United States, excluding Alaska. The temperature plummeted suddenly that day. In the morning, the temperature at Helena was –36°F (–38°C).

Dangers of the cold

Such rapid falls in temperature are extremely disruptive. Roads are blocked with snow, rail tracks are coated with ice and points freeze solid, plumbing freezes, and telephone and power lines break under the weight of snow or ice.

They are also dangerous. The 1987 European cold wave claimed nearly 300 lives, and each year cold waves kill more than 350 people in the United States. These are only the deaths directly attributable to the weather. Sudden extreme cold can accelerate the deaths of people who are already weakened by old age or sickness. In Britain it was estimated that the death rate increased by about 2,000 during the 1987 cold wave, compared with the number of deaths recorded over the same period in an average year.

It is not only humans who are at risk. Sheep suffer greatly, and severe cold spells sometimes coincide with the start of the lambing season. Wild animals may starve, because their food is frozen or deeply buried.

Cold waves have occurred throughout history. They affect only the middle latitudes and they have nothing to do with long-term climatic trends. Whether the global climate is warming or cooling, cold waves can still erupt to bring misery. It is as though the Arctic winter invades—and that is pretty much what happens.

The polar front jet stream

Middle latitudes are where polar and tropical air meet as part of the general circulation of the atmosphere (see the sidebar "General circulation of the atmosphere" on page 4). Warm air rises at the equator, cools, and loses most of its moisture from clouds that sometimes tower to 60,000 feet (18.3 km). That is why equatorial climates are wet. At high altitude, the air moves away from the equator, to north and south. Now extremely cold, at around latitude 30° N and S it meets air moving toward the equator. The converging air sinks into the subtropics, warming adiabatically as it descends. Because it lost its moisture as it cooled (see the sidebar "Why warm air can hold more moisture than cold air can" on page 18), the subsiding air is very dry and produces a belt of desert climates in both hemispheres. Some of this air flows back toward the equator at low level and some flows away from the equator. High over the poles, the air is extremely cold and dense. It sinks and flows away from the poles at low level. At around latitude 50° N and 50° S, cold air flowing away from the poles encounters warm air flowing away from the equator. The converging air rises, and at a high level some air flows toward the poles and some toward the equator.

Where the polar and tropical air meet, a boundary called the *polar front* separates them, extending all the way to the tropopause, at about 40,000 feet (12.2 km). Because the tropical air is warmer and less dense than the polar air, it extends higher and the tropopause folds over, with warm air lying above cold air. It is at the tropopause that the difference in temperature between the two types of air is most marked. This difference generates a wind, the *polar front jet stream*, blowing at all levels up the slope of the front and reaching its maximum force at the top (see the sidebar "Jet stream" on page 17).

The jet stream drives the generally westerly movement of air in middle latitudes, but its strength and location vary. In summer, when high latitudes become warmer, the temperature difference between polar and tropical air is reduced. The jet stream is generated by the difference in temperature between tropical and polar air. As this difference decreases, therefore, the westerly circulation weakens and the polar front jet stream moves toward the poles, crossing North America at about the latitude of the Great Lakes and Europe at about the latitude of Spain. In winter, the jet stream moves further toward the equator. It crosses North America from Mexico to North Carolina, and on the other side of the Atlantic it crosses to the south of the Mediterranean.

These are average positions, however, and the polar front jet stream is highly variable. In spring and fall it is on the move between its summer and winter locations and, especially in late winter, it tends to break down completely over *index cycles* lasting from three to eight weeks. Latitudinal movement is said to be *zonal*, the magnitude of the zonal component of that movement is called the *zonal index*, and the change in the zonal index is known as the index cycle. As the illustration shows, each index cycle begins as a series of undulations in the east-to-west direction of the jet stream. These grow bigger, until in some places the wind blows from the north, in other places from the south, although the overall movement of air is still from west to east. After that the westerly flow breaks up into cells, where the flow is circular. Then the jet stream ceases altogether, before establishing itself once more. This breakdown usually moves from east to west.

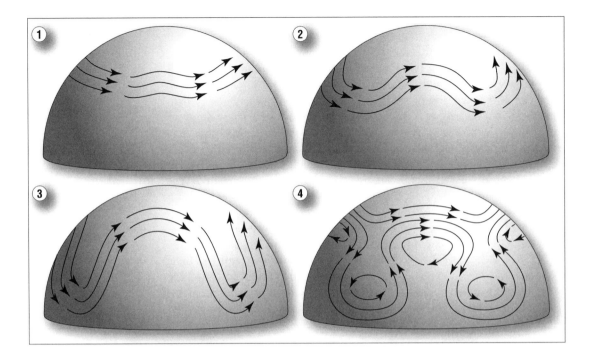

*Four stages of
the index cycle*

Drawing warm air north and cold air south

Weather systems in middle latitudes usually move from west to east with depressions following the line of the high-level, westerly jet stream. As the pattern changes and the jet stream flows across lines of latitude rather than approximately parallel to them, the movement of air and weather systems at lower levels changes with it. This means that there are places where air is being drawn from far to the north.

The jet stream flows parallel to the polar front, so in the Northern Hemisphere polar air lies to its north and tropical air to its south. As the front moves south in the fall, polar air behind it extends to cover the area north of the front. The depressions moving beneath the jet stream bring warmer air, however, and these can be extensive. They moderate temperatures, although continental climates always bring much colder winters than maritime climates.

Undulations in the jet stream mark similar undulations in the polar front. Consequently, as the jet stream and front curve to the south, they bring Arctic air to the areas north of the front. Where the front curves northward, tropical air extends over the area behind it. "Crests" in the waves, extending the front northward, are called *ridges* and curves to the south are called *troughs*. Ridges bring mild weather, owing to the northward migration of tropical air, but troughs bring Arctic air. This can extend far to the south, and cold waves due to the sudden incursion of polar air occasionally reach as far as Alabama and Florida. Indeed, they are especially dangerous there, because people are used to a subtropical climate and are not expecting them.

In 1965 a cold wave in these two states caused many deaths. Cold waves can also engulf Texas. On February 7, 1933, the temperature at Fort Worth dropped from 57°F (14°C) at midnight to 10°F (−12°C) by 8 A.M., and the following day Seminole recorded −23°F (−30°C), equal to the 1899 record low temperature.

Blocking

When the jet stream breaks down, the movement of weather systems ceases and then, too, cold waves can invade. The breakdown isolates large masses of air that remain stationary. In high latitudes these isolated masses often comprise dense air at relatively high atmospheric pressure (called *anticyclones*), and in winter this is cold, polar air. As the westerly movement of low-pressure systems resumes, these highs block their path, diverting them to north or south, and this blocking sometimes persists for weeks.

From January to early March 1963, for example, a blocking anticyclone covered the whole of the British Isles. Anticyclones bring fine weather, so skies are clear. Clear skies produce cold nights, as there is no blanket of cloud to trap heat radiating from the ground. Further south, blocking is more commonly due to stationary depressions that bring wet but fairly mild weather. As the illustration of the index cycle shows, the air flows clockwise, or *anticyclonically*, around the isolated cells to the north, producing high pressure, and counterclockwise, or *cyclonically*, around the southern cells, producing low pressure.

It is not the general weather associated with a winter anticyclone that brings a cold wave, however, but the airflow around the anticyclone. In the Northern Hemisphere, air moves in a clockwise direction around anticyclones. On the eastern side of a stationary anticyclone, the clockwise circulation draws air from far to the north. Over North America, this is cold, polar air from northern Canada and the high Arctic. In western Europe, blocking anticyclones usually occur well to the north, exposing most of the region to easterly winds along the southern side of the high-pressure center. Easterly winds draw in bitterly cold air from central Asia.

Blocking anticyclones also occur in summer, of course. Then they bring prolonged periods of fine, warm, dry weather. If blocking continues for long enough, the fine summer weather can lead to drought.

ICE STORMS

Early airplanes flew at low altitudes and took off only in fine weather. It was not until they were equipped with reliable flight instruments that pilots began to venture through clouds rather than flying around or beneath them. Once that became possible, "instrument flying" was introduced into the training of professional pilots, who were required to take off, fly predetermined courses, perform specified maneuvers, and find their way home with the windows of the cockpit covered by opaque material.

Flight instruments inform the pilot of the attitude, height, speed, and direction of the aircraft. Their introduction was a major advance that allowed planes to fly in poor weather. While this improvement was being developed, new airframe and engine designs were also making it possible for planes to fly at higher altitudes.

It was not long before a problem emerged. As planes flew through some clouds, but not all, ice would form on the wings and tail. Unless something was done to remove it, the ice could quickly grow into a layer that was thick enough to affect the airflow over the wings and control surfaces. Severely iced wings would no longer provide enough lift to keep the plane airborne and ice would jam the hinges of the control surfaces—the elevators, ailerons, and rudders. Icing caused many crashes before passenger and transport aircraft were fitted with "deicing boots." These are inflatable rubber pads along the leading edges of the wings and tail that expand and contract to break up the ice as it forms. In addition, many modern airplanes are equipped with heaters to melt surface ice. Pilots of planes lacking deicing equipment learned to identify and avoid the types of cloud that were likely to cause icing.

Research that led to rainmaking

Icing became a serious problem during World War II, and research into its causes intensified. In 1946 Vincent Schaeffer (1906–93) and Bernard Vonnegut (1914–97) were investigating icing at the General Electric Research Laboratory in Schenectady, New York. They used a refrigerated box into which they dropped particles of various substances to see whether they could induce the formation of ice crystals. In July of that year there was a heat wave and it became difficult to keep the box cold enough for their purposes. On July 13 Schaeffer used crushed dry ice (solid carbon dioxide) to reduce the temperature, sprinkling it into the box. Ice crystals formed instantly and there was a tiny snowstorm inside the box. Schaeffer had found a way to make a cloud form and then deliver precipitation—he had invented *cloud seeding* (see the sidebar). He tested the technique from

Cloud seeding

People have dreamed for centuries of controlling the weather by preventing hailstorms that damage crops and by making clouds deliver rain onto parched land. An early technological attempt began in 1891 in response to a popular belief that it often rained after a major Civil War battle. To check this, cannons were fired into clouds and kites and balloons carried explosives into low clouds, where they were detonated. Once airplanes were able to fly above clouds, people tried throwing sand into the clouds from above.

All of these experiments were aimed at making rain. Mortars were fired vertically upward into clouds to prevent hailstones forming. This technique proved popular, and by 1899 there were thousands of "hail cannons" in use all over Europe. As late as the 1960s, rockets and artillery shells were being used for this purpose in Russia.

None of these experiments succeeded. Despite the popularity of hail cannons (and rockets), they had no effect. When their use was abandoned, the frequency of hailstorms remained unchanged.

Modern cloud seeding works differently. It involves injecting suitable material into supersaturated air (air in which the relative humidity is greater than 100 percent) in order to induce condensation. Silver iodide is the most widely used substance, but solid carbon dioxide—"dry ice"—is also effective. Salt crystals, volcanic dust, dry clay particles, certain proteins, and certain bacteria are also used.

Solid particles act as cloud condensation nuclei. Water vapor condenses onto them, forming cloud droplets. Salt crystals are bigger than most cloud droplets and make bigger droplets form. These are heavy enough to fall and as they do so they coalesce with many smaller droplets. Other solid particles induce the formation of ice crystals.

Each substance works best within a fairly narrow temperature range. Both silver iodide and dry ice are most effective when the temperature inside the cloud is between 5°F and 23°F (–15°C to –5°C).

Particles can be dropped into a cloud from above or injected from ground level. Silver iodide is introduced by burning it and allowing the smoke to drift into the target cloud, where it recrystallizes as it cools.

Dry ice, in the form of pea-sized pellets, is dropped into the target cloud from above. As its temperature rises above –109.3°F (–78.5°C), the dry ice sublimes, drawing latent heat from the surrounding air. The sudden drop in temperature causes ice crystals to form spontaneously.

Hailstorms are prevented by releasing freezing nuclei—particles onto which supercooled water vapor will freeze—into clouds. An aircraft flies beneath a cumulonimbus storm cloud, releasing particles into the updrafts. The particles trigger the formation of many more ice crystals than would form otherwise, depleting the cloud of supercooled liquid droplets. The available water is converted into many small crystals and so it is not free to accumulate on ice pellets and allow these to grow into hailstones.

It is difficult to tell whether cloud seeding works, because clouds might have delivered rain in any case. The evidence suggests that cloud seeding can increase precipitation by at least 5 percent.

an aircraft over Pittsfield, Massachusetts, on November 13, 1946, and caused a snowstorm.

Shortly after Schaeffer made his discovery, Vonnegut found that ice crystals also formed when he burned silver iodide and allowed the smoke to enter the box. Silver iodide proved more convenient to use—dry ice must be kept at temperatures below –109.3°F (–78.5°C)—but today both are used.

Everyone had supposed that when water droplets cool to around 32°F (0°C) they freeze at once. Ice crystals and snowflakes present no hazard to aircraft, because they do not stick to its smooth surfaces. Icing was therefore a mystery. It should not happen. In fact, though, cloud droplets must be cooled to well below freezing temperature before they turn into ice. Supercooled droplets are common and they are what cause icing. When they collide with a surface, they freeze onto it instantly, attaching themselves firmly to it, and a plane flying through a supercooled cloud sweeps up the droplets in its path.

Icing at ground level

Aircraft icing was dramatic and at first unexpected, but a very similar kind of icing has always been familiar at ground level. Trees can be covered in a thick coating of ice, radio masts can accumulate huge masses of ice, usually on just one side, and overhead power and telephone lines can be enclosed in ice several times their own thickness. These are ice storms.

They are most likely to occur just ahead of a warm front, as illustrated in the diagram. Ahead of the front, in the cold air, the temperature is well below freezing, say at 29°F (–1.7°C), and objects in the cold air are at the same temperature. Behind the front, the warm air is just above freezing, say at 34°F (1°C), and this will be the temperature of the rain falling from the frontal cloud. The rain falls through the front and into the cold air. As it falls through the cold air, the temperature of the raindrops falls slightly, so by the time it strikes the surface, or an object projecting from the surface, the rain is at just about freezing temperature.

To produce an ice storm, the rain must be heavy and driven by wind, so it falls at an angle to the vertical. Then it will be driven against surfaces, such as the mast shown in the diagram, that are several degrees colder than freezing. As each raindrop strikes, the part of it touching the surface freezes instantly. The remainder spills to the sides and also freezes on contact. Before long, the exposed object is covered in a layer of ice.

Effects of an ice storm

The result is striking to look at. Radio masts are always located in exposed areas, on high ground, and they can accumulate an ice coating a foot (30 cm) or more thick. Ships at sea accumulate similar layers on their masts and rigging.

An ice storm produces a romantic winter scene, but it causes a great deal of damage. Ice is heavy. After a severe ice storm in southern England in January 1940, snapped telephone wires were found to be loaded with up to 1,000 pounds (450 kg) of ice between poles and some of the poles broke when their load reached 12 tons (11 tonnes) of ice.

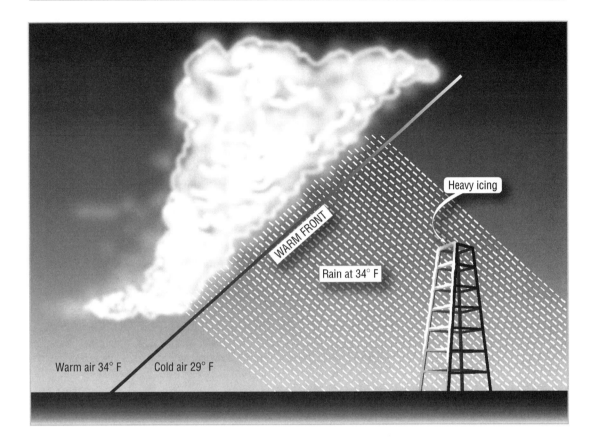

Ice storm

One of the worst ice storms of modern times lasted from January 5 through 9, 1998, and affected the northeastern United States and eastern Canada. More than 3 inches (76 mm) of freezing rain fell in some places, and the ice coating on structures was 1 inch (25 mm) or more thick. In Canada, more than 30,000 wooden utility poles and 1,000 power towers fell down, leaving more than 3 million people without power. About 100,000 people were forced to take refuge in shelters. More than 2.6 million people, amounting to 19 percent of the national workforce, had difficulty getting to work or were unable to do so at all. In upstate New York, northern New Hampshire and Vermont, and in Maine, about 500,000 people were without power, including 80 percent of the population of Maine. A total of 44 people died in the ice storm—28 in Canada, nine in New York, five in Maine, and two in New Hampshire. The ice storm caused damage costing nearly $3 billion in Canada and $1.4 billion in the United States.

The effects of ice storms on wildlife are even worse. Roosting birds have been known to freeze onto their branches, where they died from starvation, and ground-dwelling birds have remained grounded when their wings were coated with ice. Cats out on their nighttime prowls have also been stuck when their paws froze to the ground.

WIND CHILL, FROSTBITE, HYPOTHERMIA, AND SNOW CHILL

Step outdoors on a windy day in winter and the wind feels cold. Even if you know that the temperature has not fallen, nevertheless the wind will make the air feel colder than it did before the wind started, and if you move out of the wind, into a sheltered place, the air will feel warmer. While you are out in the open you are experiencing *wind chill*.

Weather forecasts often mention the "wind chill factor" as a temperature that is lower than the predicted air temperature. Obviously, since wind is simply moving air and air cannot be colder than itself, this use of temperatures can be confusing. Forecasters report wind chill as a temperature because degrees are more familiar units than those they are really using, which are calories or joules per square inch or centimeter per second. They are measuring not temperature, but the rate at which the body loses heat.

Our bodies maintain a fairly constant internal temperature and we fall sick if this varies outside quite narrow margins. Clothing keeps us warm by reducing the rate at which we lose heat through the skin. Our bodies heat a layer of air, just a few molecules thick, that covers the whole of our bodies. Clothing traps air in the millions of tiny spaces between fibers. The warm air around our bodies warms the air trapped in the fabric, and air can escape only slowly through the layers of our clothes. That is how our clothes keep us warm. If we wear too many clothes, we grow uncomfortably hot.

We are not usually fully covered by clothes, however, even when outdoors in winter. Our faces are likely to be bare and we do not always wear gloves. The face and hands can amount to as much as 10 percent of the total surface area of a human body. Bare legs can increase this to about 30 percent, but even bare skin is covered by a layer of warm air, so on a calm day we still have some protection against heat loss.

That is where the wind attacks. It sweeps away this thin layer of warmed air, first from exposed skin, but then from the fabric of our clothes. Our bodies respond by generating more heat in an attempt to replace it, but if it proves impossible to generate heat as fast as the wind removes it, the skin will grow colder and that is what we feel. The air will feel much colder than its actual temperature.

Calculating wind chill

Just how cold the wind makes us depends on the air temperature and the wind speed. The wind chill factor can then be calculated quite precisely.

With an air temperature of 40°F (4.4°C) and a wind blowing at 10 MPH (16 km/h), for example, a body loses heat at the same rate as it would if the air temperature were 34°F (1°C) and the air calm. Provided you are wearing adequate winter clothes this will not harm you, but at lower temperatures it can become serious.

Wind chill increases rapidly as the temperature drops and the wind speed rises. The effect begins when the wind speed is approximately 5 MPH (8 km/h) and increases fairly rapidly as the wind speed increases to about 15 MPH (24 km/h). After that the wind chill increases more slowly, but steadily. (See the chart showing the wind-chill effect.) For example, if you go outdoors when the thermometer reads 0°F (–18°C) and a 15-MPH (24-km/h) wind is blowing, it will feel as though the temperature is –19°F (–28°C), because your skin is cooling as fast as it would in calm air at that temperature.

Scientists at the National Weather Service have used an equation to calculate the values in the table. If you would like to check on their results, or work out the wind chill for yourself, the equation is:

$$\text{wind chill (°F)} = 35.74 + 0.6215T - 35.75(V^{0.16}) + 0.4275T(V^{0.16})$$

where T is the air temperature in degrees Fahrenheit measured 5 feet (1.5 m) above the ground (roughly the height of a human face) and V is the wind speed in miles per hour.

Wind chill

	Temperature (°F)																	
Wind (mph) calm	40	35	30	25	20	15	10	5	0	-5	-10	-15	-20	-25	-30	-35	-40	-45
5	36	31	25	19	13	7	1	-5	-11	-16	-22	-28	-34	-40	-46	-52	-57	-63
10	34	27	21	15	9	3	-4	-10	-16	-22	-28	-35	-41	-47	-53	-59	-66	-72
15	32	25	19	13	6	0	-7	-13	-19	-26	-32	-39	-45	-51	-58	-64	-71	-77
20	30	24	17	11	4	-2	-9	-15	-22	-29	-35	-42	-48	-55	-61	-68	-74	-81
25	29	23	16	9	3	-4	-11	-17	-24	-31	-37	-44	-51	-58	-64	-71	-78	-84
30	28	22	15	8	1	-5	-12	-19	-26	-33	-39	-46	-53	-60	-67	-73	-80	-87
35	28	21	14	7	0	-7	-14	-21	-27	-34	-41	-48	-55	-62	-69	-76	-82	-89
40	27	20	13	6	-1	-8	-15	-22	-29	-36	-43	-50	-57	-64	-71	-78	-84	-91
45	26	19	12	5	-2	-9	-16	-23	-30	-37	-44	-51	-58	-65	-72	-79	-86	-93
50	26	19	12	4	-3	-10	-17	-24	-31	-38	-45	-52	-60	-67	-74	-81	-88	-95
55	25	18	11	4	-3	-11	-18	-25	-32	-39	-46	-54	-61	-68	-75	-82	-89	-97
60	25	17	10	3	-4	-11	-19	-26	-33	-40	-48	-55	-62	-69	-76	-84	-91	-98

Frostbite Times: 30 minutes; 10 minutes; 5 minutes

Dangers of exposure

At any wind-chill temperature below about –17°F (–27°C), you need to be very well wrapped up, with hands and ears well protected. If you start to feel the chill, you should do something about it, because it can be dangerous if you remain exposed to it for too long. After 30 minutes you may begin to suffer from frostbite. The conditions of wind and still-air temperature producing this degree of wind chill are shown on the chart against a pale gray background.

If the wind-chill temperature falls below about –31°F (–35°C) you need to protect all of your body, leaving no bare skin exposed. In the part of the chart shown in medium gray you can suffer frostbite after 10 minutes. If the wind-chill temperature falls below –46°F (–43°C), shown with a dark gray background on the chart, you can suffer frostbite after five minutes. This is extreme cold and it can kill in a surprisingly short time.

Using the chart is straightforward, but you need to make some allowance for the wind speed quoted in weather forecasts. Close to the ground the wind is slowed by friction, especially in towns. To measure wind speed accurately and in a standard way, meteorologists mount their anemometers (instruments that measure wind speed) 33 feet (10 m) above ground level. The wind is stronger there than it is at ground level, so you can expect to experience a wind no more than about two-thirds the strength given in the weather forecast, unless the forecaster specifies that it is ground-level wind speeds that are being quoted.

You should also remember that although the air may be calm, you will feel a wind if you move about in it. If you ride a bicycle at 15 MPH (24 km/h), a 15-MPH (24-km/h) wind will blow on your face even on a windless day. If you walk briskly you will feel a wind of about 5 MPH (8 km/h). So a calm day is truly calm only if you stand still.

Frostbite

Intense cold causes injury in two ways. The first, but less dangerous, is frostbite. It is less dangerous because it is easily noticed and treated.

If you go out alone in intensely cold weather, when the wind-chill temperature is below –17°F (–27°C), always carry a small hand mirror in your pocket. From time to time, look at your face in the mirror. If you are with a friend, keep looking at one another. If you see a white patch, usually on the tip of a nose or an earlobe, that is the first sign of frostbite and you must do something about it. All bodily extremities are at risk. If you stay in the cold for long, you should also check your fingertips and toes. It is not a good idea to remove your gloves or boots and socks in subzero temperatures, but find out if you have feeling in your fingers and toes. Can you wiggle them and feel them wiggling? There is no feeling in frostbitten tissue, so your fingers and toes are safe so long as you can feel they are still there.

Frostbite occurs because heat is carried away from exposed extremities faster than it is from tissues that are better supplied with blood vessels. Blood has been withdrawn from the affected part, which is why it looks white, and cells within it are starting to freeze. This kills them, because water inside the cells expands as it freezes (see "What happens when water freezes and ice melts," page 99), bursting their walls. You will feel nothing, because the nerve endings have also lost their blood supply.

Rubbing frostbite makes matters worse. It will simply increase the damage to already injured tissue without restoring the blood supply. Instead, the affected parts must be warmed slowly and gently. Bathing them gently in cold water is usually enough to thaw them, but then the victim should see a doctor.

Hypothermia

Hypothermia is more dangerous. It develops slowly, with few early warning signs, and it can kill. *Hypo-* is from the Greek *hupo*, meaning "under," and as the name suggests, "hypothermia" simply means "low temperature." The victim has lost so much body heat through the skin that the internal, or "core" temperature has fallen. If it falls from the normal 98°F (37°C) to 90°F (32°C), the body can no longer restore it by its own efforts, and if it falls below 80°F (27°C) there is a serious risk of death.

The first sign you may notice is that the victim starts talking nonsense and seems confused and forgetful. Speech may be slurred and vision impaired. The skin will feel very cold and the face and hands may look blue. If you are out walking, the patient may complain of tiredness or even grow drowsy, and may start shivering uncontrollably. This is an added danger. Ordinarily, shivering serves to warm the body, because the rapid movement of muscles speeds up the metabolism and the rate at which blood is pumped to surface tissues. In hypothermia, however, the blood reaching the skin is chilled, returns into the body cold, and accelerates the fall in core temperature. Check the patient's pulse. Hypothermia victims have a weak pulse. If you are able to do so, take the patient's temperature. If this is below 95°F (35°C), you must take immediate action.

On no account try to warm the hands and feet. This can send cold blood to the heart, leading to heart failure. Warm the center of the body first, with your own body if necessary. Remove wet clothing and wrap the patient in whatever dry clothing or blankets you can find. Allow the patient to rest and recover slowly. If you have any warm soup, encourage the patient to take some, but the soup must be warm, not hot, and the patient should not be given any hot drink or food. On no account give the patient alcohol—it will reduce body temperature and may interfere with subsequent medication.

Meanwhile, call an ambulance or rescue service. Hypothermia is a medical emergency requiring professional treatment. If someone is suffering from both frostbite and hypothermia, deal with the hypothermia first.

Snow chill

Even when temperatures are well above freezing, wind chill can lead to hypothermia if people are exposed to it for a long time without moving, and especially if their clothing is wet. Once your clothes are sodden, the air spaces within the fabric are filled with water. Water is a much better conductor of heat than air. As you know, when you are caught in heavy rain without a coat you soon feel cold, even in summer.

This is the danger of snow. Being buried in snow can protect you from the wind, and people caught outdoors in a blizzard can often survive by digging an ice cave and sheltering inside it. Once the snow starts to melt, however, you are at risk, because the latent heat that is needed to turn ice crystals into liquid water will be taken from your body. It is you who are melting the snow, and doing so is making you colder. This is snow chill. To make matters worse, when the snow has melted, your clothes will be soaked in water that is only slightly above freezing.

WHITEOUT

A blizzard can render all our senses useless. That is one reason why blizzards are so dangerous. They also produce a strong wind-chill effect. Technically, a blizzard is defined as a snowstorm with winds of at least 35 MPH (56 km/h), a temperature no higher than 20°F (–7°C), and visibility reduced to no more than one-quarter of a mile (0.4 km). As you can see from the wind chill chart on page 159, with a wind blowing at 35 MPH (56 km/h), an air temperature of 20°F (–7°C) will chill a human body as effectively as calm air would at 0°F (–18°C).

That is very cold, but if you are caught outdoors in this kind of weather at least you may be able to find your way to shelter. Visibility will be reduced, but there is still a good chance that you will be able to see far enough to avoid becoming hopelessly lost. This is a mild blizzard, however, and blizzards can be much more severe. In a severe blizzard, the wind is at least 45 MPH (72 km/h), the temperature is no higher than 10°F (–12°C), and visibility is close to zero. Under these conditions you will be able to see no further than a few feet, and the effect of wind chill is to cool your body to a temperature equivalent to about –16°F (–27°C).

Scattering and reflecting light

We see the world around us because our eyes are sensitive to light that is reflected from objects, and most of us rely mainly on our vision to orient ourselves. Plunged suddenly into darkness we are helpless. A blizzard does not produce darkness. If it occurs during daytime the daylight remains, but the light is both scattered and reflected by the snow itself.

The light will already be diffuse. If the blizzard includes falling snow, the sky will be cloudy and light passing through it will be scattered by ice crystals or water droplets in the clouds, making the entire sky a uniform white or gray. Ice crystals and water droplets also reflect light. The thicker the layer of cloud, the more crystals and droplets there are to reflect incoming sunlight, and therefore the less light that penetrates the cloud and the darker the sky appears.

Without the airborne snow, objects would reflect this diffused light. Trees, hills, buildings, and other landscape features would be clearly visible, but they would cast no shadows because light would be shining on them evenly from all sides. The airborne snowflakes also reflect light, and because they are twisting and turning as they move they reflect it in all directions. Individual snowflakes are so small, and there are so many millions of them, that they appear as a dense, even mass of white specks. With snow falling, it is not only the sky above that is a uniform color and featureless, so is the air between the cloud and ground.

In these conditions, a flashlight or car headlights are useless, just as they are in dense fog. When you shine a beam of light ahead of you it, too, is scattered and reflected by the minute fog droplets or the snowflakes. Your light reveals nothing. Indeed, so much of it may be reflected directly back at your eyes that it dazzles you, actually making the situation worse rather than better.

Fog at least allows you to see the ground beneath your feet, but a blizzard may make even this impossible. The air is white with snow, but so is the snow-covered ground. It becomes impossible to tell where the ground ends and the sky begins. All features of the landscape are hidden and you are enclosed in a totally white world of swirling snow.

What you should do

This is a *whiteout*, and the only thing you can do is to remain where you are. Driving is impossible, because you can no longer see the road ahead of you. Inevitably you will quickly wander off it, crashing the car. If you try to walk you will become utterly disoriented. Remember the story of Lizzie and Emma (see "Snowstorms, drifting, and blizzards," page 128) who became hopelessly lost in a snowstorm as soon as they were outdoors. Pilots learning to fly in cloud, which encloses them in featureless whiteness in just the same way as a blizzard, are taught to rely wholly on their instruments. If they try to orient themselves by looking outside it will not be long before they imagine their plane is banking steeply, turning, climbing, descending, or even upside down, and when they try to correct for these false sensations they will crash. Pilots are taught to trust their instruments. People who try to walk through a severe blizzard have no instruments to help them. They do not risk becoming disoriented, they do become disoriented—and very quickly. It is inevitable.

It is possible to orient ourselves using other senses, of course, but even these are of little use in whiteout conditions. Those of use who do not see well, or at all, depend on touch and hearing. In a blizzard, hearing does not work either. A blizzard surrounds you with "white noise." The snow muffles sounds, and the howling of the wind, coming from all directions, drowns all other noises. The sense of touch remains, but it is useful only if you already have a very good idea of where you are, so you can feel your way along a wall or fence.

Many nonhumans find their way about by scent. Dogs, for example, seem to carry in their heads a map of their surroundings based mainly on odors that they, but not we, can detect and they explore their surroundings with their noses, rather than their eyes and ears. Snow buries scents, however, so even a dog cannot find its way home through a blizzard.

If you are caught outdoors in a blizzard, stay where you are. Do not go looking for shelter, but if you can see somewhere to shelter from the wind, go there. Otherwise dig a cave in the snow and shelter in it until conditions improve. From time to time clear the snow from above your body to ensure that the snow does not bury you. If you are in a car, stay with it. You will remain warmer in the car than you would be outside, and when the rescue parties come searching, a car on a road, even one that is almost completely buried in snow, is much easier to find than a person who is alone in open country.

BLIZZARDS OF THE PAST

Every winter brings blizzards to some places, although some years are worse than others. A blizzard in Inner Mongolia, China, lasted from December 31, 2000, to January 2, 2001, and was followed by freezing weather continuing throughout January. The storm and cold affected 1,640,000 people. At least 39 people died and more than 200,000 head of livestock perished.

On January 30, 2001, several villages in Khuzistan province of western Iran were buried in snow up to 6 feet (1.8 m) deep. The villages were cut off, and 28 people who ventured out in search of food were not seen again.

A snowstorm in late December 2002 covered much of the eastern United States with up to 2 feet (60 cm) of snow. That storm caused at least 18 deaths, most of them due to traffic accidents.

Blizzards are not always confined to winter. In 1989 at least 67 people died in western China in blizzards that occurred in June and July, and in 1995 blizzards began in October on the Qinghai (Tsinghai) plateau in the north-west of the country. By early February 1996 the severe weather conditions in that region had injured nearly 40,000 people and 42 persons had died.

Nor are blizzards confined to middle and high latitudes, although that is where they are most likely. Blizzards killed 47 people in the area around Alayh, Lebanon, between February 18 and 22, 1983. Many of the victims were trapped in their cars and died from cold before help could reach them. In 1992 it was the turn of southern Turkey. The storms lasted there from February 1 to 7 and triggered snowslides and avalanches that claimed 201 lives.

The 1888 American winter

There are mild winters and harsh winters, but for the United States the winter of 1888 may be the worst ever recorded. The winter promised to be mild, at least until Christmas. It was in January that cold air pushed over the Rocky Mountains, bringing a cold wave (see "Cold waves," page 149) that engulfed Montana, the Dakotas, and Minnesota.

From January 11 to 13, gales, blowing snow, and bitter cold brought these states the most severe blizzards they had ever known. Then there was a lull, but before long the winter returned with a vengeance.

From March 11 to 13 snow driven by winds gusting to 70 MPH (113 km/h) struck the eastern states, from Chesapeake Bay to Maine. Temperatures fell close to 0°F (–18°C), so the wind chill effect (see "Wind chill, frostbite, hypothermia, and snow chill," page 158) probably exposed people to temperatures equivalent to about –35°F (–37°C). The East River froze and people were able to walk between Manhattan and Brooklyn.

An average of 40 inches (1 m) of snow fell over southeastern New York State and southern New England. There were snowdrifts almost 30 feet (9 m) deep in Herald Square, a small plaza in New York City, and all roads and railroads were blocked. Fanned by the gales, fires raged intensely—and unchecked, because fire engines could not reach them. More than 400 people lost their lives in that blizzard, 200 of them in New York City. Wildlife and farm animals suffered even more. Tens of thousands of birds died, frozen to trees, and many cattle died, some of them frozen solid where they stood.

Spring blizzards

This was a spring blizzard, to which North America is especially prone. In the southeastern United States, where spring arrives early, between February 8 and 11, 1973, severe storms brought more than 16 inches (40 cm) of snow to parts of Georgia and the Carolinas. About 23 inches (58 cm) fell in Macon, Georgia.

Another spring blizzard, in March 1977, blocked 100 miles (160 km) of interstate highway in South Dakota and killed nine people in Colorado, four in Nebraska, and two in Kansas. On March 2, 1980, at least 36 people died in a blizzard that affected the Carolinas, Ohio, Missouri, Tennessee, Pennsylvania, Kentucky, Virginia, Maryland, and Florida. The northern states suffered spring blizzards on April 6, 1982.

In 1993 a blizzard comparable to the 1888 storm struck all of eastern North America. Between March 12 and 15 it killed an estimated 270 people in the United States, as well as four in Canada and three in Cuba, and caused at least $6 billion of damage.

Spring is a time of change. The polar front jet stream (see "Cold waves," page 149) is moving north, and warm, moist air from the Gulf of Mexico is following it. At the same time, as temperatures start to rise and the difference between temperatures in low and high latitudes decreases, polar air masses are likely to drift south. These two different types of air meet at the polar front, which becomes very active. The warm, moist air is lifted above the cold, dry air, becomes highly unstable, and severe storms are the result. Precipitation, formed as snow because of its altitude, falls through the cold, underlying air. Snowfall is heavy and the snow is often driven by gales generated by the storms, producing blizzards.

Winter storms

Blizzards also occur in midwinter, of course. On January 12, 1888, a blizzard swept across the Dakota and Montana territories, Minnesota, Nebraska,

Kansas, and Texas. It was called the "Schoolchildren's Blizzard," because many of the 235 persons who died were children walking home from school.

In 1891, blizzards starting on February 7 and lasting for several days caused many deaths in the central United States. A series of winter storms struck Nebraska, Wyoming, South Dakota, Utah, Colorado, and Nevada from January 2 to February 22, 1949. They brought only 12–30 inches (30–76 cm) of snow, but winds of up to 72 MPH (116 km/h) drove the snow into drifts up to 30 feet (9 m) deep. No human casualties were recorded, but tens of thousands of farm animals perished.

The winter of 1976–77 was particularly severe. For 19 states east of the Rocky Mountains, the average temperature in January and February was the lowest ever recorded. On January 28, states of emergency were declared in New York, New Jersey, and Ohio, due to blizzards and freezing. Disaster areas were also declared in several other states. These blizzards began a few days earlier in the Upper Ohio Valley and Lower Great Lakes region, then spread east. At Niagara the cold was so intense and continued for so long that the American Falls were completely covered by ice, and ice partly covered the larger Horseshoe Falls.

On January 28 the storm reached Buffalo, New York. It was the worst blizzard ever to strike the city. A total of 69 inches (1.75 m) of snow fell, driven by winds gusting to 75 MPH (121 km/h). Snow had fallen every day for nearly six weeks prior to the storm and the blizzard added to almost three feet (90 cm) of snow that had fallen already and was still lying. By the end of the 1976–77 winter, Buffalo had received a total of 200 inches (5 m). When the blizzard arrived, visibility dropped to zero in a whiteout, drifts accumulated to 30 feet (9 m) in some places, and it all happened so suddenly that thousands of workers were trapped in offices, factories, and shops. Many of those workers who set off for home were stopped by the drifting snow. Within four hours all transport came to a standstill and snowmobiles were used to rescue people trapped in cars and to ferry food and emergency supplies to those stranded in whatever shelter they had been able to find. Some 5,000 cars and trucks were abandoned. The storm lasted five days. That blizzard caused 29 deaths, nine of them of people trapped in their cars, but Buffalo was not alone. On February 1 blizzards caused more than 100 deaths throughout the northeastern states.

The Northeast Blizzard of 1978

The following winter was also severe, especially in the eastern and midwestern states. On January 25 and 26, winds gusting to 100 MPH (160 km/h) delivered about 31 inches (79 cm) of snow over Ohio, Michigan, Wisconsin, Indiana, Illinois, and Kentucky, and temperatures fell to –50°F (–45°C). More than 100 people died and damage was estimated at millions of dollars.

Then, from February 5 to 7, the "Northeast Blizzard of '78" caused chaos along the northern stretch of the Atlantic coast. According to the American Red Cross, there were altogether 99 deaths and more than 4,500 people were injured. Winds of 110 MPH (177 km/h), driving tides 18 feet (5.5 m) high, brought 50 inches (1.27 m) of snow to Rhode Island and eastern Massachusetts. New York received 17.7 inches (45 cm), and 24 inches (61 cm) fell on both Boston and Providence. The storm caused more than $500 million of damage in Massachusetts and about $94 million in New York and New Jersey.

Few winters pass without some blizzards. The eastern states often experience them and they can affect a large area. On December 17, 1973, for example, blizzards and biting cold extended from Georgia to Maine, and on February 11 and 12, 1983, a blizzard delivered at least two feet (61 cm) of snow to every city in the northeastern United States. As the winter of 1983 began, new storms began as falling temperatures reached freezing levels in air moving east from the Pacific that still held large amounts of moisture, but it was moisture that fell as snow. At least 56 people died on November 28 in blizzards that affected Wyoming, Colorado, South Dakota, Nebraska, Kansas, Minnesota, and Iowa.

The following year, 1984, blizzards occurred from Missouri to New York on February 28, and on January 22, 1987, there were blizzards from Florida to Maine. Other storms are more local. The blizzard of February 19, 1979, affected only New York and New Jersey.

After one of the coldest winters in several years, winter storms struck the eastern states again in January and February 2003. The President's Day storm, lasting from February 15 through 17, caused widespread disruption.

The 1996 storms

In 1996 the eastern states suffered what were said to be the worst snowstorms with blizzards in 70 years. They began on January 6, with thunderstorms and heavy snow, and continued intermittently for four days. The severe weather affected Alabama, Indiana, Kentucky, Maryland, Massachusetts, New Jersey, New York, North Carolina, Ohio, Pennsylvania, Rhode Island, Virginia, Washington, D.C., and West Virginia, and states of emergency were declared in Kentucky, Maryland, New Jersey, New York City, Pennsylvania, Virginia, and West Virginia.

The problems were due more to the volume of snow than to the winds. At 25–35 MPH (40–56 km/h), these produced only mild blizzards, but nevertheless the weather caused at least 23 deaths and many injuries. Roads were blocked and airports closed. Schools in New York City were closed because of snow for the first time since 1978. Icy roads also forced schools to close in Alabama. No mail was delivered in New York on January 9, and the United Nations building was closed so that staff would not attempt the almost impossible journey to work.

More snow fell on January 12, causing many roofs to collapse under the weight. Ten people were injured in North Massapequa, New York, when a supermarket roof collapsed. In Norwell, Massachusetts, a theater was condemned as unsafe after its roof collapsed, and roofs also fell at the Oakdale Mall in Tewksbury and the Bayside Exposition Center in Boston. Other roofs sagged dangerously, causing buildings to be closed. The Potomac Mills mall, in Dale City, Virginia, had to be evacuated when its roof was found to be buckling in several places.

Roofs can give way with no warning, when the weight on them stresses supporting beams or rafters beyond the load they can tolerate. A woman was killed in Berks County, Pennsylvania, when a falling beam from her barn roof struck her while she and her daughter were feeding their horses. In this case the late snow was especially dangerous, because mild temperatures added rain to the snow that was already lying, which greatly increased the weight on roofs, by adding wetter and therefore heavier snow.

President Clinton designated nine states as disaster areas. Despite the disruption, the 1996 storms were not the most costly winter storms known. Damage to property was estimated at $585 million. From that point of view, other winters have been worse.

Cold air in the West, moving south and then east, brings severe weather to the central states, and even a fairly mild blizzard can have devastating consequences. In January 1975 snow driven by 50-MPH (80-km/h) winds, but with subzero temperatures, caused about 50 deaths in these states. At least 10 people died in a more severe blizzard on November 21, 1979, when heavy snow driven by 70-MPH (113-km/h) winds crossed Colorado, Nebraska, and Wyoming. Severe blizzards affected Michigan and Minnesota on November 19 and 20, 1981, Michigan, South Dakota, Iowa, Minnesota, and Wisconsin in December 1985, and the midwestern and eastern states from January 2 to 8, 1988. All of these blizzards caused deaths.

The storms that struck the western states on November 19 and 20, 1982, also triggered tornadoes, and tornadoes in Arkansas were associated with storms in the midwestern states on December 12–16, 1987. In all, 34 people died in the 1982 storms and 73 in those of 1987. Blizzards and thunderstorms that struck the western states from March 19 to 23, 1984, did not trigger tornadoes, but they killed 27 people and at least 33 people died in a blizzard in the northwestern states in November 1985.

It is the geography of North America that makes blizzards a feature of most winters. The landmass is so large that the interior experiences a continental type of climate (see "Continental and maritime climates," page 1), with extremes of summer and winter temperatures, and from time to time the movement of air over the Rockies draws cold air masses south from the Arctic. At the same time, the narrowing of the continent in the south exposes the interior to tropical air from the Gulf of Mexico. No other continent has this combination of features, but that does not mean other continents escape blizzards, and it sometimes happens that a severe winter in North America is also severe elsewhere.

Blizzards in Europe

The blizzards of 1891, for example, were not confined to the eastern United States. They struck there in February, but on March 9 they reached southern England. From then until March 13, snow driven by winds that reached almost hurricane force (75 MPH; 121 km/h) swept eastward along the English Channel. More than 60 people died on land and more than a dozen ships were destroyed, and many of their crew members perished.

Britain has suffered many blizzards, but there, as elsewhere in the world, detailed information about them is slowly lost over the years. In February 1762, for example, there was a blizzard in England that lasted for 18 days and caused nearly 50 deaths. In 1674 a blizzard in the border region between England and Scotland began on March 8 and lasted 13 days, but we know no more about them than this.

More recent storms are documented more thoroughly. From January 9 through 12, 1982, most of western Europe was exposed to snow driven by gales. The blizzards were most severe in the west. Wales, bordering the Irish Sea on the western side of Great Britain, was completely cut off from England by snowdrifts up to 12 feet (3.7 m) deep that blocked all the roads. Those blizzards caused casualties, as blizzards always do, and at least 23 people died. Western Europe suffered again in 1984. That year the blizzards struck on February 7, and 13 people lost their lives.

There were several periods of very severe weather over Europe during the winter of 1995–96. In late December temperatures plummeted and there were blizzards everywhere from Britain in the west to as far east as Kazakhstan and Bangladesh. More than 350 people died, many of them in Moscow.

The 1996 storms reach Europe

Later, as the eastern United States recovered from the blizzards of January 1996, the storms struck Britain. Early in February most of the country suffered and parts of it were paralyzed by low temperatures and heavy snow sometimes driven by fierce winds. To add to the misery, there was freezing fog in many places.

The Sellafield nuclear reprocessing plant, in Cumbria, had to close because snow blocked all the roads leading to it. About 1,000 workers were unable to get home and had to spend two nights at the plant. A state of emergency was declared in Dumfries and Galloway, in southwestern Scotland, when hundreds of motorists were trapped by the snow on local roads. When snow blocked the A74M, one of the main roads between England and Scotland in the east of the region, more than 1,000 motorists were stranded in their vehicles for 22 hours before rescuers were able to move them to emergency centers. Some of the victims had to spend most of a second night at the centers before the northbound side of the road was cleared around 4 A.M. and others were there even longer, waiting for the southbound side to reopen.

A train became stuck in a snowdrift in the same area and its crew and passengers had to be rescued by helicopter. All over Britain gale-force winds and snow brought down power lines, leaving tens of thousands of homes without electricity.

Hardly had the February blizzards abated before the harsh weather returned. On March 12, Scotland and England north of the Midlands were brought to a standstill again. Blizzards even closed the Scottish ski resorts, and the crews of North Sea oil rigs were stranded. The helicopters that supply them were grounded by 100-MPH (160-km/h) winds.

Blizzards are always disruptive and always dangerous. Roads and rail tracks are blocked, power and telephone lines broken, and people are stranded. Every year, at any time between fall and spring, there are severe storms somewhere, and it is not only northern regions that are at risk. Places as far south as Florida and the eastern Mediterranean can be affected, often with consequences that are more serious where such conditions are unfamiliar and unexpected.

WILL CLIMATE CHANGE BRING FEWER BLIZZARDS?

Over the last few years there have been many newspaper and TV stories describing how climates of the world are growing warmer. This change is attributed to the *greenhouse effect* and it happens because we are releasing into the air certain gases that absorb heat, the most important of these being carbon dioxide.

It is tempting to suppose that despite all the problems such a widespread change may bring, there will be at least one consolation. Blizzards will be much rarer in a warmer world. After all, it does not snow when the weather is warm. It is not that simple, however. Climates work in a complicated way.

All the estimates of future temperatures refer to what may happen if the atmospheric concentration of carbon dioxide doubles compared with the amount that was present in the air prior to the Industrial Revolution. In 1750 carbon dioxide accounted for 0.028 percent of the air by volume. Today it accounts for 0.0367 percent, an increase of 31 percent. Obviously, if more or less than a doubling of carbon dioxide accumulates in the air, the predicted temperature changes will be different.

Most climatologists (scientists who study climates) agree there is a strong chance that average temperatures will rise over the next century. Small airborne particles, mainly of dust and sulfate, will counter part of this warming, because they reflect sunlight and cool the surface. When this effect is taken into account, the temperature rise scientists anticipate by the year 2100 is between about 2.5°F and 10.4°F (1.4–5.8°C). This is a very wide range, reflecting the great uncertainty. In fact, since the late 1970s when the present warming began, the average global air temperature has been increasing by about 0.027°F (0.015°C) a year, or 2.7°F (1.5°C) a century. This is the change measured by satellite instruments, with an accuracy of 0.02°F (0.01°C), of the air between 5,000 feet (1,525 m) and 28,000 feet (8,540 m). It is a more reliable measure than surface measurements, which are unevenly distributed, with many more being taken on land than over the sea.

Why worry?

An increase in temperature of less than about 3.6°F (2°C) would have very little effect. Any larger increase, on the other hand, might have serious consequences. As the seas warmed, for example, they would expand to occupy more space, because water expands when it is warmed. At the same time, glaciers would retreat, releasing some of their water into the oceans. Together, these would cause sea levels to rise. Rising sea levels will increase erosion on some coasts and some unprotected low-lying areas may be flooded.

During an ice age, huge amounts of water accumulate as ice. This water is taken from the oceans, and so sea levels fall. When the ice age ends and the ice starts to melt, sea levels rise again. At the same time, the land itself rises and falls. Ice is heavy, and the ice sheets depress the Earth's crust, so that the fall in sea level during an ice age is partly offset by the fall in land levels in places beneath the ice. Similarly, the sea-level rise as the ice melts is accompanied by a rise in land level. Scandinavia and Scotland are still rising as they rebound following the last ice age.

Over the 20,000 years since the coldest part of the most recent ice age, the sea level has risen by an average 394 feet (120 m). At present, the average sea level is rising by about 0.03 inch (0.7 mm) a year. If the climate warms by 2.5–10.4°F (1.4–5.8°C) by 2100, the sea level then is likely to be 4.3–30 inches (11–77 cm) higher than it is now, according to the Intergovernmental Panel on Climate Change (IPCC). This rise takes account of expansion due to the warming of ocean water and the melting of glaciers. The Greenland and Antarctic ice sheets may shrink very slightly, contributing to a rise in sea level, but alternatively they may thicken, removing water from the oceans. If the temperature increases by no more than 2.7°F (1.5°C) by 2100, the sea-level rise will be much smaller.

Warmer weather sounds pleasant. So far, the warming that has occurred has resulted mainly in milder winters in northwestern North America—Alaska and the Yukon—and northeastern Siberia. Overall, two-thirds of the warming has taken place in winter. This has resulted in fewer early and late frosts, so the growing season for crops is several days longer. Not everywhere has become warmer. There has been no warming over most of the eastern United States, for example, and temperatures have fallen over southern China and the Indian subcontinent. The Antarctic Peninsula has grown considerably warmer, but the interior of Antarctica has been cooling for several decades.

If the rate of summer warming should increase, however, the effect might be different. The amount of water available to plants depends on the ratio of the amount of precipitation that falls to the rate at which water evaporates from the ground surface. If these are in balance, so that rainfall is sufficient to replace the water lost by evaporation, plants will thrive. If they are not, and water evaporates faster than precipitation can recharge the water below ground, then the land will dry out. A rise in temperature is likely to be accompanied by an increase in precipitation because water evaporates faster into warmer air. Precipitation over the United States has increased by about 10 percent over the past century. If the temperature rises more than a certain amount, however, evaporation will exceed precipitation. Some climate scientists fear there may be more droughts in the interior of continents.

The enhanced greenhouse effect

The warming of which scientists warn is due to an *enhanced greenhouse effect*, and their concern about it is not new. As long ago as 1827, the French mathematician Jean-Baptiste Fourier (1728–1830) suggested that the temperature of the air is affected by its chemical composition. In 1896 the Swedish chemist Svante Arrhenius (1859–1927) calculated that if the atmospheric concentration of carbon dioxide were to double, average temperatures would rise by 8.9°F (4.95°C) at the equator and 10.89°F (6.05°C) at latitude 60° N and 60° S. Arrhenius believed that such an increase would be due to volcanic eruptions.

Today it is not volcanic eruptions that are seen as the problem, but carbon dioxide released when fuels containing carbon are burned. Other gases also contribute. The principal ones are methane (CH_4), nitrous oxide (N_2O), chlorofluorocarbons (CFCs), and carbon tetrachloride (CCl_4). Methane is released by bacteria in the digestive systems of cattle and sheep, and in rice fields. It also escapes from leaking gas pipes. Nitrous oxide is released from some factories and from automobile engines fitted with catalysts. Carbon tetrachloride is a solvent, formerly used for dry cleaning, and CFCs were used as propellants in aerosol cans, in foam plastics, and in refrigerators, freezers, and air conditioners. The use of carbon tetrachloride and CFCs is being phased out, so the effect of these will be less serious in years to come, and most governments are now committed to reducing emissions of the other "greenhouse gases."

Greenhouse gases have an effect rather like the glass in a greenhouse. That is how they, and the "greenhouse effect" they cause, earned their name. Greenhouse glass is transparent to sunlight, but not to radiant heat. Sunlight can enter freely and warm the contents of the greenhouse. These then start to radiate heat, but this heat cannot pass through the glass. It is trapped inside. The description is a little misleading, however, because the temperature inside a greenhouse rises mainly because warmed air cannot escape and be replaced by an inflow of cooler air.

Scientists have measured the amount of energy radiated by the Sun and can calculate the proportion of that energy that strikes the Earth. At the top of the atmosphere, it is about 12.7 calories per square inch per minute (1.367 kW m^{-2}). This is called the *solar constant*. Some of this radiation is absorbed as it passes through the atmosphere, but most reaches the surface and warms it. The warmed surface radiates its heat back into space at a rate that can also be calculated precisely. These calculations show that the average temperature at the surface should be –9°F (–23°C). In fact, the average surface temperature is 59°F (15°C), and the difference between the two, of 68°F (38°C), is due to the fact that certain constituents of the air absorb some of the outgoing radiation. This is the greenhouse effect. It is entirely natural. Without it the air would be too cold to hold more than a trace of water vapor and probably there would be no liquid water at the surface anywhere except, perhaps, near the equator. All seas and lakes would be covered in a thick layer of ice and many of them would be frozen solid. Life would be extremely difficult if not impossible. So the greenhouse effect is entirely beneficial in itself.

It is not the greenhouse effect that is undesirable, but the enhancement of it that may result from human activities. This is why, strictly speaking, scientific predictions of climate change are based not on the greenhouse effect, but on an enhanced greenhouse effect.

How the atmosphere absorbs heat

The greenhouse effect is due to the behavior of particular molecules when radiation strikes them. Light and heat are both forms of electromagnetic radiation, varying only in their wavelengths. Most of the radiation we receive from the Sun is at short wavelengths (see the box). Air molecules scatter it (especially blue light, which is why the sky is blue), but they are the wrong size and shape to hold and absorb it. Outgoing radiation, on the other hand, is at very much longer wavelengths. It ranges from about 4–10 μm with a strong peak at about 10 μm. Molecules larger than those of nitrogen and oxygen absorb radiation at these wavelengths. This makes them move faster and collide more often and more violently with other molecules. Eventually they lose their excess energy, but in doing so they warm the air.

Different molecules respond to different wavelengths. Carbon dioxide, for example, absorbs radiation at wavelengths of about 5 μm and also at 15–18 μm. Carbon dioxide is the most abundant of the greenhouse gases. The effect of other gases is calculated as their *global warming potential* (GWP) compared with carbon dioxide, which is given a value of 1. On this scale, methane has a GWP of 11 (meaning it is 11 times more effective than carbon dioxide), nitrous oxide of 270, and the various CFC and related compounds values of 1,200 to 7,100. Water vapor is the most effective of all greenhouse gases, absorbing strongly in several wavebands, but the amount present in the air varies widely from place to place and time to time and is beyond our control.

Fortunately, there is a radiation "window" at 10 μm. No gases absorb at this wavelength, so outgoing radiation at the peak wavelength is not trapped.

Tracing the emissions

All the calculations depend on knowing how much of each gas is emitted and what happens to it. We release carbon dioxide by burning fossil fuels, manufacturing cement, and by the way we manage the land. Burning fossil fuels

The solar spectrum

Light, radiant heat, gamma rays, X rays, and radio waves are all forms of electromagnetic radiation. This radiation travels as waves at the speed of light. The various forms differ in their wavelengths, which is the distance between one wave crest and the next. The shorter the wavelength, the more energy the radiation has. A range of wavelengths is called a *spectrum*. The Sun emits electromagnetic radiation at all wavelengths, so its spectrum is wide. The diagram shows how solar radiation is divided into the types of radiation forming the solar spectrum.

Gamma rays are the most energetic form of radiation, with wavelengths of 10^{-10}–10^{-14} μm (a micron, μm, is one-millionth of a meter, or about 0.00004 inch; 10^{-10} is 0.0000000001). Next come X rays, with wavelengths of 10^{-5}–10^{-3} μm. The Sun emits gamma and X radiation, but all of it is absorbed high in Earth's atmosphere and none reaches the surface. Ultraviolet (UV) radiation is at wavelengths of 0.004-4 μm; the shorter wavelengths, below 0.2 μm, are absorbed in the atmosphere but longer wavelengths reach the surface.

Visible light has wavelengths of 0.4-0.7 μm, infrared radiation 0.8 μm–1 mm, microwaves 1 mm–30 cm, and radio waves have wavelengths up to 100 km (62 miles).

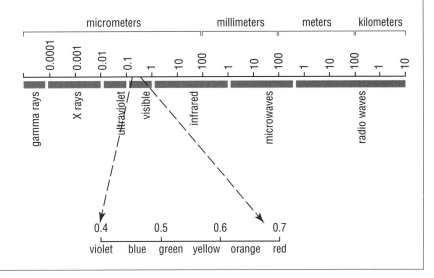

The solar spectrum

releases an average of about 6.7 billion tons (6.1 billion tonnes) of carbon into the air each year and cement making releases about 220,000 tons (199,760 tonnes), making a total of about 6.9 billion tons (6.26 billion tonnes). Changing the use of land, for example by converting forest to farmland by burning surface vegetation, releases 1.9 billion tons (1.7 billion tonnes) of carbon a year into the air, but farming and forestry remove 2.1 billion tons (1.9 billion tonnes) from the air. Plants need carbon dioxide for photosynthesis, but at present the air contains such a small amount that many plants are unable to achieve their full growth potential. Adding carbon dioxide therefore stimulates plant growth—it is called *carbon dioxide fertilization*.

About 2.1 billion tons (1.9 billion tonnes) of carbon dioxide dissolves into the oceans and land plants take up a similar amount. This leaves approximately 2.1 billion tons (1.9 billion tonnes) unaccounted for. No one knows where it goes.

Although the amount of carbon dioxide we emit increases year by year, the rate at which the gas accumulates in the atmosphere has slowed. In the 1980s, when emissions averaged 5.9 billion tons (5.36 billion tonnes) a year, carbon dioxide was accumulating at about 3.6 billion tons (3.3 billion tonnes) a year. In the 1990s, however, when emissions were 6.9 billion tons (6.3 billion tonnes) a year, the gas was accumulating at about 3.5 billion tons (3.2 billion tonnes) a year. No one is certain why it is accumulating more slowly.

Methane is also accumulating in the air at a decreasing rate and the concentration may be stabilizing. The amount in the air is increasing at about one-quarter the rate of the 1980s.

A rise in temperature will cause more water to evaporate. Water vapor is a powerful greenhouse gas, so increasing its concentration may accelerate the warming effect. Water vapor condenses, however, so the more of it that the air contains, the more clouds there are likely to be. Condensation releases latent heat, adding to the warming, but low-level clouds cool the surface by shading it, although high-level clouds made from ice crystals absorb radiation and warm the air. Working out just what type of clouds will form where and when is extremely difficult, but very important if predictions are to be at all reliable.

Estimating the effects

If a general warming occurs, this is expected to be most marked in high latitudes. Equatorial temperatures will change little. The effect will be to shift the climate belts of the world. Tropical conditions will extend into the southern parts of middle latitudes, what is now a great belt of coniferous forest across northern North America, Europe, and Asia will experience more temperate conditions, and the coniferous forests will expand into what is now tundra.

Again, there are many uncertainties. Some scientists fear that any widespread melting of permafrost (soils that are permanently frozen below the surface) could stimulate bacterial activity and release a large amount of methane. This would add to the enhanced greenhouse effect and might accelerate the warming.

Then again, what if plants were unable to tolerate their new climates? The trees of the high-latitude coniferous forest are adapted to a long winter, when the ground is frozen and liquid water is not available. If winters became shorter and wetter they might die. Eventually, trees from lower latitudes would replace them, but this would take time and meanwhile large areas of forest would simply disappear. As the dead trees decomposed, a huge quantity of carbon dioxide would be released into the air, because the organisms responsible for decomposing dead vegetation feed on the carbon and obtain energy by oxidizing it to carbon dioxide. This would also accelerate the warming that killed the trees in the first place.

High-latitude warming would reduce the temperature difference between polar and tropical regions. The polar front and its associated jet stream (see "Cold waves," page 149) would then lie further north than they do now. In winter they might be somewhere just to the south of the Great Lakes and across the central United States. The fiercest storms follow tracks a little to the south of the jet stream, so this might increase the risk of blizzards over much of the country, especially if increased evaporation made the air to the south moister than it is now. There is no reason to suppose there would be any diminution in the violent weather produced when warm air from the Gulf moving north meets cold air moving south, so spring blizzards would probably continue, although the southern states might escape them more often than they do now.

Thermohaline circulation

Combined with a general warming, a large increase in the amount of precipitation might trigger a change that would offset some of the warming. The last time the world grew rapidly warmer, at the end of the last ice age, about 12,000 years ago, the warming went abruptly into reverse. Around 11,000 years ago extremely cold weather returned and lasted for about 1,000 years. Scientists believe this reversal was caused by changes in the circulation of ocean currents.

At the edge of the North Atlantic sea ice, very dense water sinks all the way to the ocean floor, becoming the *North Atlantic Deep Water* (NADW). It does so because as water freezes, substances dissolved in it are squeezed out of the ice. The salt that has been removed enters adjacent water, making it saltier and therefore denser. Freshwater reaches its maximum density at about 39°F (4°C), but seawater is densest at about 32°F (0°C), and freezes at about 28°F (–2°C). This is about the temperature of the water at the edge of the ice. The dense water sinks beneath less dense water further from the edge of the ice and flows as a slow-moving current all the way to Antarctica. It then flows through the other oceans, rises to the surface and is warmed at the equator, and returns to where it began, completing the loop. The current is known as *the Great Conveyor;* its scientific name is the *thermohaline circulation.* The Gulf Stream and its extension, the North Atlantic Current, form part of this system of currents.

From time to time, large amounts of freshwater from Canadian rivers or less saline water from the Pacific (which is less salty than the Atlantic) flow into the Arctic Ocean and from there into the North Atlantic. The less saline water floats above the denser Atlantic water and, because it freezes at a slightly higher temperature, it extends the area of sea ice. This alters the formation of NADW and the way ocean water circulates. The North Atlantic Drift no longer reaches northwest European shores, and air crossing the Atlantic is chilled by contact with ice and colder water.

Eleven thousand years ago, the melting of the Laurentide ice sheet, covering much of North America, released vast amounts of freshwater and plunged Europe back into almost ice-age conditions. This time it could be increased rainfall, although the effect would be less dramatic. Scientists calculate that even if the thermohaline circulation shut down altogether, western Europe would continue to grow warmer, although at a much reduced rate.

Common sense suggests that blizzards will be rarer in a warmer world, but common sense is not always a reliable guide. Global warming might have little effect on the frequency and severity of North American blizzards. If the North Atlantic Drift ceased to flow, northwestern Europe might even suffer more of them.

FORECASTING BLIZZARDS

Throughout history, people have gazed at the sky and tried to predict the weather. They have studied plants and animals in search of clues and learned to recognize those signs that are often followed by certain kinds of weather. A red sky at sunset usually means the following day will be fine, for example, and when sailors see high, wispy, cirrus cloud swept out into "mares' tails" they expect strong winds a few hours later. Many of these observations are preserved as rhymes. "Red sky at night, shepherd's delight..." and, for the sailors, "Trace in the sky the painter's brush: The winds around you soon will rush."

Sayings such as these are often reliable, but not all of them are and, in any case, there are not many of them, so as a forecasting method they are very limited. They work because the conditions producing the visible signs are centered a long way away, often hundreds of miles, and they are approaching. A red sunset, for example, is caused by the scattering of sunlight by dust particles. When the Sun is low in the sky, its light has to pass through much more air than it does when the Sun is overhead. Blue and green light are scattered most, so we see mainly the red and orange light that remains. Dust means that the air is dry, and because weather systems in middle latitudes move generally from west to east, the dry air will probably reach us by the following morning, bringing a clear sky and fine weather.

A red sky in the morning is produced in the same way, but this time in the east. The fine weather is retreating—because the weather system is moving eastward—and wet weather may well follow behind it, so the day will be wet. This is less reliable than the red sunset, because wet weather does not necessarily follow fine weather. We might get lucky and have another fine day!

The signs tell us about conditions before they arrive and obviously that is the only way weather can be predicted. Weather forecasting is possible only if we can examine entire weather systems and air masses and do so quickly enough to predict the weather before it arrives. No one is much interested in a method that takes four hours to calculate what the weather will be like two hours ahead!

Problems of scale

Weather systems are huge. There is nothing unusual in a low-pressure system, with its associated fronts, that covers almost all of North America, from the tip of Florida to the far north of Canada and from the Atlantic coast almost to the Rocky Mountains. Prior to 1844 there was no way a system even a fraction of this size could be studied as a whole until long after it had disappeared. Observers could record the pressure, temperature, winds, clouds, precipitation, and so forth, at the same time in many different places, so the information needed to compile an overall picture could be obtained, but then they were stuck. Their measurements and observations could be sent to a central point only at the speed of a horseback rider. Collecting all the data in one place would take days if not weeks.

What happened in 1844 was that the first telegraph line was built. It ran only between Baltimore and Washington, but it changed everything. Within two years, preparations were being made to gather meteorological data from all over the United States by means of the telegraph. At the Great Exhibition, held in London in 1851, one of the exhibits was the first weather map to show readings taken simultaneously in many different places and assembled at a central point. Modern forecasting soon followed, the first daily bulletins being issued in 1869 and the first three-day forecasts in 1871, both from the Cincinnati Observatory.

Improved communications also allowed scientists to study the way weather systems work. Little by little they came to understand better not only how weather develops and moves, but what is happening inside the mass of air to make it do so.

Weather stations, balloons, and satellites

Forecasts and meteorological studies still rely on direct observation, and new technologies have added greatly to what can be observed. Thousands of surface weather stations all over the world—many of them fully automated—continue to collect data at regular hourly or six-hourly intervals and transmit them to forecasting centers. Some stations report only the conditions at ground level; at others meteorologists launch *radiosondes*—balloons carrying instruments to take measurements in the upper atmosphere that radio data to the ground receiving station. Meteorologists track the balloons with radar to measure the wind speed and direction at different heights.

Since the first one was launched in 1960, orbiting satellites have been transmitting photographs, some taken with cameras sensitive to infrared wavelengths, as well as a variety of measurements of the atmosphere. Between them, meteorological satellites now provide continuous observation of the entire Earth.

As they arrive at forecasting centers, the data are fed into supercomputers that display them as detailed and constantly changing weather charts that can be related to the satellite images. What forecasters see on their monitors is very detailed. They can call up three-dimensional images showing cloud, temperature, and wind to a height of about 8 miles

(13 km) over a particular locality and, within clouds, the regions where vertical air currents are strongest and icing is most likely. This is vital information for airlines.

Forecasting

Forecasts are made by several different methods, usually in combination. In some, experienced meteorologists use their own judgment to assess how a weather system will develop and the direction and speed of its movement. Others, based on numerical forecasting, use the laws of physics to calculate what will happen from the measurements fed into the computer. The number of calculations needed is vast. The numerical forecasting method was devised in 1922 by the English mathematician and meteorologist Lewis Fry Richardson (1881–1953), but it did not become practicable until meteorologists had really fast computers to help.

Despite the computing and observational power at their disposal, forecasters can predict the weather for only a week or so ahead. Long-range forecasts, for weeks or months ahead, are impossible to make and may always remain impossible. This is because differences that are too small to be noticed magnify rapidly as a weather system develops and moves. Consequently, two systems that appear identical at one time may be entirely different from one another a few days later. There is no way of telling in advance what they will do and weather patterns never repeat themselves precisely, although they often do so approximately. Weather is said to behave *chaotically*. This does not mean it behaves in a random fashion, but only that after about a week it will have diverged from any prediction of its behavior by an amount that will make the forecast useless. Weather systems are acutely sensitive to minute differences in their initial conditions.

Chaos, as a mathematical concept, was discovered by the American meteorologist Edward Norton Lorenz (born 1917). Lorenz was one of the first scientists to use computer models to study the way weather systems evolve. One day in 1961 he ran a particular program for a second time, using what he thought were the same starting conditions as he had used first time, but for convenience he shortened some of the values he fed into the model from six to three decimal places. To his surprise, the weather system developed in an entirely different way—those three decimal places had made a huge difference. On December 29, 1979, Lorenz presented a paper describing what had happened at the annual meeting of the American Association for the Advancement of Science. He called his paper "Predictability: Does the Flap of a Butterfly's Wings in Brazil Set Off a Tornado in Texas?" Since then, this kind of chaotic unpredictability has been described as the "butterfly effect."

Long-range forecasts are impossible, but short-term forecasts are now fairly reliable. The shorter the forecast period, the more reliable they are.

If the forecasters tell you there are severe winter storms heading your way, you should believe them.

The forecasters look first for clues in the distribution of air pressure. These reveal fronts and areas of low pressure, and if the isobars surrounding a low are packed tightly together, it means that the pressure changes rapidly with horizontal distance. In other words, there is a steep pressure gradient, and a steep gradient indicates strong winds. So the winds are the first thing to be identified and their actual speed can be calculated from the surface pressures. Weather systems are usually moving, and details of the pressure distribution also allow forecasters to calculate their direction and speed.

Reports from weather stations tell the forecasters how much cloud and precipitation are associated with the low. Satellite images confirm this, and provide a clear picture not only of the extent of the cloud, but also of its thickness and type around the low and along fronts associated with it. Not all fronts are active, and well away from the low there may be little cloud or even none. Water droplets strongly reflect radar at wavelengths of about 10 centimeters, so radar is used to detect precipitation.

By this point the forecasters know the size of the weather system, its direction and speed of movement, the force and direction of winds around it, and the amount of precipitation it is producing. Next they need to know the type of precipitation. This will depend on the cloud type, which they have already identified, and temperatures inside the cloud and between the base of the cloud and the ground. If the temperature in the lower part of the cloud and in the air beneath the cloud is below about 39°F (4°C), precipitation will fall as snow. If the winds around the low exceed 35 MPH (56 km/h), that snow will arrive as a blizzard, and if light, powdery snow is already lying on the ground the wind will be strong enough to raise it.

Warnings

Once the forecasters have identified severe winter weather they begin to issue warnings. In the United States these are broadcast on radio and television and also by the Weather Radio run by the National Weather Service of the National Oceanic and Atmospheric Administration (NOAA). In other parts of the world, warnings form part of the routine weather forecasts broadcast on radio and TV.

Forecasters start to issue warnings as early as they can to allow people as much time as possible to prepare. The warnings themselves are graded and specific. A *winter weather advisory* warns of weather that is bad enough to cause inconvenience, especially to motorists, and that is possibly dangerous.

A *frost–freeze warning* means temperatures are expected to fall below freezing in areas that are not expecting such cold weather. Some horticultural and garden plants may be harmed and should be protected. People living in homes without heating should check that portable heaters are working properly and they have adequate stocks of blankets and warm clothing.

The most serious warnings are called *winter storm watch*, *winter storm warning*, and *blizzard warning*. A winter storm watch is issued a day or two before severe weather is expected to arrive in a specified area. It allows time for everyone to prepare. As the weather system draws closer, a winter storm warning is broadcast. This means the bad weather is already beginning or that it will arrive in a matter of hours.

A blizzard warning is the most serious of all. It is issued when the combination of snow and wind is likely to produce deep drifts, dangerously low wind-chill temperatures (see "Wind chill, frostbite, hypothermia, and snow chill," on page 158), and visibility reduced almost to zero.

SAFETY

Every winter, bitterly cold weather, snowstorms, and blizzards cause deaths wherever in the world they occur. Of all those who die from the cold, one in five is indoors at home, half are more than 60 years old, and three-quarters are men. Most of those who die outdoors are also men more than 40 years old, but only one-quarter of the deaths are of people caught in the open. About 70 percent of those are of people trapped in their cars.

Death is a serious risk, but it is not inevitable. You can survive severe winter weather, provided you are prepared. The secret of good preparation is that it begins long before the bad weather arrives and information is one of its key ingredients. Your chance of surviving any catastrophe increases greatly if you know what to do and do it calmly. Do not panic, because panic, too, is a killer.

A severe winter storm may hold you trapped at home for several days. Power and telephone lines may be out of action, so you may have no electricity and no direct contact with the outside world by land-line telephone. It may not be this bad, of course, but this is the situation for which you should prepare. Your preparations should begin as soon as you hear a winter storm watch alert. This will give you no more than a day or two, so do not waste time.

Lay in supplies

Probably you will need to shop for supplies. As you do so, tell your friends and neighbors what you are doing and why. They may not have heard the alert.

You will need lighting, heating, food and a means for cooking it, and access to information from outside. Check first that all battery-operated equipment is working and you have spare batteries. In particular, you will need a battery-operated radio or TV and flashlights. Then check that you have kerosene lamps and candles, and matches to light them.

Make sure cell phones are working and that their batteries are fully charged.

Check that you have ample kerosene, wood, or coal for heating. Once the storm arrives, deliveries may cease and the household boiler may stop working, either because components freeze or because it relies on electrically operated thermostats or pumps. You can use camping stoves, powered by bottled gas, for essential cooking and for heating water. Have spare gas bottles available, but store them well away from where you will use the stoves.

Make sure that all stoves, fireplaces, or other devices that burn fuel are working properly and that ventilation is adequate. Inadequate ventilation can allow carbon monoxide to accumulate in the air. This gas is colorless, odorless, and poisonous.

Using these fuels creates a risk of fire. Make sure fire extinguishers are easily accessible and in working order, and that smoke alarms are working. If necessary, change the batteries in the alarms. A bucket of sand (or cat litter) is useful for smothering fires. On no account should you pour water onto a kerosene or electrical fire.

You will need enough food to last for several days. Choose items that do not need to be stored in a refrigerator and, so far as possible, foods that need no cooking. Make sure you have ample supplies of food and other items for any babies in your household. Lay in a supply of high-energy foods, such as peanuts, chocolate, and dried fruit. When buying food, do not forget the needs of your household pets. A large ball of string may also prove useful.

The water supply may fail. You can store water in the bathtub. If you use bottles, allow one gallon (3.78 liters) for each person per day and store enough for three days.

If anyone in your home is taking medication, make sure you have enough. Make sure everyone knows where first aid supplies are kept.

If you have to drive

If you have to drive during a winter storm, prepare your car or truck. Fill the tank with fuel. As well as preventing you running out, this will stop ice forming in the tank and fuel pipes. If power supplies fail, gas stations may close, because the pumps are driven by electricity.

Then pack a survival kit. For each person you will need a sleeping bag or blankets; food such as chocolate, candies, peanuts, or dried fruit; and a change of clothing and footwear. Your survival kit should also include a flashlight with spare batteries; a first aid kit and manual; coins to use a pay phone; candles and waterproof matches; a sharp knife; a can in which you can melt snow to provide drinking water; a tow rope; booster cables (known in Britain as jump leads); a windshield scraper and brush; sand or gravel and a shovel in case your tires slip on ice; a bright red cloth and, if your vehicle has no radio antenna, a long stick; and a large, covered bucket and paper towels for sanitary use.

Before setting out, make sure you have all the maps you will need and a compass. If you need to use the compass, stand outside the vehicle to do so, because the vehicle's metal and electrical systems will make the reading unreliable. Tell someone where you are going, the route you plan to follow and alternative routes you will take if the preferred route is blocked, and the time you expect to arrive. Do not travel alone if you can avoid it.

When you hear the warning

From the time you hear the winter storm warning, stay indoors if you are at home. Do not set out on any journey except in an emergency. If you are outdoors when you hear a blizzard warning, seek shelter at once. If you are caught outdoors in a blizzard you may die.

At home, close off rooms you are not using and stuff towels or blankets beneath the doors. This will conserve heat. Keep windows closed and cover them at night. Several layers of warm clothing give better heat insulation than one layer, and loose-fitting clothes are better than tight ones. If you feel too warm, remove a layer. Avoid perspiring. Eat regularly and drink plenty of water.

Outdoors

When the storm eases it will be safe to go outdoors, provided you are physically fit and take sensible precautions. Avoid overexertion. Shoveling snow is very hard work and, unless you are young and fit, shoveling too enthusiastically can cause heart attacks. Wear mittens that fit snugly around the wrists, a hat (half the heat lost from your body can be through the top of your head), earmuffs or some other ear protection, and cover your mouth and nose to warm the air you inhale before it reaches your lungs. If you grow warm from physical exertion, remove a layer of clothing; perspiration can make your clothes damp, which will chill your body.

If anyone has to go outdoors during heavy snow or a blizzard, however briefly, attach them to a lifeline. Use the ball of string from your emergency stores and tie one end around the person's waist (do not rely on them holding the end, because they may lose it). Then pay out the string from inside the house. When visibility is reduced almost to zero people become disoriented and lost very quickly.

You may be outdoors and far from any building when the storm begins. In that case you must aim to shelter from the wind and keep dry. Use whatever material you can find to build a windbreak. If the snow is deep enough, dig a shelter in that. If you can find anything that will burn, try to light a fire; as well as keeping you warm it may attract attention. If you can find rocks, place them around the fire; they will absorb heat and make the fire feel hotter. While you are working, remove a layer of clothing if you start to feel warm, to avoid perspiring.

While you are sheltering, cover all exposed parts of your body. Keep your gloves or mittens on and pull your scarf over your face to cover your nose and mouth. Do not eat snow. It will lower your body temperature. You can use snow for drinking only if you melt it first.

If the car is stuck

If you are driving when the storm begins and the vehicle becomes stuck in the snow, stay where you are. On no account leave the vehicle and try to make your way to safety unless you can see your destination clearly and are able to reach it easily. A car is much easier for rescuers to find than a person who is alone in the countryside, and in poor visibility you will soon become disoriented.

Make the vehicle as conspicuous as you can. Tie a red cloth to the antenna or a long stick so it waves above the roof. Leave the inside roof light on at night and if you have a dome light, turn it on at night when the engine is running.

Run the engine for no more than 10 minutes each hour, with the heater on full. This will conserve fuel for what may be a long wait. While the engine is running, open the windows slightly to prevent carbon monoxide accumulating to dangerous levels. Before starting the engine each time, check the exhaust pipe is not blocked with snow. Otherwise, stay in the vehicle.

While you are waiting, exercise to keep warm. Clap your hands, stamp your feet, and swing your arms. Wiggle your fingers and toes as vigorously as you can. Eat and drink water regularly. You can drink melted snow, but do not eat snow.

Stay awake. When you sleep, your body core temperature falls and in extreme weather this is dangerous. Listen to the radio, sing, shout, and do everything you can to avoid falling asleep, especially at night when temperatures fall even further.

Provided you stay awake and remain in your vehicle, and are dressed for the weather, you can survive a surprisingly long time. Remember that people are searching for you. If you left details of your route, rescuers will be following it. If not, they will be combing the entire surrounding area. You are unlikely to be the only stranded driver, so help will reach you eventually.

Almost all deaths from cold could have been avoided. Prepare thoroughly and before storms or blizzards reach you. Know what to do and do it. Dress appropriately. Take care and when at last the wind drops, the snow stops falling, and the temperature starts to rise again, you will be none the worse for your experience.

BEAUFORT WIND SCALE

Force	Speed mph (kmh)	Name	Description
0	0.1 (1.6) or less	Calm	Air feels still. Smoke rises vertically.
1	1–3 (1.6–4.8)	Light air	Wind vanes and flags do not move, but rising smoke drifts.
2	4–7 (6.4–11.2)	Light breeze	Drifting smoke indicates the wind direction.
3	8–12 (12.8–19.3)	Gentle breeze	Leaves rustle, small twigs move, and flags made from lightweight material stir gently.
4	13–18 (20.9–28.9)	Moderate breeze	Loose leaves and pieces of paper blow about.
5	19–24 (30.5–38.6)	Fresh breeze	Small trees that are in full leaf sway in the wind.
6	25–31 (40.2–49.8)	Strong breeze	It becomes difficult to use an open umbrella.
7	32–38 (51.4–61.1)	Moderate gale	The wind exerts strong pressure on people walking into it.
8	39–46 (62.7–74)	Fresh gale	Small twigs torn from trees.
9	47–54 (75.6–86.8)	Strong gale	Chimneys are blown down. Slates and tiles are torn from roofs.
10	55–63 (88.4–101.3)	Whole gale	Trees are broken or uprooted.
11	64–75 (102.9–120.6)	Storm	Trees are uprooted and blown some distance. Cars are overturned.
12	more than 75 (120.6)	Hurricane	Devastation is widespread. Buildings are destroyed and many trees are uprooted.

AVALANCHE CLASSES

(There are five classes. Each class is ten times stronger than the one preceding it.)

Class	Damage	Path width
1	Could knock someone over, but not bury them.	10 m (33 ft.)
2	Could bury, injure, or kill someone.	100 m (330 ft.)
3	Could bury and wreck a car, damage a truck, demolish a small building, break trees.	1,000 m (3,330 ft.)
4	Could wreck a railroad car or big truck, demolish several buildings, or up to 4 ha (10 acres) of forest.	2,000 m (6,560 ft.)
5	Largest known; could destroy a village or up to 40 ha (100 acres) of forest.	3,000 m (9,800 ft.)

SI UNITS AND CONVERSIONS

Unit	Quantity	Symbol	Conversion
Base units			
Base units			
meter	length	m	1 m = 39.3701 inches
kilogram	mass	kg	1 kg = 2.205 pounds
second	time	s	
ampere	electric current	A	
kelvin	thermodynamic temperature	K	1 K = 1°C = 1.8°F
candela	luminous intensity	cd	
mole	amount of substance	mol	
Supplementary units			
radian	plane angle	rad	$\pi/2$ rad = 90°
steradian	solid angle	sr	
Derived units			
coulomb	quantity of electricity	C	
cubic meter	volume	m^3	1 m^3 = 1.308 yards^3
farad	capacitance	F	
henry	inductance	H	
hertz	frequency	H_z	
joule	energy	J	1 J = 0.2389 calories
kilogram per cubic meter	density	$kg\ m^{-3}$	1 $kg\ m^{-3}$ = 0.0624 lb. ft.$^{-3}$
lumen	luminous flux	lm	
lux	illuminance	lx	
meter per second	speed	$m\ s^{-1}$	1 $m\ s^{-1}$ = 3.281 ft. s^{-1}
meter per second squared	acceleration	$m\ s^{-2}$	
mole per cubic meter	concentration	$mol\ m^{-3}$	
newton	force	N	1 N = 0.225 lb. force
ohm	electric resistance	Ω	

SI UNITS AND CONVERSIONS (*continued*)

Unit	Quantity	Symbol	Conversion
Derived units			
pascal	pressure	Pa	1 Pa = 0.145 lb. in.$^{-2}$
radian per second	angular velocity	rad s^{-1}	
radian per second squared	angular acceleration	rad s^{-2}	
square meter	area	m^2	1 m^2 = 1.196 yards^2
tesla	magnetic flux density	T	
volt	electromotive force	V	
watt	power	W	1 W = 947.82 Btu h^{-1}
weber	magnetic flux	Wb	

PREFIXES USED WITH SI UNITS

Prefixes attached to SI units alter their value.

Prefix	Symbol	Value
atto	a	× 10^{-18}
femto	f	× 10^{-15}
pico	p	× 10^{-12}
nano	n	× 10^{-9}
micro	μ	× 10^{-6}
milli	m	× 10^{-3}
centi	c	× 10^{-2}
deci	d	× 10^{-1}
deca	da	× 10
hecto	h	× 10^2
kilo	k	× 10^3
mega	M	× 10^6
giga	G	× 10^9
tera	T	× 10^{12}

Bibliography and further reading

Allaby, Michael. *Dangerous Weather: A Change in the Weather.* New York: Facts On File, 2004.

———. *Facts On File Weather and Climate Handbook.* New York: Facts On File, 2002.

———. *Deserts.* New York: Facts On File, 2001.

———. *Encyclopedia of Weather and Climate.* 2 vols. New York: Facts On File, 2001.

"Antarctica: The End of the Earth." Available on-line. URL: www.pbs.org/wnet/nature/antarctica. Accessed October 29, 2002.

Antarctic Connection. "McMurdo Station." Available on-line URL: www.antarcticconnection.com/antarctic/stations/mcmurdo.shtml. Accessed November 13, 2002.

———. "Researchers Describe Overall Water Balance in Subglacial Lake Vostok." *Antarctica News Archives.* Available on-line. URL: www.antarcticconnection.com/antarctic/news/2002/03230202.shtml. Posted March 23, 2002.

Arnett, Bill. "Ganymede." Available on-line. URL: http://seds.lpl.arizona.edu/nineplanets/ganymede.html. Last updated October 31, 1997.

"Avalanche Awareness." National Snow and Ice Data Center. Available on-line. URL: http://nsidc.org/snow/avalanche. Accessed February 11, 2003.

Barry, Roger G., and Richard J. Chorley. *Atmosphere, Weather & Climate.* 7th ed. New York: Routledge, 1998.

Bentley, W. A., and Humphreys, W. J. *Snow Crystals.* New York: Dover Publications, 1990.

British Antarctic Survey. Natural Environment Research Council. Home page available on-line. URL: www.antarctica.ac.uk/Living_and_Working/Stations. Accessed November 13, 2002.

Bueckert, Dennis. "Ice Storm Damage Tallied." *CNews,* December 15, 1998. Available on-line. URL: www.canoe.ca/CNEWSIceStorm/icestorm_dec15_cp.html.

Bunce, Nigel, and Jim Hunt. "James Hutton—the Father of Geology." The Science Corner, College of Physical Science, University of Guelph. Available on-line. URL: http://helios.physics.uoguelph.ca/summer/scor/articles/scor164.htm. Accessed November 19, 2002.

Calder, Nigel. "Some context." Available on-line. URL: www.wmc.care4free.net/sci/iceage/calder.context.html. Accessed November 20, 2002.

Claypole, Jim, and Yvonne Claypole. "Jim's Diary." Available on-line. URL: www.sofweb.vic.edu.au/claypoles/diary/jim33.htm. Accessed May 19, 1999.

Connolley, W. M. "Antarctic Weather." Available on-line. URL: www.nbs.ac.uk/public/icd/wmc/Blueice/weather.html. November 22, 1995.

Dennis, Jerry. "Nature Baroque: Snowflakes & Crystals." *Northern Michigan Journal.* Available on-line. URL: www.leelanau.com/nmj/winter/nature_baroque.html. Accessed February 11, 2003.

"General Circulation of the Atmosphere." Available on-line. URL: http://cimss.ssec.wisc.edu/wxwise/class/gencirc.html. October 2002.

"Greenland Guide Index." Available on-line. URL: www.greenland-guide.gl/default.htm. Accessed October 29, 2002.

Hall, Dorothy, Nick DiGirolamo, George Riggs, and Janet Chien. "Below-average Snow Cover over North America." *Visible Earth*. NASA. Available on-line. URL: http://visibleearth.nasa.gov/cgibin/viewrecord. Accessed November 22, 2002.

Hamilton, Calvin J. "Ganymede: Jupiter III." Available on-line. URL: www.solarviews.com/eng/ganymede.html. Accessed October 31, 2002.

Hardy, Doug. "Kilimanjaro Summit Measurements: Climate and Glaciers." Available on-line. URL: www.geo.umass.edu/climate/tanzania/synopsis.html. Updated May 1, 2002.

Harper, Lynn D., and Greg Schmidt. "Lake Vostok May Teach Us about Europa." *Astrobiology: The Study of the Living Universe*. NASA. Available on-line. URL: http://astrobiology.arc.nasa.gov/stories/europa_vostok_0899.html. Posted August 5, 1999.

Hartwick College. "Ice Ages and Glaciation." Available on-line. URL: http://info.hartwick.edu/geology/work/VFT-so-far/glaciers/glacier1.html. Accessed November 19, 2002.

Heidorn, Keith C. "Lake-Effect Snowfalls." *Weather Phenomenon and Elements*. February 26, 1998. Available on-line. URL: www.islandnet.com/~see/weather/elements/1kefsnw2.htm.

Helfferich, Carla. "A Farewell to All Six Sides of Ice and Snow: Article # 1180." Alaska Science Forum, University of Alaska, Fairbanks April 21, 1994. Available on-line. URL: www.gi.alaska.edu/ScienceForum/ASF11/1180.html.

Hoffman, Paul F., and Daniel P. Schrag. "The Snowball Earth." Harvard University. Available on-line. URL: www.eps.harvard.edu/people/faculty/hoffman/snowball_paper.html. August 8, 1999.

Holland, Earle. "African ice core analysis reveals catastrophic droughts, shrinking ice fields and civilization shifts." Available on-line. URL: www.acs.ohiostate.edu/researchnews/archive/kilicores/htm. Updated October 17, 2002.

Houghton, J. T., et al. *Climate Change 2001: The Scientific Basis*. Contribution of Working Group I to the Third Assessment Report of the Intergovernmental Panel on Climate Change. Cambridge, U.K.: Cambridge University Press, 2001.

"Ice." Available on-line. URL: www.glacier.rice.edu/land/5_tableofcontents.html. Accessed October 28, 2002.

Jet Propulsion Laboratory. "Moons and Rings of Jupiter." Available on-line. URL: http://galileo.jp1.nasa.gov/moons/europa.html. Accessed October 31, 2002.

Kendrew, W. G. *The Climates of the Continents*. 5th ed. Oxford, U.K.: Clarendon Press, 1961.

Kennedy, Martin. "A Curve Ball into the Snowball Earth Hypothesis?" *Geology*, December 2001. Geological Society of America. Summary available on-line. URL: www.sciencedaily.com/releases/2001/12/011204072512.htm. December 4, 2001.

Kid's Cosmos. "Channeled Scablands." Available on-line. URL: www.kidscosmos.org/kidstuff/mars-trip-scablands.html. Accessed November 20, 2002.

Lamb, H. H. *Climate, History and the Modern World*. 2d ed. New York: Routledge, 1995.

Libbrecht, Kenneth G. "Snow Crystals." California Institute of Technology. Available on-line. URL: www.its.caltech.edu/~atomic/snowcrystals. Accessed February 11, 2003.

Lutgens, Frederick K., and Edward J. Tarbuck. *The Atmosphere*. 7th ed. Upper Saddle River, N.J.: Prentice-Hall, 1998.

Nakaya, Ukichiro. *Snow Crystals: Natural and Artificial*. Cambridge: Harvard University Press, 1954.

National Science Foundation. "Lake Vostok." NSF Fact Sheet. Office of Legislative and Public Affairs. Available on-line. URL: www.nsf.gov/od/lpa/news/02/fslakevostok.htm. May 2002.

National Weather Service. "Lake Effect Weather Page." Available on-line. URL: www.erh.noaa.gov/er/buf/lakeeffect/index1k.html. Accessed February 14, 2003.

Newitt, Larry. "Magnetic Declination: What Do You Mean 'North Isn't North'." Geological Survey of Canada. Available on-line. URL: www.gerolab.nrcan.gc.ca/geomag/e_magdec.html. September 8, 1999.

New Scientist. "Snowball Earth." Available on-line. URL: http://xgistor.ath.cx/files/ReadersDigest/snowballearth.html. November 6, 1999.

Nicosia, David. "The Blizzard of 1993: One of the Worst in Modern Times." National Weather Service Binghamton. Available on-line. URL: www.erh.noaa.gov/er/bgm/news/mar02.txt. Accessed February 6, 2003.

Oliver, John E., and John J. Hidore. *Climatology, An Atmospheric Science.* 2d ed. Upper Saddle River, N.J.: Prentice Hall, 2002.

"Original Bentley images." Jericho Historical Society. Available on-line. URL: http://snowflakebentley.com/snowflakes.htm. Accessed February 11, 2003.

Priscu, John. "Exotic Microbes Discovered Near Lake Vostok." Science@NASA. Available on-line. URL: http://science.nasa.gov/newhome/headlines/ast10dec99_2.htm. December 10, 1999.

Scientific Committee on Antarctic Research. "Stations of SCAR Nations operating in the Antarctic Winter 2002." The International Council for Science. Available on-line. URL: www.scar.org/Antarctic%20Info/wintering_stations_2000.htm. Last updated November 8, 2002.

Sheldon, Addison Erwin. "History and Stories of Nebraska: Great Storms." *Oldtime Nebraska.* Available on-line. URL: www.ku.edu/~kansite/hvn/books/nbstory/story38.html. Accessed February 13, 2003.

"Significant Scots: John Playfair." Electric Scotland. Available on-line. URL: www.electricscotland.com/history/other/playfair_john.htm. Accessed November 19, 2002.

Sohl, Linda, and Mark Chandler. "Did the Snowball Earth Have a Slushball Ocean?" Goddard Institute for Space Studies. Available on-line. URL: www.giss.nasa.gov/research/intro/sohl_01. Last modified November 12, 2002.

Spokane Outdoors. "Channeled Scablands Theory." Available on-line. URL: www.spokaneoutdoors.com/scabland.htm. Accessed November 20, 2002.

Tew, Mark. "National Weather Service Plans to Implement a New Wind Chill Temperature Index." Office of Climate, Water, and Weather Services. Available on-line. URL: http://205.156.54.206/om/windchill. Updated October 29, 2001.

"Three-Cell Model." Available on-line. URL: www.cimms.ou.edu/~cortinas/1014/125_html. October 2002.

Tindol, Robert. "Snowball Earth Episode 2.4 Billion Years Ago Was Hard on Life, but Good for Modern Industrial Economy, Research Shows." Caltech Media Relations. Available on-line. URL: http://pr.caltech.edu/media/Press_Releases/PR12031.html. February 14, 2000.

USA Today. "Weather Basics." Available on-line. URL: www.usatoday.com/weather/tg/wamsorce/wamsorc1.htm.

"Vladimir Zenzinov Papers: Vladimir Zenzinov Biography." Available on-line. URL: www.amherst.edu/~acrc/zen/zenbio.html. Accessed February 6, 2003.

Waggoner, Ben. "Louis Agassiz (1807–1873)." University of California, Berkeley. Available on-line. URL: www.ucmp.berkeley.edu/history/agassiz.html. Accessed November 19, 2002.

———. "Georges Cuvier (1769–1832)." University of California, Berkeley. Available on-line. URL: www.ucmp.berkeley.edu/history/cuvier.html. Accessed November 19, 2002.

Wyhe, John van. "Georges Cuvier (1769–1832), leader of elite French science." The Victorian Web. Available on-line. URL: 65.107.211.206/victorian/science/cuvier.html. Accessed November 19, 2002.

———. "Charles Lyell (1797–1875), gentleman geologist." The Victorian Web. Available on-line. URL: http://65.107.211.206/victorian/science/lyell.html. Accessed November 19, 2002.

"Wilson A. Bentley: The Snowflake Man." Jericho Historical Society. Available on-line. URL: http://snowflakebentley.com. Accessed February 11, 2003.

Index

Page numbers in *italic* refer to illustrations.